How to
Meet Standards,
Motivate
Students,
and *Still*
Enjoy Teaching!

Second Edition

Dedicated to Steve, my husband and constant support system

How to
Meet Standards, Motivate Students, and *Still* Enjoy Teaching!

Second Edition

Four Practices That Improve Student Learning

Barbara P. Benson

CORWIN PRESS
A SAGE Company

For information:

 Corwin Press
A SAGE Company
2455 Teller Road
Thousand Oaks, California 91320
www.corwinpress.com

SAGE India Pvt. Ltd.
B 1/I 1 Mohan Cooperative
    Industrial Area
Mathura Road, New Delhi 110 044
India

SAGE Ltd.
1 Oliver's Yard
55 City Road
London EC1Y 1SP
United Kingdom

SAGE Asia-Pacific Pte. Ltd.
33 Pekin Street #02-01
Far East Square
Singapore 048763

Printed in the United States of America.

Library of Congress Cataloging-in-Publication Data

Benson, Barbara (Barbara P.)
How to meet standards, motivate students, and still enjoy teaching!: Four practices that improve student learning / Barbara P. Benson.—2nd ed.
    p. cm.
Includes bibliographical references and index.
ISBN 978-1-4129-6366-4 (cloth : acid-free paper)
ISBN 978-1-4129-6367-1 (pbk. : acid-free paper)
    1. Effective teaching—United States. 2. Education—Standards—United States.
3. Educational tests and measurements—United States. I. Title.

LB1025.3.B465 2009
371.102—dc22

2008025493

This book is printed on acid-free paper.

08 09 10 11 12   10 9 8 7 6 5 4 3 2 1

Acquisitions Editor:	Carol Chambers Collins
Associate Editor:	Desirée Enayati
Production Editor:	Eric Garner
Copy Editor:	Dorothy Hoffman
Typesetter:	C&M Digitals (P) Ltd.
Proofreader:	Carole Quandt
Indexer:	Molly Hall
Cover Designer:	Monique Hahn

Contents

Foreword   vii
  Spence Rogers

Preface to the Second Edition   viii

Acknowledgments   xii

About the Author   xiv

Introduction: Focusing on Standards in the Classroom   1
  A Positive View of Standards   2
  Taking a Big-Picture Look at Standards   2
  Standards and the Classroom   10
  Four Practices That Meet Standards and Motivate Students   11
  Ideas for Teachers   13
  Ideas for Administrators   16

1. Creating a Community of Learners   21
  Why Do I Need a Community of Learners in My Classroom?   21
  The Helpless and the Hopeless Students   22
  Help Students Become Self-Directed Learners   24
  Have an Interactive Classroom   27
  Helping Students Work Cooperatively   35
  Strategies for Group Work in a Community of Learners   36
  A Quality Focus   37
  The Community of Learners, a Final View   53
  Ideas for Teachers   53
  Ideas for Administrators   54

2. Making Reflection Routine   56
  Teacher Reflection   57
  Student Reflection   62
  Concluding Reflection   73
  Ideas for Teachers   73
  Ideas for Administrators   74

3. Teaching Content and Process   76
  The Learner Actions   77
  Using the Learner Actions to Meet Standards   80
  Analyzing Lessons to See Who Is Doing All the Work   82
  Ideas for Teachers   98
  Ideas for Administrators   98

4. Developing More Authentic Tasks and Assessments   **100**
    What Type of Work Should Students Be Doing?   100
    Performance Tasks   102
    Designing Tasks   106
    Assessment and Evaluation   121
    Assessing and Evaluating Performance Tasks   123
    Tasks and Assessment: Final Thoughts   126
    Ideas for Teachers   127
    Ideas for Administrators   128

**Conclusion: Implementing the Four Practices in
a High-Stakes Test Environment**   **130**
    What About the Tests?   131
    If Tests Don't Always Match the Standards,
        Why Do We Have Them?   131
    Teach Past the Tests to the Standards   132
    Don't Ignore the Tests, But Don't Obsess Over Them   133
    Teaching the Learner Action Verbs in the Standards Is Test
        Preparation   134
    Final Thoughts   136

Resources: Reproducible Forms   **137**

References and Further Readings   **182**

Index   **186**

Foreword

"How can we possibly get all kids to reach standards?" is a question I am frequently asked in my effective teaching, learning, and assessment workshops, institutes, and seminars. Thanks to outstanding educators like Barbara Benson, we are accumulating significant resources to help answer this critical question.

In my work teaching how to effectively build a context for learning and how to provide classroom instruction and assessments that are successful with virtually all students, I am always searching for practical resources. This latest book by Barbara Benson has a wealth of essential tools that she has perfected with her years of experience as a teacher of both adolescents and adults.

I first met Barbara when she was an exceptional secondary language arts teacher for both gifted and at-risk students. She was a participant in my week-long summer training on increasing student achievement. We quickly connected, found we had much in common philosophically and pedagogically, and began a meaningful friendship based on a shared commitment to success for all kids.

When Barbara asked me to write the foreword for her new book, I was so honored that I agreed to do it before I even read the manuscript. I knew that any book written by her would be effective, well-researched, and good for teachers and kids. Barbara did not let me down. *How to Meet Standards, Motivate Students, and Still Enjoy Teaching!* is a truly outstanding, practical resource that should be in every educator's professional library. It succeeds beautifully with the complex challenge of defining a classroom in which standards come alive for teachers and students in a "doable manner."

Barbara has developed an easy-to-understand, comprehensive model for enhancing success for students that is unusually refreshing. Through real classroom stories, she effectively presents four practices to improve student learning. Her easy, step-by-step approach for both teachers and administrators is sound, her strategies are clearly presented, and her advice is practical and based on real experience.

Thousands of students have been profoundly affected by Barbara's work, and with this "must read" new book, she is continuing to expand her reach. Read it, use it, and discover how it can help you make an even greater difference for kids, reach the standards, and enjoy teaching even more.

—Spence Rogers, Founder and Director
Peak Learning Systems
Author of *The High Performance Toolbox*,
Motivation & Learning, Teaching Tips, and *Teaching Treasures*

Preface to the Second Edition

■ WHY IS THIS BOOK NEEDED AND WHO SHOULD READ IT?

When this book was first published, many state standards were still in development and the full impact of No Child Left Behind had not been realized. I felt the book was needed to help teachers organize all of the knowledge and programs they had in a way that was logical and would lead to student success in meeting the emerging standards. As accountability processes have been solidified, the pressure on teachers has only increased as districts, desperate to improve test scores, have bombarded teachers with programs that promise immediate success but are layered over existing programs and instructional habits. This piling on of approaches to teaching only makes the classroom teacher's job more chaotic and increases the feeling of too much to do with too little time. Therefore, I think this book is more needed than ever because it intends to help teachers focus on what is important: motivating students to learn and remember what the standards say they need to know to be successful as well as enjoying the process.

This book originated from 15 years of presentations, workshops, classroom observations, problem-solving sessions, and planning meetings with teachers and administrators in school systems across the United States and Canada. During that time, I have watched educators working to ensure that all of their students get the best opportunity to meet the national, state, and/or local standards for learning that No Child Left Behind requires. As I work with teachers and administrators, however, it is evident that they are often overwhelmed by the demands being made on schools today. One reason for this is that teachers have been given mandates but very few practical methods or structures for implementing the standards in real classrooms. My intentions in writing this book remain the same:

- to share a clear perspective on what the standards mean for daily practices in public education,
- to offer teachers and administrators a four-part structure for organizing classrooms for teaching the standards, and
- to give them specific, usable strategies for helping students reach the higher requirements of the standards now in place across the United States.

However, in this revised edition there are some additional features:

- Clearer instructions for designing performance tasks
- Additional references
- Resource samples for easier reproduction and adaptation

This book is based on the recognition that standards are a reality and that the pressing issue for teachers is not Where did these standards come from? but How will I implement them in my classroom? I will not, therefore, be discussing the history of the standards movement. There are already many excellent sources that trace the origins and development of national and state standards if a reader needs this information.

My audience is mainly teachers who are working in K–12 classrooms across this country, and who are struggling to help their students succeed on mandated standards and tests. But I am also addressing principals and other administrators who support teachers in their efforts to create appropriate classroom experiences for students. Some teachers are lucky enough to be working in schools or systems that have visionary leaders and have already instituted the changes needed to help teachers create standards-based classrooms. But, for both teachers and principals, who feel alone and overwhelmed by the demands in this era of increased accountability, this book is for you.

I taught in public middle and high schools for 26 years in both rural and urban communities, and I know how hard it is to teach all types of students in the same class, how impossible new curriculum and assessment demands can feel, and how lonely it can be in a room full of children or young adults when you are the one responsible for all of them. I also know how miraculous it is when a group of students begin to take ownership of their learning, how exhilarating it is to realize that lesson plans are working even better than I had hoped, and how energizing it is to see students excited by what they are learning in my class. For these reasons, my heart is always in the classroom as I talk and write about instruction and assessment. When I do presentations to groups who are not classroom teachers, I always tell them that I am a teacher first and that what I will be sharing is the "down and dirty" view of standards. We teachers need to understand what we are doing and why, but the bottom line is, if the ideas and strategies won't work with 27 kids on Monday morning, they aren't useful. The ideas for the classroom that I share here do work with students.

Although many instruction and assessment strategies are included here, this book is not intended to be a collection of strategies. Rather, it offers a productive way of thinking about standards and a structure for organizing your classroom practice to give all students the best possible chance at success. The many teachers I have worked with over the last 15 years have found this approach to standards very useful. They often tell me that they have gained ideas and strategies to use in class tomorrow and a lot to think about as they plan future lessons and assessments. And, best of all for me, an experienced teacher who knows what classroom "burnout" feels like, veteran teachers have said that these ideas gave them hope and got them excited about teaching again.

Even though this book is for teachers, building administrators can also use it as they work with teachers to ensure all students learn well. Since principals now must be instructional leaders, they need to know what the standards-based classroom should look like. This book offers building administrators a view into that world, and at the end of each chapter, I give principals ideas for using the information in their roles as school leaders. Administrators can use the four components of the standards-based classroom

to determine staff development needs for their schools,

to model instructional strategies for teachers,

to facilitate change in classroom practice,

to support teachers who are working to make their classrooms standards-based, and

to create appropriate teacher observation and evaluation forms for the classroom that standards demand.

Using this book to start dialogue in schools about standards and what they will require of educators can give principals and teachers a common view of what is needed to meet standards in their schools and a common vocabulary so that everyone can communicate more productively.

One important feature of the information this book offers is that the four practices discussed in the text can be applied to K–12 classrooms in all content areas. In fact, the components are more powerful when a district uses them as a framework for classroom instruction and assessment and for professional development for all of their teachers. If we are to be successful in this era of increased expectations for all students, we must work together from the first day a student enters school until the day she walks across the stage to receive a diploma. That is the main reason this book is aimed at all public school educators and administrators rather than addressing only one content area or grade level. Teachers in various states with differing standards have applied the strategies successfully and benefited professionally from working together across grade levels and content areas to meet state mandates. To illustrate the universality of the ideas presented, the book offers examples of how teachers at various grade levels have applied them.

It is my hope that this book will help educators see the positive side and daily implications of the new content standards. Also, by offering the four practices for classrooms, I wish to give teachers and administrators a usable structure for synthesizing best teaching practices and working together productively to help students succeed in school and in the world beyond.

■ HOW IS THE BOOK ORGANIZED AND WHAT IS IN IT?

This book is organized around a logical process that begins by examining the implications of standards for the classroom. Then it explores the four components of a classroom that is aligned with what standards demand

and discusses various ways to use this information to improve student learning. Each section begins from the classroom perspective because that is where the major work of learning takes place and where the standards must be implemented. After listing specific ideas for teachers, ideas are offered for administrators to use in their role of facilitating the development of this type of classroom practice.

The Introduction, using sample student learning standards from numerous states, looks at the wide-ranging implications of what the standards are demanding of students. I offer processes for analyzing the specific standards that a teacher or system must meet and for communicating to students, parents, and the wider community about the standards and changes that are needed in the classroom for students to meet expectations. This analysis of the standards is necessary because it is the rationale for the ideas put forth in the rest of the text.

The Introduction also gives a picture of the type of classroom that is most likely to help students meet the demands standards make on them. It lists the four components that must be in place in a classroom that is aligned with standards and leads into the detailed discussion of these components in Chapters 1 through 4.

In Chapter 1, I discuss the importance of creating a Community of Learners in the classroom. The chapter explores the many facets of creating this community and discusses existing practices and new strategies for doing so.

Building the habit of reflection, the second component needed in a standards-based classroom, is the subject of Chapter 2. As in Chapter 1, we look at the rationale for including reflection and many ways to involve teachers and students in reflection.

Chapter 3 is about the third practice, the necessity to teach both the content and the processes included in the standards. Since schools should already be teaching the essential content, I focus on how to teach the processes that are now mandated in the standards along with content. I explain a learning cycle that includes all of the processes represented by the verbs imbedded in the standards. This chapter also discusses a lesson analysis/planning method based on the learner action cycle.

The final component of a standards-based classroom is the subject of Chapter 4: creating more authentic students tasks and assessments. This discussion clarifies the meaning of "assessment" and "evaluation" as they relate to classroom practice and offers a method and template for teachers to use to design quality performance tasks.

The Conclusion summarizes the previous four chapters and discusses the connections between the standards, the classroom, and the high-stakes tests being used to assess student learning. The topic of this book is the standards and their implications for classroom practice, not the tests. The tests, however, are a reality that cannot be ignored. Therefore, I illustrate that if a teacher uses the four components discussed in the text, students will learn and retain more content, and perform better on mandated testing.

In addition to a list of Resources, the volume also contains sample forms for teachers and administrators to use in implementing the ideas discussed in the chapters.

Acknowledgments

I would like to thank all the special people who have contributed to my thinking, my experiences in education, and my work on this book. I have been blessed with years full of wonderful students, who touched my life in my own classroom, and dedicated teachers, who have energized my work as a consultant. First, a huge thank you, Sherri Carreker, for being the visionary principal who dragged me out of my classroom in 1990 to go to a three-day workshop that changed my life, and then for being so supportive as I began to rethink how I would run my classroom and set off in directions that were pretty scary sometimes. I couldn't have learned and innovated and explored better teaching without your encouragement and help.

Susy Barnett, my sister-friend, how can I ever thank you enough for always being there when I needed to say some new idea aloud or struggle with how to make something work in my classroom? Thank you for all the years we worked side by side to implement the vision we had for our students, and traveled to share the dream with other teachers all over the United States and Canada.

Thank you, Dr. Bill Spady, for the vision of what school can and should be. Spence Rogers, Dr. Kit Marshall, Dr. Helen Burz, and Dawn Shannon, thank you for years of think tank sessions and work that asked the right questions and struggled with how to make learning happen in classrooms. Dr. Barbara Skipper and Uvalde ISD, Uvalde, Texas, I am so grateful to you for giving me the opportunity to see the impact of these ideas with all grade levels over a period of years. Linda Steinbruck and Susan Stone in Uvalde, Texas, thank you for being wonderful teachers who enhanced my ideas in your classroom by adding your own energy and creativity. To Dr. Mike Stevens, Pat Stone, and Ingrid Hollister in Shenendehowa CSD, Clifton Park, New York, I am in your debt for helping me refine the process for designing and using performance tasks. Thank you, Dorothy Dirks, of Elementary School District #20 in Hanover Park, Illinois, for breaking the trail with me in assessing more than content. Ellen Edmond, I appreciate you so much for believing in the vision and doing the wonderful follow-up needed to help support teachers. Thank you, Carol Scearce, for pushing me to take the learner actions into lesson planning so they were easier to use on a regular basis. A big thank you, also, to all the great teachers who have taken these ideas and gone back to classrooms and gotten students involved in and excited about learning. You are what it is really about. Bless you!

Finally, and especially, thank you Steve for encouraging my dreams and living patiently all these years with a committed teacher who always has some "school stuff" that needs to get done.

Corwin Press gratefully acknowledges the contributions of the following individuals:

Joan E. Anderson, Reading
    Instructor
Oakridge Middle School
Naples, FL

Katherine Avila, Mathematics
    Teacher
Tewksbury Memorial High School
Tewksbury, MA

Marsha Basanda, Fifth Grade
    Teacher
Bell's Crossing Elementary School
Simpsonville, SC

Randy Cook, Chemistry and
    Physics Teacher
Tri County High School
Morley, MI

Laura Cumbee, Special Education
    Math Teacher
Cartersville Middle School
Cartersville, GA

Linda C. Diaz, Program Specialist
    for Professional Development
Monroe County Schools
Key West, FL

Dixie Dastis, Mentor Teacher
Mukilteo School District
Everett, WA

Jolene Dockstader, Seventh-Grade
    Teacher
Jerome School District #261
Jerome, ID

Lynn Freeman, Leadership
    Facilitator
Georgia Department of Education
Marietta, GA

Shirley Gholston Key, Associate
    Professor of Science Education
University of Memphis
Memphis, TN

Sharon Kane, Professor of
    Curriculum and Instruction
State University of New York
Oswego, NY

David Moursund, Professor of
    Teacher Education
University of Oregon
Eugene, OR

Ellen Reller, Mathematics Teacher
San Francisco Unified School
    District
San Francisco, CA

Pauline E. Schara, Retired Principal
Linda Vista Elementary School
Yorba Linda, CA

David Scheidecker, Academic
    Facilitator
Neuqua Valley High School
Naperville, IL

Joseph P. Schmidt, Biology Teacher
Payson High School
Payson, AZ

Pearl Solomon, Professor Emeritus
    of Education
St. Thomas Aquinas College
Sparkill, NY

Catherine Thorne, Staff
    Development Coordinator
Lake County Regional Office of
    Education
Grayslake, IL

Amy Massey Vessel, Assistant
    Professor of Elementary
    Education
Louisiana Tech University
Ruston, LA

Lois Williams, Adjunct Faculty
Mary Baldwin College
Staunton, VA

About the Author

 **Barbara P. Benson** is, first of all, a teacher. She has taught middle school, high school, and university classes. As a public school teacher, she won local and state recognition for her innovative work with student portfolios, performance assessment, and service learning. In addition to teaching English, social studies, and humanities, she taught education courses at Appalachian State University and supervised secondary student teachers. She has an AB degree in English and history from High Point University in High Point, NC, a MA degree in English from North Carolina State University in Raleigh, NC, and advanced Certification in Teaching Gifted and Talented Students from Appalachian State University in Boone, NC.

Since 1991, she has been an educational consultant for schools and districts across the United States and Canada. She has also presented at the annual conferences of the National Staff Development Council and the Association for Supervision and Curriculum Development on various topics. She has published articles on classroom practice, edited *The Performance-Based Classroom*, a national newsletter for teachers, and co-authored *Student-Led Conferencing Using Showcase Portfolios* (2nd edition, 2005) with Susan Barnett.

After full-time consulting and leading professional development sessions nationwide with teachers and administrators in the areas of implementing standards, classroom instructional and assessment practices, rubrics, portfolios, student-led conferencing, performance task design, and improving student writing, Mrs. Benson returned to the classroom as a middle school teacher for three years. This was a reality check, if you will, for all of the ideas she has about teaching and learning. This led her into work with Expeditionary Learning Schools/Outward Bound where she is now a School Designer for schools in North Carolina. In all her work, the focus is always on the classroom and improving student learning, and her heart is with the teachers who have the awesome responsibility of teaching all children well.

Introduction

Focusing on Standards in the Classroom

In this time of standards for student learning, high-stakes testing, and accountability for all, teaching has become more challenging than ever. I know of no educators who would disagree with the previous statement! Without a doubt, the pressure to teach the standards (see Box 0.1 for a definition) and to have all students succeed on the tests has complicated the already-complex task of teaching children. So, as one teacher asked me recently, "How do I do it all and still enjoy the journey?"

Box 0.1

Standards

Standards are statements by national organizations, states, and local school districts to clarify the expectations for student learning. They state what students are expected to know and be able to do with that knowledge when they reach a benchmark or exit the system.

I do believe that it is possible to implement standards in the classroom, motivate students to become engaged in their learning, and enjoy the process of teaching at the same time. The first step is to get a clear picture of what the standards demand of students and how these demands will impact the way we teach and assess students on a daily basis. The second step is to incorporate four major components into classroom instruction and assessment. These components are a synthesis of many best practices already available for effective teaching, and, when in place, they create the type of classroom that will be necessary for implementing state content standards. This four-part approach also offers a broad enough frame to allow teachers to add new research-based methods as they become available. The best part, though, is that in this type of classroom, teaching is fun again.

The premises in this book are based on the states' standards documents and how they should guide classroom instruction and assessment. I am not ignoring the fact that states are using high-stakes tests to measure student learning, but I believe the standards are the bigger picture and come closer to describing what students will need to know and be able to do to succeed in school and beyond. If students do, in fact, learn what is in the standards, they will be able to succeed on the tests. They could, however, pass many of the tests now being used and not meet the standards in their states. For additional discussion of high-stakes testing and its relationship to standards and classroom practice, please see the Conclusion.

■ A POSITIVE VIEW OF STANDARDS

As we approach discussions on standards, we should be positive. Realizing that these statements of what students should know and be able to do when they reach a benchmark or leave school are a step in the right direction and will help us ensure student success. They can guide us toward some of the things we want most from our students and our schools—the development of successful, responsible adults who will take active and positive roles in our communities. As Mizell (2000), director of the Program for Student Achievement at the Edna McConnell Clark Foundation, said in a speech to a conference of representatives of states, school systems, and schools participating in the Making Middle Grades Matter initiative of the Southern Regional Education Board on July 10, 2000:

> Standards . . . are not the enemy. Fear of change is the enemy. Weak curriculum is the enemy. Lack of will and effort is the enemy. But standards are not the enemy. They can be a useful weapon. What makes the difference is how you think about standards and use them. Standards are not for the purpose of punishing students for their academic deficiencies. Standards are not an excuse for narrowing a teacher's instruction to prepare students to pass a high-stakes test. (p. 5)

I agree with Mr. Mizell because I believe that the standards are for the purpose of helping schools and teachers coordinate their efforts to prepare students well for their futures. Clear learning standards for students can help us see where we are now, what our goals need to be, and what steps we need to take to meet those goals. Standards are an opportunity for us all to work together for the good of students, and if we could see standards in this positive light, we would have a much better chance of helping students meet the higher expectations.

■ TAKING A BIG-PICTURE LOOK AT STANDARDS

To deal rationally with the current pressure to meet standards, educators need practical ways to determine just what the standards mean for students, for teachers, and for administrators. Teachers who are teaching specific grade levels or content areas where the state tests occur are certainly experts in their own segment of expectations for students. But they need to see the big picture, to know what the end result of the child's learning should be, and to recognize their own part in creating the graduate that can meet the learning standards.

Clarifying what the standards really demand of students is crucial to being able to create the type of classroom needed to meet these demands. Therefore, I am offering a process for examining state standards for student learning to determine their implications in the classroom. As a group goes through this process and looks at their local expectations for student learning, they must answer three significant questions (see Box 0.2) to clarify what should be done at the local level to address the standards. The first question is, What are these standards demanding of students? After these demands have been noted, we have to ask, How are they different from what was demanded of students in the past? The differences between previous expectations and standards students must now meet will be the driving force for change in classrooms and schools. Because of this, Question 3 is, What are the implications of these demands and differences for classroom and school practices? Having teachers, administrators, students, parents, boards of education, and the community surrounding the school answer these questions is essential for building a rationale and support for school change that is aligned with national, state, and local student learning standards.

Box 0.2

Three Questions to Ask About Standards

1. What do the standards demand of students?

2. How are these demands different from what was required in the past?

3. What are the implications of these differences on classrooms and schools?

What Do Standards Demand of Students?

To answer this question, we need to look at some sample standards representing different content areas. As a teacher, I would look at my own state's standards, but for our purposes, I have chosen sample standards in the various content areas from different locales (Box 0.3). The sample standards in Box 0.3 represent exit standards that would be expected of a graduate from high school. I feel all teachers, K–12, should be examining and discussing the kind of graduate being required so that they can do their part in contributing to that result.

To see how this exercise works, please take a moment to consider the samples offered. Do not look for specific pieces of content that students must know but at the demands that transcend content areas and, therefore, must be addressed by all who are teaching students. It is these common strands, in fact, that are the major differences between these standards and what we have always taught and tested in schools. As you look at these sample student learning standards, note the common threads and common language used. What do you see being required of students? You can use the space below the standards to record your observations if you like. You can also compare your responses to those from a teacher group in

Box 0.3

Sample Student Learning Standards

Sample 1

New York State Learning Standards and Core Curriculum in Mathematics (Rev. 2005), fifth grade, Problem Solving strand
Students will apply and adapt a variety of appropriate strategies to solve problems.

- 5.PS.10: Work in collaboration with others to solve problems.
- 5.PS.11: Translate from a picture/diagram to a number or symbolic expression.
- 5.PS.12: Use trial and error and the process of elimination to solve problems.
- 5.PS.13: Model problems with pictures/diagrams or physical objects.
- 5.PS.14: Analyze problems by observing patterns.

Retrieved February 24, 2008, from http://www.emsc.nysed.gov/ciai/mst/math.html.

Sample 2

Illinois Learning Standards for Social Science (Illinois State Board of Education, 1997)
State Goal 16: Understand events, trends, individuals, and movements shaping the history of Illinois, the United States, and other nations.
Late High School: 16.A.5a Analyze historical and contemporary developments using methods of historical inquiry (pose questions, collect and analyze data, make and support inferences with evidence, report findings).
Retrieved February 23, 2008, from http://www.isbe.net/ils/social_science/standards.htm.

Sample 3

Science Content Standards for California Public Schools (California State Board of Education, 2000), Grades 9–12: Investigation and Experimentation

1) "As a basis for understanding this concept and addressing the content in the other four strands (physics, chemistry, biology/life sciences, and earth sciences), students should develop their own questions and perform investigations." For example, item i states, "Students will analyze the locations, sequences, or time intervals that are characteristic of natural phenomena (e.g., relative ages of rocks, locations of planets over time, and succession of species in an ecosystem)." (p. 52)

Retrieved February 23, 2008, from http://www.cde.ca.gov/be/st/ss/scinvestigation.asp.

California State Board of Education 1430 N Street, Suite #5111 Sacramento, CA 95814

Sample 4

North Carolina Standard Course of Study in English Language Arts, English IV 9 (North Carolina Department of Public Instruction, 2004)

- Competency Goal #2: The learner will inform an audience by exploring general principles at work in life and literature.
- 2.01: Locate, process, and comprehend texts that explain principles, issues, and concepts at work in the world in order to:
  - ○ relate complex issues from a variety of critical stances.
  - ○ discern significant differences and similarities among texts that propose different ideas related to similar concepts.

Retrieved February 23, 2008, from http://www.dpi.state.nc.us/curriculum/languagearts/scos/2004/30english4.

Sample 5

Texas Essential Knowledge and Skills for Health Education Grades 7–8 (Texas Education Agency, 1998)

1) Health information. The student comprehends ways to enhance and maintain personal health throughout the life span. The student is expected to:
   - ○ analyze the interrelationships of physical, mental, and social health;
   - ○ identify and describe types of eating disorders such as bulimia, anorexia, or overeating;
   - ○ identify and describe lifetime strategies for prevention and early identification of disorders such as depression and anxiety that may lead to long-term disability; and
   - ○ describe the life cycle of human beings including birth, dying, and death.

Retrieved February 23, 2008, from http://www.tea.state.tx.us/rules/tac/chapter115/ch115b.html#115.23.

Texas (Table 0.1). They were looking at the *Texas Essential Knowledge and Skills* (Texas Education Agency, 1996, revised 2001) document, but you may be surprised to see similarities with your own responses. One observation I have had as I worked with various state standards is that, although the language varies in the documents, they seem to be making similar demands on students.

Standards Are Connecting Content Areas

One of the first things teachers comment on as they analyze their state standards is that the boundaries between content area disciplines are blurring. This is appropriate because if we want to prepare students for success in a complex world, we must see that discipline knowledge is not used in isolation. In fact, real-world problems are, by their very nature,

Table 0.1   Demands, Differences, and Implications of Texas Standards

Demands	Differences	Implications
* Think critically * Solve open-ended problems * Communicate in many ways in all content areas * Analyze information * Identify patterns * Apply concepts * Predict results * Demonstrate knowledge * See real-world connections * Use technology * Work independently and with others * Gather information * Connect one discipline with others * Present data * Critique ideas and works * Organize data	* Less memorization and more *thinking* * More student responsibility for their learning * More application of what is learned * Use of technology * More connection between content areas * Expectations that students write in all classes, even math * More connections to the work outside school * Expectations of active learning * Students working together and talking about what they are learning—class not always quiet	* Different teaching style: fewer lectures, more discussion * Cooperative learning strategies * Students writing in all classes * Teachers connecting content to real world * Teachers learning about technology and planning for kids to use it * Teaching of critical thinking * More staff development about how to get kids doing more * More current resources for content areas

interdisciplinary. To illustrate this move toward integration, the New York State Education Department (2005), for example, has listed math, science, and technology in one curriculum document.

Standards Require More Than Memorizing

Another observation about the standards is that complex critical-thinking processes are demanded along with content knowledge. Students cannot meet the standards simply by memorizing facts. They must also be able to pose questions, analyze data, make and support inferences, comprehend texts, relate complex issues, discern significant differences and similarities, organize, and interpret. We always worked with students to see that they could do these things, but, in the past, most curriculum documents did not require such skills.

Perhaps the most obvious demand of the standards is, however, that students are expected to be able to apply the content they have learned in complex ways. The standards' statements have a large number of action verbs, and they all say, "the student/learner will. . . ." These facts make it clear that the students are expected to *do* something with the information they have been taught. The ability to use content knowledge in unpredictable situations is a survival skill in the adult world. In the mid-1990s, Daggett (1994), an international expert on standards and assessment, pointed this out by presenting a new taxonomy for learning that was based on the context in which learners could apply content knowledge. He called it the Application Taxonomy and said that it used the real-world context that students would be operating in as adults to set levels of competence (Box 0.4). The highest level of learning, according to this model, is having the ability to use content information in a complex and unpredictable situation in the world beyond school. Judging from the wording of standards, they also require the ability to apply content knowledge in complex situations.

Box 0.4

Application Taxonomy

Level 1: Knowledge of one discipline

Level 2: Application of that knowledge within that discipline

Level 3: Application of that knowledge across disciplines

Level 4: Application of that knowledge to real-world, predictable problems

Level 5: Application of that knowledge to real-world, unpredictable problems

Sample of Leveled Tasks Using Map Skills

1. Student knows, can name, and can explain map symbols.

2. Student can read a map and answer questions about it in a geography class.

3. Student uses map-reading skills learned in geography to read a topographic map of land forms in earth science class.

4. Student plans a family trip from Denver, Colorado, to St. Louis, Missouri.

5. Students use a road map to figure out where they are in New Orleans and how to get back on the proper road when lost.

SOURCE: Adapted from W. Daggett (1994, July 6–10), *Designing curriculum for today's and tomorrow's labor market demands.* Materials from workshop presented at the Reaching New Heights in Learning conference, Vail, Colorado.

How Are These Demands Different From What Was Required in the Past?

After creating a list of what standards demand, it is important to determine how these are different from what was expected of students in the past. This is a very interesting question, and answers will vary somewhat based on a person's experience in school as well as on the nature of the student learning expectations in a particular school community. Some people will look at the standards and remark that they match what was expected of students when they went to school or began teaching. Most, however, will immediately exclaim that these standards don't really look like what they had to do to graduate from high school. In fact, many will admit that they really did not have to do very much in school other than memorize and stay out of trouble.

There are many differences between the student learning standards at the beginning of the 21st century and what was officially expected of the last generation of public-school students. Admittedly, individual teachers throughout the ages have expected their students to do more than simply memorize factual information, but statewide school systems did not legislate these expectations as they have done with modern standards documents. Some of the differences in past and present expectations may vary in degree, depending on which state's standards you are reading, but the following list gives some of the main ways that current standards change the type of graduates we want from our school systems.

Students are now

- Expected to do critical thinking as opposed to only memorizing facts
- Expected to ask questions as well as answer them
- Held accountable for all communication skills—listening and speaking, understanding information communicated through various mediums, and reading and writing
- Asked to integrate curriculum areas and relate pieces of discrete information to a bigger picture instead of just knowing a finite list of facts
- Expected to take more responsibility for their learning and to become actively involved in the learning process instead of sitting quietly and passively in class
- Required to deal with and understand broad concepts in discipline areas instead of only small, isolated facts
- Asked to gather and organize data instead of just taking in information that has already been collected and sequenced for them
- Required to learn and use technologies that were not even on the horizon when their parents were in school

Another significant difference between the standards and what was officially expected of students in the past is that the requirements are for all students. It used to be accepted that only certain students would meet high-level academic requirements. In the past, for example, New York State demonstrated this expectation by granting Regents and non-Regents diplomas. The Regents diplomas required that students take a challenging curriculum and pass Regents exams in different content areas. Now all students must pass the Regents exams to receive a high school diploma. States may have to modify their criteria for high school graduation as the implications of the high-stakes tests are felt by students and parents, but the learning expectations put forth in the standards documents currently illustrate a version of something reformers have been saying for the past few years: "All students can and will learn."

What Are the Implications of These Differences for Classrooms and Schools?

We do not have to worry about the things in the standards that are the same as what we are already doing. It is the differences between the standards and previous expectations for student learning that will drive change. With that in mind, let's go back and take a look at just one of the differences listed in Table 0.1 to see what changes it might initiate. The first item in the list states that students must now be skilled at critical thinking. Implications of this single difference for the traditional classroom, where the teacher gives out information and the students absorb it without question, are enormous. Critical thinking involves open-ended and messy processes that are difficult to teach, control, measure, and grade—all things that teachers spend a great deal of class time doing.

Implications of Just One Demand: Critical Thinking

For the purpose of illustration, we will look, in Box 0.3, at just one of the critical thinking skills evident in the sample standards: Students should be posing questions as well as answering them. For students to be able to ask good questions, they have to be taught to recognize different types of questions, and they need to have practice creating, asking, and answering their own questions. For teachers, this means that some lessons might be about the art of questioning instead of content-specific facts: For example, teaching Bloom's Taxonomy could give students a way to classify questions and analyze what information they need to supply to answer various test questions well. Teachers will also need to plan for students to spend less time answering the questions supplied by texts or teacher-made tests and more time generating and answering their own questions. In addition, teachers will need to model various questioning techniques for students, including the use of open-ended questions. Open-ended questions rarely have one correct answer and may, in fact, lead to other complex questions before any logical answer is possible. This means teachers will need to be flexible in how they assess and evaluate student knowledge when students are struggling with complex questions.

When students do start generating substantive questions on their own, these questions are often open-ended and can easily go beyond the teacher's realm of expertise or the school's resources. So teachers must be able to help find the answers or teach students strategies for getting information when the answer is not apparent and resources are not immediately and easily available.

Continuing to follow this one demand for students to demonstrate critical thinking through creation of good questions, let's see what it could mean even beyond the type of lessons and classroom assessments teachers will have to create. If a teacher does not know how to question effectively, he will need to work on this skill in professional-development activities sponsored by the school. If there are limited print resources for specific content areas where students are involved in seeking answers to complex questions of their own creation, the school budget may need to include fast Internet access to allow for worldwide exploration of resources. Maybe this budget item will be more significant in helping students meet the district's learning goals than a full set of texts for the class. If that is the case, parents will need to be included in the decision so they understand why each student may not need to have a book to bring home in all classes and why homework assignments may appear to parents to be very untraditional. Looking at just this one example of what standards demand, it becomes obvious that the shift in what students must know and be able to do will have many implications for what teachers must know and be able to do and for how classrooms and schools will operate.

To illustrate the impact I believe the standards will have on education, I often compare it to someone dropping a stone in a still pond. Initially, the action seems harmless, but, in time, the ripples will spread out in concentric circles that disturb the whole pond and splash on the banks far from where the stone was dropped. We don't know the full impact of the standards yet, because the implications are just beginning to be understood; the ripples are just beginning to be felt.

■ STANDARDS AND THE CLASSROOM

The relationship between the content standards and classroom practice is direct and complex. The standards tell us what to teach—both content and competencies that are represented by the action verbs in all content areas—but they do not tell us how to teach. Teaching all the required content and competencies, however, will require a synthesis of existing best practices and new strategies crafted to facilitate and assess learning in an active, student-centered classroom. So, the required content and the methods necessary to be sure all students learn well are closely connected (see Figure 0.1).

Figure 0.1   Two Facets of Standards-Based Classrooms

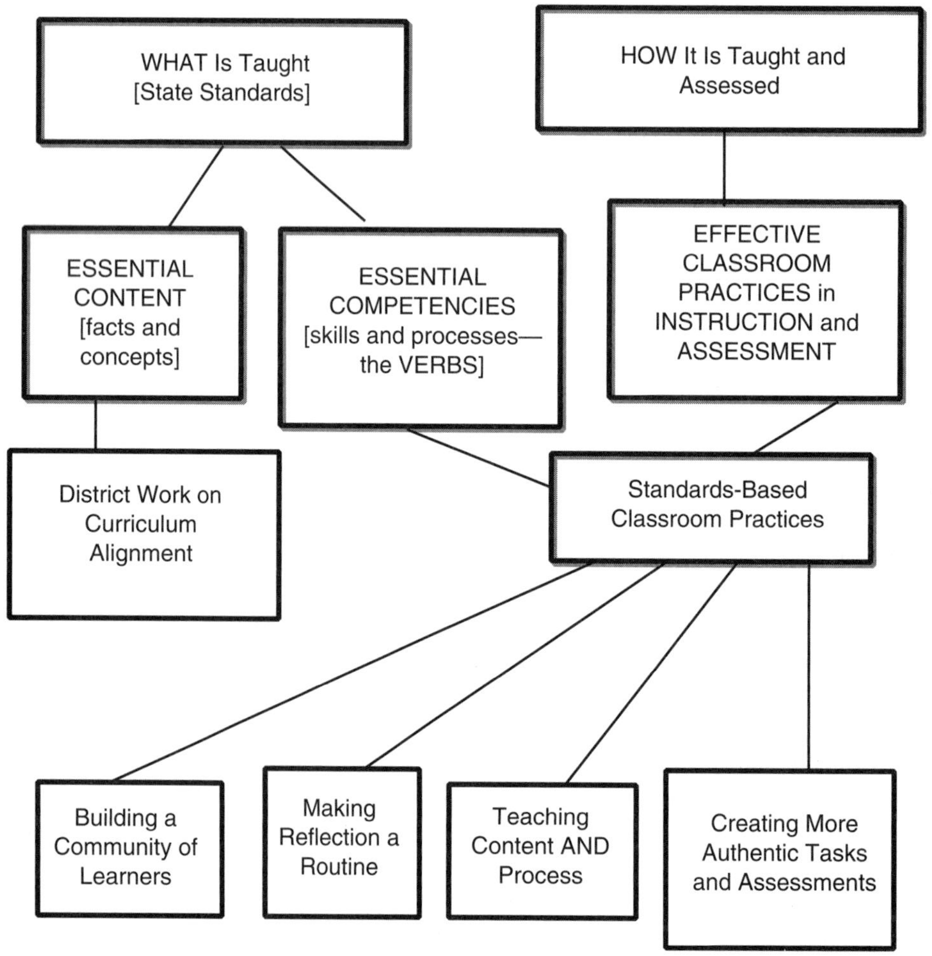

Aligning a district curriculum with new state standards is usually the first step districts take when new state standards go into effect. This step is necessary because what teachers are teaching must coincide with what is now demanded of students, but aligning curriculum is just the beginning. As many teachers and administrators are discovering, despite the fact that the district has spent a lot of time to get an appropriate curriculum guide, students are still not reaching targets for learning and the schools are not reaching Annual Yearly Progress goals set forth by No Child Left Behind. What is the problem?

First, the problem is multifaceted. The standards tell us what to teach, but they do not tell us how, and we will need many, many methods and strategies if we are to teach all students the amount of content that may be in a standards-aligned curriculum. With all good intentions, teachers are often working very hard doing the same things they have always done in school and expecting to produce a different result, a new type of graduate the state wants. Teaching the essential content facts and concepts in a traditional way is not going to be enough, because the student is still a passive learner. Educators and experts in teacher training, Wong and Wong (1991) tell new teachers, "It may be dangerous to teach as you were taught" (p. 28). We were taught when content knowledge was enough, so in today's environment, when students must have knowledge and skill and where accountability is a reality, Wong and Wong are certainly correct.

Because of the requirement that students be competent at applying knowledge, the standards-based classroom will be a very different place from the one we remember from our own schooling. Looking in on this classroom (see Table 0.2), one sees the increase in student involvement and the fact that every day is not the same. One day the teacher may be lecturing while students take notes, but on another day, students may be accessing information in many different ways, both individually and in small groups. The secret to this classroom will be that it engages students in their own learning and balances whole-group activities with those tailored to meet individual needs.

FOUR PRACTICES THAT MEET STANDARDS ■
AND MOTIVATE STUDENTS

The truth is that it will take a different type of classroom and different types of student work to teach both the content and the process skills represented by all the verbs embedded in the content-specific objectives of the standards. Creating this type of class will initially feel uncomfortable because it is different from what we experienced. In a classroom where students are actively involved in their own learning, the teacher's role changes to facilitator, and even if we see the need to create different learning experiences for students, we are sometimes not sure how to do it. This problem is compounded by the fact that so many programs promised to help students meet standards, and each one seemed to exclude the practices of the one that came before it. Teachers often refer to this situation as the flavor-of-the-month phenomenon. In workshops, they make comments like, "Last year it was cooperative learning, and this year it is brain compatible classrooms. Which does the district want me to do now, and what will it be next year?"

Table 0.2   Snapshots of the Standards-Based Classroom

The Classroom

- Might have desks in rows but more often desks will be clustered to allow interaction, or there will be tables for students to use
- Might be noisy as students talk and work together
- Might look messy as students are involved in complex, long-range tasks involving multiple activities
- Should be full of student work for viewing
- Will offer working areas that are comfortable and have varied resource materials
- Will have evidence of student collaboration in posted lists, signs, rules, mementos, and presentations

The Students

- Will sometimes be working alone but more often will be working in groups
- Will be able to explain what they are doing and why
- Will be glad to include a visitor in their activity or explain their work
- Will be respectful to each other and any adults in the room
- Will be collaborative rather than competitive with classmates
- Will ask questions as often as answer them
- Might be involved in different activities at the same time as they work to complete a complex task
- Will have goals and be focusing on doing quality work, which means they are constantly trying to improve
- Will be able to discuss what they are learning and how they can use it
- Will use rubrics to self-assess as they do their work

The Teacher

- Might be hard to find among the students
- Will be facilitating student learning—sometimes by direct instruction and lecturing but more often by coordinating group and individual activities
- May be assisted by other adults in the classroom
- Will be interacting with students in a respectful and encouraging way
- Can explain what students are doing and why
- Can discuss the alignment of student activities and tasks with district and state standards
- Does not give students all the answers
- Asks open-ended questions and helps students learn the processes needed to problem solve for answers
- Has a professional portfolio with collected artifacts and reflections on the year's activities

The Student Work

- Might be graded in a traditional way or might be assessed with descriptive rubrics using categories like "Excellent," "Acceptable," or "Not Yet Acceptable," to give improvement-focused feedback to students
- Will often be evaluated with rubrics developed by the teacher and/or students
- Might integrate content areas
- Might be leading to a complex student demonstration of learning
- Might involve experts from the community
- Might deal with a real community problem
- Will often be accompanied by student and teacher reflection on the process and product
- Will often depend on the work of other students and contribute to a larger task the class is completing
- Will be public and available for others to view, critique, and enjoy

In reality, the best analogy might be that all the programs we have tried in the past are tools in our toolboxes for successful teaching. We will need to be able to select from all the good ideas and strategies we have available rather than only use one program at a time. Therefore, what teachers need is a simple structure to help synthesize prior knowledge and practices with new information, to help organize strategies, to help make decisions about classroom practices and staff development needs, to help design lessons, and to help create appropriate classroom assessments. We need a practical way to organize our thinking and practices so that we can help students meet both facets of the standards—the content and the competencies.

The four components of a standards-based classroom offer just such an organizational structure for creating a classroom to implement standards. A classroom that offers the best opportunity for all students to learn the content and competencies required is one where the teacher is following the curriculum set out by the standards and is

1. Creating a community of learners who are self-directed, interactive, cooperative, and focused on quality

2. Making reflection a routine for everyone

3. Teaching content *and* process

4. Developing more authentic student tasks and assessment methods

These four components need to be in place in classrooms from kindergarten through 12th grade, in all content areas. When present, they create the necessary environment for everyone to take risks as they explore new ideas and skills, learn from mistakes that will happen when we are doing something new, and benefit from the richness of working with others toward worthy goals. Teachers as well as students need this type of learning place as they struggle to raise standards for everyone.

IDEAS FOR TEACHERS   ■

To Focus on Standards

Whether teachers like it or not, they are the local representatives for the district or state agencies that may have imposed the standards for student learning that affect students in their schools. I'm sure they have realized this whenever a friend who has some concern about her child's school or teacher has accosted them in a grocery store or dry cleaners. So teachers need to be prepared to help their students and their parents understand and accept the requirements that the student will have to meet in school. Here are some ideas to assist you, as a teacher, in this task:

• Be sure you understand the standards in your state and can discuss them comfortably in simple terms with your students' parents.
• Become very familiar with the learning expectations your students must meet, and connect these to the assignments you give students.

Be sure to share this information with your students so they know what and why they are learning.

- Help your students understand what is expected of them, both at their grade level and beyond. Young students can examine what will be needed to pass the grade they are in. For example, on the first day of fourth grade, one teacher gave her students the task of discovering what would be needed to get to fifth grade. They determined what they needed to know, where they might find out, and how to begin. They interviewed fourth- and fifth-grade teachers and fifth-grade students. They examined the state learning standards for fourth grade and looked at the textbooks in their classroom. They discovered that they would have to pass the state tests in reading, writing, and math. Then they wanted to talk to "the test guy," so the teacher invited the district test coordinator to come and be interviewed. By the end of the first week of fourth grade, these students had a good idea of what they were expected to do, had developed a plan to get started, and were ready for the challenge.

- If students are older, take them through the Big Picture activity. (See Resources, Samples 1 and 2, for the process and a work page.) This will give them an idea of what is expected of them and help them understand *why* you will be asking them to learn in new ways.

- Whenever possible, communicate positively with parents about the standards that will affect their children. For example, in notes, letters, or regular communications you send parents include one standard and a sample assignment that students have been working on that meets this standard.

- Ask students to talk to their parents and share their work and the standards it addresses.

- Invite parents to your classroom to see the work students are doing, and post standards being met as students work in certain centers or complete projects that might be on display in the room.

To Create a Standards-Based Classroom

For years, we have heard that a teacher should be not the "sage on the stage" but rather the "guide at the side," and now the standards are requiring just that. If a teacher has been the one who dispensed all the knowledge while students soaked it up, her role will change. Now she must be the one who plans and facilitates the learning experiences for students. She won't have to throw out everything she is already doing and start over, but she will have to assess all that she does to see if it is getting the students actively engaged in learning. She will need to combine best practices from the past with emerging knowledge about learning. She will also have to be prepared to be a learner, because this classroom is not like the ones in which she was taught and trained (see Box 0.5). The professional teacher of the 21st century must be an expert at using what works, balancing multiple approaches so that the various needs of students are met, and continuing to explore the changes taking place in the world students will enter as well as any new research about the process of learning.

All this work and effort will not be in vain, because the teacher's expertise is the key ingredient to student success. Olson (1998) cites William Sanders of the University of Tennessee, who researched what impacted

Box 0.5

Building a Standards-Based Classroom

Building a standards-based classroom doesn't mean starting over! Use the tools you already have, and work to get the ones you are missing by

- Reading
- Attending workshops
- Starting study groups with other teachers (in-house or a teacher learning network with other schools or districts)
- Using grade-level, content-area, and staff meetings for discussion, sharing ideas and experiences, and problem solving as you try new strategies
- Doing formal lesson study, which is defined by Stigler and Hiebert as "a collaborative process in which a group of teachers identify an instructional problem, plan a lesson (which involves finding books and articles on the topic), teach the lesson (one member of the group teaches the lesson while the others observe), evaluate and revise the lesson, teach the revised lesson, again evaluate that lesson, and share the results with other teachers" (cited in Sparks 1999, p. 2)
- Doing action research, which Caro-Bruce defines as "a process where participants—who might be teachers, principals, support staff— examine their own practice, systematically and carefully, using the techniques of research" (cited in Richardson, 2000, p. 1)

student learning and reported, "The single greatest effect of student performance is not race, it's not poverty, it's the effectiveness of the individual classroom teacher" (p. 27). What teachers do matters! Following are some suggestions to help teachers get started on creating the classroom that standards demand:

- Assess classroom practices by looking through the descriptors in Snapshots of a Standards-based Classroom, (Table 0.2), and checking the ones that a visitor might see in your classroom.
- Now, go through the list again and put a star next to any that you *wish* described your classroom. These can become the source of goals for you, and you can begin to search for staff development opportunities, reading material, study groups, or courses that would help you gain strategies to make these items part of your practice.
- Use the lists of staff development programs that complement the four practices of a standards-based classroom to take inventory of knowledge-base and learning needs. (See Resources, Sample 3, for a list.) Check any of the programs you have attended or studied in the last five years. Now, put a star next to the ones you are using on a regular basis with your students. Look over what you have marked to determine areas of expertise that you could share with colleagues and areas of need where you should be learning more. The areas of need could be included in your own professional development plan for future growth.

- Start collecting classroom strategies that you could use in all four of the components of the standards-based classroom. Write these on your classroom computer for quick access or on cards in a box or on a Rolodex so they are available to you at a moment's notice as you plan and teach. (See Resources, Sample 5, for instructions.)
- When you attend staff development sessions, be sure to have a blank page with you entitled "Ideas and Strategies I Can Use." As you listen to the information and observe the presenter's methods, jot down ideas and interactive learning strategies you can use with *your* students. This way you have separated out items you might want to implement so that you can find them quickly. You could put this page in your plan book for easy access. Once you have tried a strategy and like it, you can add it to the list of ideas you keep on your computer or elsewhere.
- Once a week, try at least one new strategy that will actively engage students in their own learning.
- Work together with other teachers to build trusting, collaborative relationships so that you can share ideas, critique student work, plan together, and support each other.

■ IDEAS FOR ADMINISTRATORS

To Focus on Standards

Since you are the leaders in schools and systems, you are essential in initiating the process of meeting standards. Without focused discussion, educators and school communities will waste time needed to work toward student success. As you no doubt already know, people will not do what needs to be done unless they feel the need to do it. If you tell them what the standards mean and demand that they do what is necessary, chances are good that real change won't be occurring in all the classrooms in your school. Teachers must see the need to change and say in their own words what needs to happen. So, your task is to facilitate this discussion. Following are some ideas to help you:

- In order to help people see the purpose for the standards—to help students succeed in the world once they leave school—get some good pictures of children of different ages. Make some color transparencies or put these on a computer to be projected at meetings as you discuss the origin of the standards movement and the intent of clarifying learning expectations for students.
- Facilitate the Big-Picture activity to help the group get a quick grasp of the standards' demands and impact on their schools. (See Resources, Samples 1 and 2, for instructions and a worksheet.) I have done this activity with many groups of students, parents, teachers, administrators, and community members, and it has always delivered the same type of information on the demands, differences, and implications of the standards. The responses you get to these three questions are the rationale for changes that will be needed.

- Be sure that what teachers are teaching is what is demanded in the standards at their grade level. If your state standards only give learning expectations for benchmark and testing years, have curriculum committees made up of teachers representing all grade levels create curriculum guides of essential content and competencies—the skills represented by the verbs in your standards—for teachers of all grades to use. Once these are created, be sure they are put into practice.
- Communicate in positive ways about standards with parents and your community at every opportunity: in school newsletters, in news releases, at parent meetings, at school board meetings.

To Facilitate and Support Standards-Based Classrooms

You will need to be an instructional leader for your teachers if you wish to have a school where classrooms have the components needed to achieve student success on standards. According to David Holdskom (cited in Checkley, 2000), assistant superintendent for research, development, and accountability in Durham (NC) public schools, it makes sense that, "As we redefine what teachers do as professionals, we must, by necessity, redefine how school leaders operate" (p. 1). If you are looking for new ways to lead and support teachers as they implement standards, following are some ideas for beginning the process:

- The four practices for a standards-based classroom can be used to unify staff development opportunities with school improvement plans. The current focus on research-based programs for school reform and test-driven professional development has helped, but for far too long, school staff development has been a scattered affair. Teachers went to whatever they chose with little guidance from or accountability to the school or district. Or the district brought someone in to present training to teachers in the deadly two hours after a full day of school. In both cases, the message was that this learning and new classroom practice was not really important, was not connected to the school improvement document that sat on shelves in offices throughout the district, was not expected when administrators observed classes, and, therefore, made no measurable difference in student learning. I agree with Richardson (2001), director of publications for the National Staff Development Council, that, "If the school is not integrating its school improvement plan and its staff development plans, it is not likely to move forward" (p. 1). Figure 0.2 shows the four practices for a standards-based classroom as the steel skeleton of a skyscraper. To take stock of how your school's staff development connects to these components, write in all the initiatives and staff development programs that teachers have been involved in or attended in the last five years. See which of the four girders they connect to, and see if your school or system has not addressed adequately one or more of these components. If so, that is an area you might want to target for the coming year in your school improvement plan and staff development offerings.

Figure 0.2   The Standards-Based Classroom and School

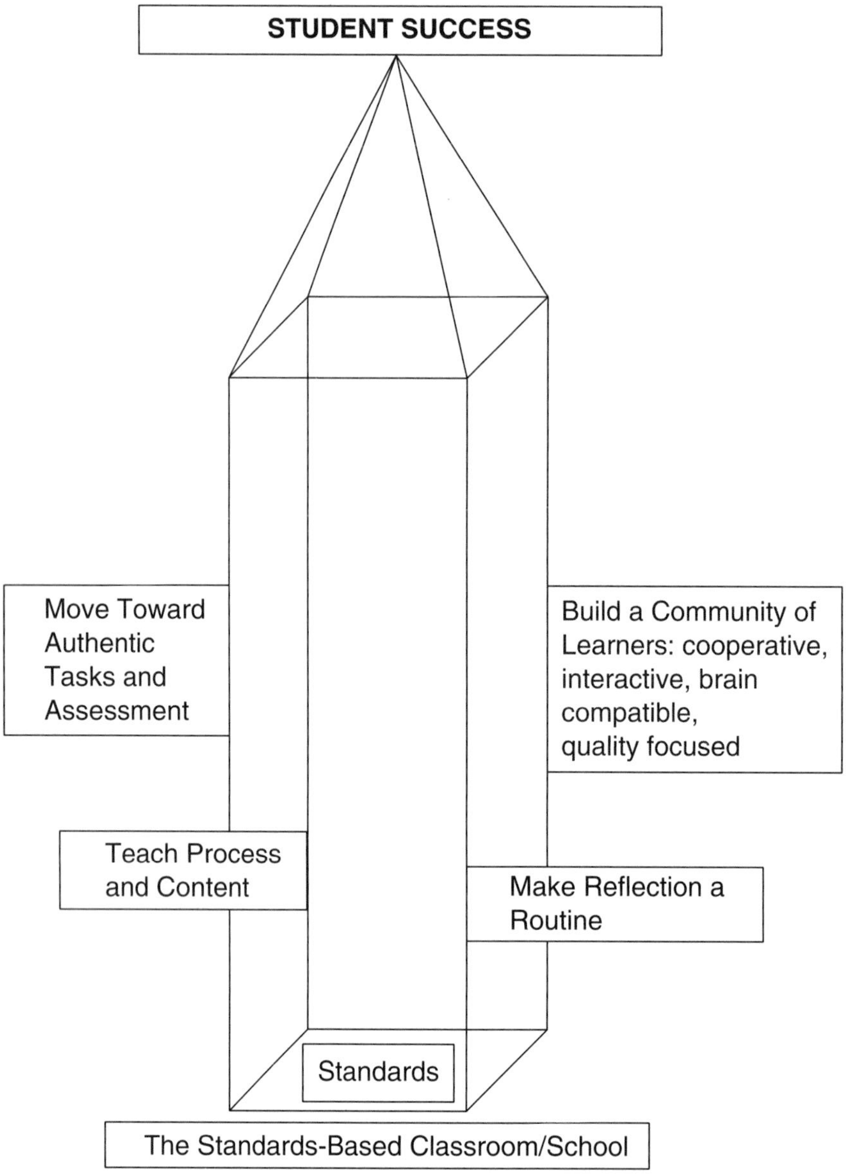

SOURCE: B. Benson, *Teaching in the Changing Classroom.*

- Consider the Staff Development Survey, Sample 3, in the Resources, which lists some training programs that relate to the four practices of a standards-based classroom. You might want to add other programs or titles that you know have been available in your area to the list. Then ask teachers to check the topics they have been exposed to or studied. Also ask them to put a star beside the ones that they use regularly in their classes. Collect these surveys and list the teachers who are using appropriate programs in their classes. This list can be distributed to all teachers and become an in-house resource for teachers to use to learn about practices they need. They might ask for help from these experts or go and see their classes in operation. If you have areas that are not in practice, these are the topics that your teachers need to investigate and that should be offered as staff development sessions in your school or district.

- Help your staff make use of the in-house experts the survey identifies. If teachers want to visit classes, make that possible. If grade-level or content-area groups want to meet and discuss strategies, help them arrange for time in the school day and for credit for this work. If there is schoolwide interest in one particular topic, make arrangements for your experts to offer professional development sessions and compensate them in some way.
- Give the survey forms back to the teachers so that they can use them to set professional development goals addressing areas where they need more information.
- Once you have determined areas of need in your school and district, create staff development request-and-reflection forms for teachers to use when they wish to attend learning opportunities outside the district (see Resources, Sample 4).
- Be sure to maximize the impact of any professional development that is sponsored by the school or district or to which teachers are sent (see Box 0.6). Remember, the purpose of teacher learning is to impact and improve student learning.
- Take time in all faculty meetings to share and discuss articles or strategies that address targeted areas of need. If the announcements could be placed on the agenda, and everyone was asked to read

---

Box 0.6

How to Maximize the Impact of Professional Development: Getting the Biggest Bang for Your Buck

- Have clear district and school goals for improving student learning and be sure the professional development activities are aligned with these goals.
- Have specific goals for teachers who attend staff development and be sure teachers know what these expectations are.
- Attend sessions with your teachers so you will know what they may be trying in their classes and can support their efforts.
- Send teachers to professional development sessions in teams to improve the chance they will implement new strategies in their classes and to give them a support system to help them sustain any new practices.
- Have a form for teachers to request release or support for professional development activities they wish to attend on their own.
- Create a reflection sheet that teachers must complete after they have attended professional development. This sheet should require that teachers reflect on their learning in sessions they attend, on how they plan to use their new ideas with students, and on the impact of the new methods on student learning.
- Have teachers share their information with colleagues.

them ahead of time and then sign in to indicate that they had done so, it would be easier to provide time for professional discussions. Teachers could have been given articles in advance so small group discussions could be organized in the staff meeting. Teachers could also take turns bringing material or classroom strategies to share.

- Help interested faculty start professional study and discussion groups to address areas they wish to learn more about. Allot time in the school calendar for these gatherings and attend them if asked. Allow teachers who take part in a study and discussion group to have that count as professional development activity to address their own professional development plans and requirements. Ask these groups to share with the whole faculty what they are learning and doing differently in their classrooms as a result.

- Go through the Snapshots of a Standards-Based Classroom (Table 0.2), and check the ones that describe the majority of classrooms you see in your own school. Then put stars beside the ones that you would really like to see more of when you visit teachers' rooms. The ones you have starred can be the focus of goal setting for your school or individual teachers. Once you have selected areas that need improvement, you can offer information or staff development activities to address these. You can also begin to include these items in conversations with teachers after observation visits.

- As the instructional leader, you will need to have a repertoire of classroom strategies that address the four components of classrooms you want in your building. You will need these strategies so you can model them in staff meetings and share them with teachers who need to change how they teach and assess student learning. Start collecting good strategies as you continue to read this book, observe teachers, do other professional reading, and attend meetings and professional development sessions. Keep a running list handy when you are planning meetings with staff, observing teachers, and conferencing with teachers (see Resources, Sample 5).

- Model classroom strategies in meetings you conduct. Teachers are more likely to use a new method if they have experienced it themselves and know how it will work. If they see you use a strategy to enhance the interaction of a faculty meeting, they will know that you understand how that strategy might look in the classroom. They will have more confidence to try it and know that you will understand what is going on if you see it in their classrooms.

- Start a support group to help you implement these ideas in your school. Find other administrators who are working to align the classrooms in their schools with standards, and plan to meet together regularly to problem solve and celebrate successes. Depending on where your school is at the beginning of this process, you may need to make some drastic changes, and you will need a support group of your own to help you get the job done.

1

Creating a Community of Learners

First, what do I mean by a community of learners? A community of learners is a group of people who support each other in their collective and individual learning. They are cooperative and can work productively together. Individually, they are motivated and strive to do quality work. Since they know they are going to be encouraged to take risks and be supported if they do not succeed the first time they try something new, they challenge themselves, and they view mistakes as learning experiences, which will make their later attempts successful. A community of learners can include all levels of learners, because everyone is learning, not competing. And, best of all, a true classroom community of learners allows the teacher to learn as well as the students. Such a classroom will be absolutely necessary if all students are to learn what the standards demand, because teachers alone cannot possibly meet all the needs of all learners. Teachers need the supportive community of students helping each other succeed.

WHY DO I NEED A COMMUNITY OF LEARNERS IN MY CLASSROOM? ■

There is really no secret to getting a community of learners in the classroom. It has to do with how we as teachers conduct our classes. We are the ones who set up the conditions that will create and support the community we need to help students meet standards. Wong and Wong (1991), in their book for new teachers, define classroom management as "all of the things that a teacher does to organize students, space, time, and materials so that instruction in content and student learning can take place" (p. 84). I would like to add that learning is enhanced even more when classroom management is not just skill in the efficient manipulation of resources, space, and people but is also centered on creating a supportive environment for learning.

Recent brain research by many neuroscientists and educators supports the need for a nonthreatening place to learn. Unfortunately, the traditional classroom was often based on stress and fear of punishment. Sylwester (2000), one expert in how the brain learns, states that a classroom based on fear goes against what we now know about what a brain needs to learn well. He maintains, "To create a chronically stressful school environment to increase learning is thus biologically both counterproductive and irresponsible" (p. 41). A more productive learning place than the one operating on fear and stress is one where all learners feel challenged but encouraged and confident that they can succeed if they work at it.

An added benefit of this kind of classroom environment is that it is an enjoyable place for the students and the teacher. I saw a wonderful example of this as I visited in a first-grade classroom one morning. As students entered for the day, they said hello to the teacher and went directly to their cubbies to put away their coats and lunches and get out what they were to begin working on that day. They spoke to each other and drifted a little bit before settling into their seats to begin the day's work. There was no tension or need for the teacher to yell, because everyone was settled within five minutes of the bell to start class. The teacher had time to take roll and speak to parents and students as they came into the room. The environment was orderly, relaxed, and productive. It reminded me of an office where workers come in every morning, get a cup of coffee, and, after greeting colleagues, settle in to work. It was a community of six-year-old learners who knew why they were there and were ready to go about the business of learning. What teacher wouldn't enjoy this type of class?

In recent years, as we have tried to determine what must be done to raise the learning curve for students, researchers have documented the impact of the classroom environment on student success. For example, Marzano et al. (1992) say that students' attitudes about learning, which are strongly influenced by the classroom environment, are the first dimension that surrounds all others (p. 5; see Box 1.1). If a student does not have a positive attitude about the possibility of learning all the required content, the chances of success are slim.

■ THE HELPLESS AND THE HOPELESS STUDENTS

Unfortunately, too many of our students do not have the positive attitudes toward school and learning that are necessary to successfully meet standards. Instead, they feel helpless and hopeless when they enter a classroom, and we must do something to help students believe that they can succeed before we can teach them anything. This came home to me when one of my at-risk high school students announced that I couldn't teach the class strategies for "doing school" because there weren't any. He said that

Box 1.1

In Order to Learn, Students Must

- Feel accepted in the classroom
- See the classroom as physically and emotionally pleasant
- Perceive the classroom as orderly
- View the tasks as valuable and relevant
- Believe they have the ability to do the tasks
- Understand clearly what they are expected to learn and do

SOURCE: Adapted from R. Marzano et al. (1992, pp. 18–30).

whether or not you could do it was "gunetic" (genetic). He said that his mama didn't graduate from high school, his daddy didn't graduate from high school, and the longer he stayed the worse school got. He also observed that there were "some kids who already knew how to do everything when they got here."

I realized that before I could really help him, I had to deal with his hopelessness, but at least we had made a first step. He felt comfortable enough to let me know how he viewed his chances. Now I had a basis for working with him, and the environment I established in the classroom was obviously going to be crucial in creating a supportive place for him to risk trying school one more time.

No doubt readers can remember a pleasant or unpleasant personal experience in a classroom and how it colored the way they viewed their ability to learn or their interest in the content being taught at the time (see Box 1.2 for one of my school memories). Feeling the power of these experiences on our own learning, it becomes obvious that to succeed at difficult school tasks and learn the increasingly more sophisticated content demanded by state standards, students need a safe, supportive place. They are not the only ones. Teachers and administrators are also learning new roles and struggling with new accountability requirements. Everyone within the school walls will need a safe place to risk, to make mistakes, and to grow. A true community of learners who are working together toward meeting standards can create just such a place.

The type of classroom that encourages student involvement, a necessary component for teaching students the competency skills in all content areas of the standards, is one where *students are taught how and expected to be self-directed, interactive, cooperative, and focused on quality.* It is a place where teachers use all the best information about how the developing brain learns so they can create lessons that work with the brains in the room instead of against them. We already have a lot of information about how to create this type of community in a classroom. Over the last 20 years, many educators have put forth methods for involving students in their own learning and offered teachers excellent strategies for creating student-centered lessons. I will, therefore, discuss each facet of the community of learners only briefly and encourage my readers to pursue the many excellent resources available to gather additional ideas for how to make this happen in their own classrooms.

Box 1.2

Algebra Class Memory

The Impact of a Class Environment on Learning

One of my memorable school moments occurred when I was in eighth grade, and my family moved from Virginia to a suburb of Boston. The school year had already started, and being a rather shy 14-year-old, I was very unhappy about going into a new school.

On my first day as the new kid in school, I entered algebra class and took the seat the teacher assigned me without comment. Later in the hour, he called on me to give an answer for a problem on the board. I prefaced my answer with, "Yes, sir," as my southern parents had taught me.

Before I could get any further, the teacher spent 5 minutes berating me for being "smart" with him. He said he did not allow that kind of sarcasm in his class and wanted me to know right off the bat that I would be in trouble if I didn't straighten up. I have rarely been as embarrassed as I was that day. I wanted to crawl in a hole and disappear.

From that moment on, whenever I went into his or any other math class, I was terrified. I tried to make myself small and never volunteered an answer. For all practical purposes, my learning in mathematics stopped in eighth grade. To this day, I become anxious and confused when I am faced with multiple numbers on a page. As an adult, I have come to understand that it probably isn't because I am stupid and could not have learned math. It is, instead, a direct result of associating math with personal humiliation and fear.

Barbara Benson

■ HELP STUDENTS BECOME SELF-DIRECTED LEARNERS

If I ask any group of teachers what they would wish for in their classes, one thing they will definitely say is, "I would love to have a class full of responsible and motivated students!" What they are asking for is a class of self-directed learners who have goals and are driven to achieve them, who are curious about the world and want to learn, who take responsibility for their own actions and work to improve both how they work and the products they produce. This description fits perfect students and adult lifelong learners. This is also the type of students we must have if we are to teach them the complex content required in the standards.

What would a classroom of self-directed learners be like? One spring, as my at-risk high school students were working to finish a major class project, the creation of a video on local environmental issues, which they wanted placed in all the county elementary school libraries, I got a real glimpse of what a group of motivated and responsible students can be like. I had to be out of school for a day as we were pressing to finish the project. When I returned, the substitute teacher told me a fascinating and remarkable story. She reported that when the students arrived for first-period class, they told her that she could go to the teachers' lounge and have a cup of coffee because they didn't really need her. They said they all had their jobs for the day and would be busy.

She knew a lot of these students and, as any good substitute should be, was very skeptical, to say the least. She said she did step out into the hall to see what would happen, and, to her amazement, every one of the 26 students in the class got busy! Some were working in groups writing the script and planning the camera shoots while others were working alone on their particular tasks for the day. She didn't go get that coffee, but she said they really didn't need her much during that class period.

I was delighted to hear how they had behaved and really gave some thought as to why these students, who were some of the worst discipline problems in the school, would have been so focused on getting their work done that they didn't require supervision. First, they were motivated because they were working to produce something they felt was relevant and important to their community. Second, they were responsible to the group for getting their part of the project done well, and they were rising to my expectations that they do quality work. Finally, we had spent a lot of the year working toward this type of task. They had other experiences throughout the year to prepare them for working independently and in collaborative groups. They had become a true community of self-directed learners and, because of that, they were succeeding at a very complex task designed to meet a number of our language arts standards.

Even though the ideal is that students can work on their own, with or without the teacher standing over them, all teachers know that when the school year begins, few students can do this. In fact, depending on how they have worked during the year and what the teacher has taught and expected, they still may be totally passive and dependent students in June. If a teacher really has not expected students to be self-directed and has not worked to give them the skills and experience to become independent, chances are good they will be satisfied to sit back and let the teacher do all the work and carry all the responsibility. Such passive students will not have learned what is necessary to meet standards that require application of content in complex situations.

Goal Setting as a Beginning

So the challenge becomes how to help develop self-directed students. Teachers should start the year by having students reflect on their role as learners and set goals for their own learning. (See Table 1.1 and, in Resources, Sample 6, for a sample Goal Card.) On the first day of school, students should be asked to discuss or write about who they are and why they are in school. Even if the responses are initially rather shallow, it will be clear to students from day one that the teacher regards them as individuals and is expecting them to take responsibility for their own learning. Even the youngest students can express who they are and why they have come to school. They can draw self-portraits if they are unable to write, and they can dictate information to accompany their pictures.

In addition to telling who they are, students should be asked to set a goal and give at least one strategy they will use to reach their goal. When teachers first ask students to set goals, they will need to discuss the nature

Table 1.1   Instructions for Having Students Create Goal Cards

- For Primary Students
  Ask them to draw a self-portrait and then script what they say about their goals or discuss these as a group.
- For Elementary and Middle School Students
  Create a goal sheet for them and ask them to fill it out.
- For High School Students
  On the first day of school, give all students large index cards for name tents. Have them fold the cards horizontally and write their names on both sides of their tent. They should place the tent in front of them on their desks. At the end of each class, take up the name tents. You can use them to learn students' names by returning each tent to the proper student when they return to class the next time. Some time during the first week, ask students to open their tents and answer the following questions inside: Who are you and why are you here? What are your goals for this class, month, week? What strategies can you use to meet your goals?

of realistic goals and strategies, because this process will be new to most students. Many students might initially set unrealistic goals and thus fail to meet them. For example, one six-year-old told her teacher on the first day of school that she was there "to learn to read—today!"

For elementary, middle school, and immature secondary students, the goals should be short term. This way, students and teachers can monitor these goals regularly and adjust strategies if necessary. Also, the students may see some early success and be encouraged to try harder, like one middle school student who set a goal of passing the next class test. His strategy was to find his long-lost textbook. When he took the next test, he did raise his score from a low 40% to a mid 60%. He had not yet reached his goal of passing a test, but he had made quite a leap and was close. When the teacher asked if he had found his book, he said yes and then went on to add that he had been thinking about what he would do next. His next strategy was to know what day the teacher was giving the next test.

As you see from this example, many students really do not know how to "do school" and find it almost impossible to be self-directed about their learning. But, as this young man illustrates, when they get a little success as a result of their own effort to use learning strategies, they begin to look for other strategies and feel more hopeful about their chances to reach their goals. Now, like the student above, they are on the way to becoming self-directed learners.

Getting Honest Goals and Real Strategies

Another point to be aware of is that when a teacher first asks students for this type of information, students usually say what the teacher wants to hear rather than really think for themselves and verbalize personal goals. As an example, the first time I asked a group of high school seniors to do this, almost all of them said their goal was to get an A in the class and their strategy was to "study real hard."

Since this was an at-risk class, I knew they had not really given me their goals. I returned their goals and strategies to them the next day and asked them to be honest about what they would like to achieve. After one brave soul admitted that her goal was to get a D, others agreed. I had them write that goal down, and then we brainstormed strategies for getting a D. As you would expect, they listed the same things I might have said to them: come to class, listen, do homework, pass tests, and so on. Now, however, they wrote down at least one of the strategies they came up with and were much more likely to use it than if I had told them what to do. Naturally, I wanted them to want more than a D, but I knew that when I first ask students to be honest about what they want and will do to ensure they meet their goals, I have to take them where they are.

This class was full of the helpless and hopeless, and they needed several things before they could succeed academically. They needed to know that I respected them enough to expect them to be responsible for their own learning. They needed to set some realistic goals for themselves and understand that goals are no good without practical strategies to reach them. Finally, they needed some success before they would ever believe that they could do better than they had always done, a D. So I had to take the first honest goals and work to raise their expectations for themselves as the year progressed. We repeated the process of goal setting, monitoring progress, adjusting or adding strategies, and celebrating success throughout the year. I am happy to report that by June, almost all the students had raised their expectations for themselves, and 25 students in that class of 27 achieved grades above D.

Having students introduce themselves by sharing who they are and why they have come to school and asking them set goals and identify strategies for reaching these goals is just the beginning of developing self-directed learners. Helping students see themselves as in control of their own learning and success is a long, complex process that spans many years and requires multiple strategies and much patience. Many of the other components of the standards-based classroom will contribute to the development of independent learners who are confident and motivated, the type of student who can learn anything and is ready to tackle the demands of the challenging content standards.

HAVE AN INTERACTIVE CLASSROOM   ■

An interactive classroom is a place where students talk with each other and where students and the teacher communicate on a regular basis. Sizer (1999), founder of the Coalition of Essential Schools and an expert on secondary education, says, "We cannot teach students well if we do not know them well. At its heart, personalized learning requires profound shifts in our thinking about education and schooling"(p. 6). I agree wholeheartedly and feel that this statement really captures the essence of what I mean by an interactive classroom—one where the teacher knows the students well. It is only then that the teacher can individualize instruction and support to help all students learn the enormous amount of content being required in state standards.

Just knowing the students well, especially in secondary classrooms, would make a world of difference in how students view themselves as learners. One problem in making this happen is the still-common practice of having a middle or high school teacher working with over 100 students per day. It is not only challenging but also virtually impossible for one teacher to have substantive interactions with this many students in a day. Middle schools that use the middle school model do have students in smaller groups for learning. Also, some high schools, especially those following the Gates model, are attempting to help with this situation by creating smaller schools, stressing relationships, and setting up structures like advisory or CREW, a group of 7 to 10 students (Farrell, 2000), which allow the students to get to know each other, build relationships with a small, supportive group of students, and have an adult mentor who will accompany them through the difficult high school years.

CREW is a particular structure used in Expeditionary Learning Schools K–12 based on the ideas of Kurt Hahn, founder of Outward Bound. Emily Cousins supports the notion of classroom community by explaining that Expeditionary Learning Schools focus "on the architecture of community because we believe that learning happens best in an atmosphere of trust and sustained caring" (1998, p. 21). She admits, however, that building this community is not easy. I agree that even in a school that has specific time allotted for small groups such as CREW, classroom teachers will still need multiple strategies for creating community in their classes, for finding out where students are at the beginning of new learning, what they are learning along the way, and what difficulties they may be having.

Teacher and Student Interaction

There are many strategies for gathering information about what students have learned, but we often neglect the type of conversations with students in which we want to know what they know at the beginning of the learning and what they are understanding or questioning as the learning progresses. The goal-setting strategy mentioned earlier can give the first insight into the individual student and offer the first conversations between the teacher and students about learning.

Other strategies can let students talk about what they already know or think they know about a topic that is going to be studied in class. For example, K–W–L (What I know–What I want to know–What I learned) (Ogle, 1986), a strategy often used in elementary and middle school classrooms, is one strategy to get information from students before the teaching begins. I am including it here to illustrate the point that we already have a lot of good strategies we can use to help students meet standards. K–W–L, when used appropriately, is a good interactive method for finding out what prior knowledge students have on a subject, and, unfortunately, many secondary teachers may not be aware of the strategy or the fact that they could use it effectively in a high school class (see Box 1.3). If students create their own "know" list, or put a group list on flip-chart paper, at least the teacher now has some information to go on when planning lessons. The questions that students want to know the answers to can also be the lead-in to students accessing information about the topic on their own. For instructions on how to do K–W–L and how some teachers have adapted the strategy, see the Web site Instructional Strategies on Line, http://olc.spsd.sk.ca/DE/PD/instr/strats/kwl/ (retrieved February 9, 2008).

Box 1.3

K-W-L

1. To do a K-W-L, make a chart or handout that has three columns with headings: "What I Know," "What I Want to Know," and "What I Have Learned."

2. Ask students to brainstorm what they know about the topic and write their responses in that column. As the students work through the unit of work, be sure to keep their K-W-L chart posted or handy so it can be referred to easily. If some of the things students think they know are in error, write them on the list anyway, and as soon as that information is covered in the unit, have students go back and amend their original information to correct any errors.

3. Based on what they know, ask students to list things they would like to know. These could be in the form of questions. Use these questions to begin the study of the topic. Students can be responsible for finding the information for specific questions as the class goes through the unit work.

4. As the students go through the unit or after they have finished, have them fill in the third column listing the things they have learned. At the end of the work, the whole K-W-L could be used to sum up the unit and review for the test.

A personalized graphic organizer for prior knowledge, learning, and questions generated during and after a unit of study might be even more useful in helping a teacher communicate with individual students. Activities like an Into-Through-and-Beyond learning map are good for this purpose (see Box 1.4). If students have never used strategies like these, it will be essential for the teacher to model how they would work and teach students to use them well. Otherwise, as Kane (2007, p. 104) confirms, "you can imagine that seventh or eighth graders, when asked by a teacher or textbook what they want to learn about almost any topic . . . might feel inclined to answer, 'Nothing.'"

Encourage Questions

Another strategy for conversing with students is using Think Pads to encourage them to ask questions about the content being studied (see Box 1.5 on page 32). We know from observation in the classroom that by about Grade 6, many students stop asking questions because of peer pressure or because they have made the decision that they are dumb, and it won't help anyway. Interestingly, many academically gifted students stop asking questions because they think they will be the only ones in the class who don't know the answer. Since standards require critical thinking skills such as being able to ask "pertinent questions" (Massachusetts Department of Education, 1994) and then pursue answers, it is imperative that teachers encourage questions from students. The North Carolina

Box 1.4

Into-Through-and-Beyond

This is a great strategy for accessing prior knowledge, asking questions, recording learning, connecting ideas, and applying content knowledge.

Into

1. Ask student to draw four to six circles on a blank piece of paper. The number of circles can vary depending on the material you will be working with and the length or complexity of the segment of content to be studied. Be sure to tell students to make the circles large enough to write something in but not so large that they fill the whole page, since they will be adding squares and triangles later.

2. Tell students to write what they know about the topic in the circles. If they don't know very much about the topic, they can write questions in the circles. Remind them that this is not a test and that you have no correct answers that you are looking for. If you plan to collect these papers when students are done, do not grade them for the quality of the answers, but you can give students credit for completing the assignment.

3. It is a good idea to have a look at these papers to get a sense of where students are and what they already know as you begin the new material. If there are errors in the information students give you, do not mark them. The students will be making their own corrections as you go through the unit of study. Once you have looked at them, you can return them to students, but tell the students that they will need the papers again about halfway through the unit of study. If you have any fear that students may lose their papers, take them up and save them for later.

Through

1. Approximately halfway through the material students are learning, ask them to put four to six rectangles on their Into-Through-Beyond paper. These shapes should be large enough to write in but not so large that they fill the space.

2. Before students write anything in the rectangles, they should reread what they put in their circles to see if they need to make any amendments to the information. Often what students think they know about a topic is incorrect, and this step gives students a chance to self-assess and fix any misconceptions. If students had questions and now have the answers, they should write those in the circle where the question appeared.

3. Have students write what they have learned so far inside the rectangles. They can also write any new questions they now have in the rectangles.

4. Ask students to put their papers away until later, or collect them and save them for your students until you are ready to finish the activity. Again, it is useful for you to look over these papers to see if students are getting the key concepts and ideas from the material you are teaching. If not, you can adjust instructional strategies at this point.

Beyond

1. When the unit of study is over, have students take out their sheets and look over what they wrote in the rectangles and any questions they had not answered in the circles. They can now amend any errors they made and supply answers to the questions they had.

2. Now students should add four to six triangles to their page. Keep the number of shapes the same as you move through the process. So if you had students start with five circles, they should have five rectangles and five triangles. Inside of the triangles, they should write *any* new information they have learned since the rectangles, any new questions they now have, and ways they might use the information they have gained.

3. After filling in the triangles, students could be asked to draw lines connecting any of the shapes that contain related information. For example, if they had a question in a circle and the answer is in a triangle, they could connect these two. If they do this, they will have created their own web of what they have learned. This personal-learning graphic organizer can now be used as a study guide for tests on the material, as a basis for discussing what they have learned, and as evidence of their participation in the class learning activities.

Special Note: In early elementary classrooms where students do not yet know how to write, this activity can be done as a class with the teacher recording student responses on large flip chart paper.

SOURCE: Adapted from S. Rogers, J. Ludington, & S. Graham (1997, p. 173).

Department of Public Instruction (1999) even specifies that, "The teacher will facilitate the development of information acquisition skills as students use questioning skills" (p. 20). Therefore, having strategies that encourage students to ask questions is necessary in a standards-based classroom.

One no-risk way to encourage questions and have other means of interacting with students is, then, to give each of them a Think Pad—a small pad of paper to use to jot down questions during the class. They should be instructed to keep the question in front of them until there is a good time to ask it. Often, they will find the answer as the class progresses, and whether they do or not, they will be paying more attention because they have something they want to know.

If students' questions are not answered in class, they should be told to put their names on the paper and give it to the teacher as they leave. This will allow the teacher to write a response and return the paper to the

Box 1.5

Think Pads

- Have a small pad of paper on each student's desk or table.
- Tell students to write their questions on their pad as the class progresses.
- If they do not get an answer during class, ask them to sign the paper and give it to you on the way out.
- Respond to questions and return, or date and save questions to document active participation.

The same pads, made from cut and stapled recycled paper, can be used

- For students to write responses the teacher will circulate and check
- For students to signal whether or not they understand
- For students to write a ticket in or out of the door
- For students to record responses they will share with others

This strategy is appropriate for third-grade students and up who can write. Students who cannot write can have colored squares of paper to hold up to indicate they understand and are ready to move on. For example, red cards might mean, "Stop, I'm confused." Green cards mean, "I understand. I'm ready to move on." And, yellow cards mean, "Slow down. I have a question." Or students could have cards with different symbols: a smiley face to indicate, "I understand and am ready to move on," and a question mark to show, "Wait. I have a question."

SOURCE: Adapted from High Success Network. (1994, April). Prompt Cards. *The High Success Connection, 2,* 5–6.

student at the beginning of the next class. The questions and responses from the teacher, whether they are written or verbal, can really open up the lines of communication and give the teacher a lot of insight into whether or not students understand the content being taught.

Sometimes, teachers may get a number of similar questions on one day. This tells them to begin class there on the next day because the students didn't hear or understand the information. There are several added bonuses to this strategy. One is that a student who would not ask questions in class will realize that the teacher does want questions and will not be judgmental, and therefore the student may begin to ask questions during class. Another is that this can be used to discourage blurters, those students who yell out questions constantly. The teacher can ask them to write the questions down to be answered later, assuring them that they will get an answer. In addition to recording questions, these Think Pads can be used for communication between students and teachers in many other ways as well.

All these interactive strategies help students develop skills the standards require and help teachers plan effective lessons to teach standards. They also give teachers information about whether or not students understand the concepts being taught so that specific re-teaching or remediation can occur if necessary.

Students Interacting With Each Other

In an interactive classroom, students should also be talking to each other, a lot. This goes against the grain of the traditional classroom, where students spent most of their time listening to the teacher do the talking and were severely chastised for talking to each other. Meier (1995), a master teacher, administrator, and innovator who founded and for many years led Central Park East Secondary School in New York City, says, "Teaching is not talking and learning is not listening: instead, it may be in fact that teaching is mostly listening and learning is mostly talking" (p. xi). In my own classes, I have observed that students retain more content information not when I am talking about it but when they are actively engaged in talking, discussing content, and doing something with it. If teachers ask themselves when they really learned the content they teach, they will admit that it wasn't in "teacher school." It was when they had to teach the information to their own classes. At that point, they had to say it and do it themselves, and that was how they made meaning and remembered the information.

Therefore, if we want students to remember the content so that they can recall it for state tests at the end of the year, they need to be talking about it as much as possible. We know they are not likely to leave the classroom and organize discussion groups about algebra, the exploration of the American West, or Willa Cather's *My Antonia,* so we had better have them talking about the required content while they are in class.

To make these discussions efficient and effective, teachers need a lot of strategies for student interactions, and they will have to train students to use discussion time productively. The first step is to inform the students about why they need to talk about what they are learning. Share research and anecdotal proof about how the brain processes information when we have to put it into our own words. Ask students how they learn and remember best. Many will undoubtedly say they need to talk about it or listen to peers. If students understand the purpose and value of the discussion time, they are more likely to stay on task.

Organize the Talking Time With Discussion Appointments

Second, teachers will need to train students and develop some routines for discussion. One method that is versatile and can be used at *any* grade level is to have students sign up for discussion appointments with each other. (See Box 1.6 for instructions, and Resources, Sample 7, for a model of an appointment sheet for students discussing the solar system or related topics.) Once appointments for discussions are set, the teacher can ask students to meet with one another for their appointments for various types of conversations about content. (See Box 1.7 for ideas.) Having a specific classmate to talk to helps make the process more efficient for students. Every teacher has seen class members waste a lot of time just finding a person or small group to work with on a task, and knows that there is no time to waste if the class is going to get through all the information they need to learn in a year.

In a true community of learners, any one individual can work productively with any of the others. This should always be a goal for a class,

Box 1.6

Instructions for Discussion Appointments

1. Create a discussion appointment sheet with two to five appointments on it. Be sure that you use a visual that is related to the important content you are teaching at the time. For example, an elementary teacher could use a calendar or colored geometric shapes. Determine the number of appointments by how long you want to use the same sheet and how experienced your students are in moving and working together.

2. Give students the sheet and tell them they will have a set amount of time to sign up, with one person per appointment. Tell them to write on their sheets in the correct place the name of the person with whom they have the appointment.

3. Also ask them to come to you if they cannot find a person with whom to have an appointment for one of their slots. If you have an uneven number of students, one student at each appointment will not be able to get a partner. That will be okay, because as you use these appointments over time, some students will be absent, others will have lost their sheets, and some will come into class having missed the sign-up time. When students don't have an appointment, if they come to you, you can match them with others in the same situation, or you can ask them to join a pair and form a committee of three. This process is usually very efficient, and everyone can begin their work quickly.

Box 1.7

Students Can Use Discussion Appointments to

- Develop questions to ask the teacher
- Analyze a problem
- Test each other
- Respond to a teacher's question
- Compare notes taken in class
- Quiz another pair
- Review for a test
- Discuss a short, written document
- Interview each other
- Critique or edit each other's work
- Question each other about reading assignments or lecture information
- Recap a lesson or class session
- Read a passage together

SOURCE: Adapted from unpublished work by B. Benson with C. Scearce of Enlightening Enterprises.

because it will increase the amount of support the group can offer and decrease the need for the teacher to supply everyone with the information and help they might need on a given assignment. Using Discussion Appointments mixes students from different class cliques and increases the probability that students will get to know each other and be willing to work with anyone in the classroom on standards-based assignments by the end of the year.

Since there are lots of ways to use these Discussion Appointments as a class works on content objectives, it is important to give students a conversation task that is appropriate to their age and experience. Students will need practice and time to learn how to stay on task and be efficient. So, if it does not work exactly the way a teacher hoped the first time, he should not give up, but should keep using the strategy on a regular basis until the students are accustomed to what they must do. If teachers expect students to get better at these short conversations, and keep the discussions focused and timed, students will become efficient at moving and talking about what the teacher wants them to discuss—content required in the standards being taught.

A particularly interesting thing often happens when the strategy works and all the students are on task as they meet with their partners. The teacher may feel uneasy because she has nothing to do. If she is particularly conscientious, she feels as if she is not earning her money, not teaching. At this point, she might begin talking to some of the kids and literally take them off task. I had to warn my students that I might do this so that they could just gently tell me to leave them alone to do their work! While students discuss, the teacher can circulate and be sure students are on the right track as they complete tasks and can also meet with individual students who may need special attention.

HELPING STUDENTS WORK COOPERATIVELY   ■

In the world beyond school, working productively in teams is a basic skill necessary for success. Many state and local standards even include teamwork in the skills students need to develop. We also know that cooperative groups are a powerful tool for enhancing learning and retention of content (see Box 1.8). As Darling-Hammond (1997), codirector of the National Center for Restructuring Education, Schools, and Teaching at Teachers College, Columbia University, states, "Learning-centered classrooms feature student talk and collective action" (p. 129). For these reasons, the teacher must teach cooperative work skills and give students practice in working productively together.

There are many long-established programs to help teachers learn *ways* to use and manage cooperative groups, but implementation has still been uneven. There are still far too many teachers who do not use student groups in their classrooms, who do not realize that cooperative skills must be taught and practiced, or who continue to believe that having students work together is inefficient at best and cheating at worst. If a school wishes to implement standards, however, classrooms should be places where students often work together and teachers are good at facilitating such work.

Box 1.8

Why Work in Groups?

- People in groups can lend their strengths to other people in their areas of weakness.
- Some students need other students to explain the work; they didn't get it when the teacher explained it.
- Working in groups is common in the working world because businesses have learned that problems can be more creatively solved in this way.
- People working together can solve a problem they couldn't solve individually because the process of sharing ideas will spark the solution.
- If you teach others—you will learn it yourself!

SOURCE: California Model Technology High School, Alhambra, California.

I am offering some basic strategies to help teachers get started, but I suggest that they search for additional information, training, and strategies to increase their own ability to manage this type of student work well.

■ STRATEGIES FOR GROUP WORK IN A COMMUNITY OF LEARNERS

- Have students generate guidelines for group work.
- Create a generic task sheet (see Resources, Sample 8, for a model) students can use to organize work, record the task answer or results, assess their effectiveness and efficiency as a group, and make plans for improvement the next time they work together.
- Train students in group strategies by using tasks outside your content area (example: The Mystery Box, Box 1.9).
- Assign students specific jobs in their group, such as Liaison (contact person between the group and the teacher), Recorder (writes the group's responses), Reporter (shares group's responses with the class), Bouncer (keeps the group on task and on time), Supply Officer (gathers whatever the group needs to work), and Morale Officer (keeps everyone pleasant and positive), and insist that they rotate jobs with each task. Be careful, however, that students do not become so focused on the roles that they do not really engage in the good conversations and collaboration needed for productive group work.
- After some initial training in home groups, vary the makeup of groups regularly to get students used to working with everyone in the class. If a group has problems working well together and can't solve them, however, you may need to act as mediator.
- Set up various organized and efficient ways to group students.
- Instead of always using the group process to get a group answer or product that will give a group grade, use the process more often to help all students learn more content so that when they have individual, graded assignments they will do better.

Box 1.9

The Mystery Box

- Create boxes—one for each group of four students—that have seven items in them and are then wrapped tightly with duct tape so students cannot open them.
- Number the boxes and record on a sheet of paper what is in each box.
- Give each group of students a task sheet and a box. They have 5 to 10 minutes to brainstorm everything they think might be in the box and then select the seven most likely items. They can do this work on the back of the task sheet. Since this is a noncontent activity to teach cooperative skills, the items are not connected to any particular content or topic. Students are limited only by their imaginations and what could possibly fit in the box, weigh what the box weighs, and make the noises they hear when they shake the box.
- Then they must complete the task sheet before you reveal what is in each box.
- *Everyone* needs to understand that the purpose of this activity is not to win by guessing the most items but to work well together.

- When there will be an important graded product, if possible, allow students to decide whether to work alone or in groups. If they choose a group, require the group to submit a plan stating what each member will do and how they will document their work.
- Have individual students regularly assess their own performance in group situations, and designate strategies they will use for improvement.
- Do not encourage competition between groups within your class.
- Always set a time limit for group work. Set it for less time than you think the task will take. Check with the groups when the time is up, and give a few more minutes if needed.

Since state standards include ideas that suggest students should study and work effectively both independently and in groups, teaching cooperative skills is teaching to the standards, no matter what content area is being studied. In standards-based classrooms, teachers are helping students develop cooperative working skills and giving students many opportunities to interact with each other.

A QUALITY FOCUS ■

Higher standards are requiring that everyone involved in schools strives to improve the quality of student learning and performance. For teachers attempting to get students to meet higher standards, it makes sense to use some of the ideas of Dr. W. Edwards Deming, the international expert on quality control, creating quality processes, and improving the quality of results. Although his work is not the most recent on quality in education, his ideas are the basis for current authors such as Bonstingl (2001), an internationally recognized expert on quality, who applies quality philosophy to running schools. I am therefore returning to the source on quality and using Dr. Deming's theories (cited in Aguayo, 1990) as they apply not just to whole school organization but also to the day-to-day function of individual classrooms.

Applying the concepts of improving quality in the work world to classrooms is very appropriate as we face the challenge of improving student motivation and learning. Dr. Deming (Aguayo, 1990) said quality is "pride of workmanship" (p. xi), which comes from a commitment to continuous improvement, the kind of commitment schools are being asked to make in the current climate of standards and accountability. Students also need to become committed to continually improving their performances if we are to make any real headway in helping them meet content standards. Dr. Deming's theories about how to help people do better quality work certainly offer teachers some good guidelines for improving the quality of student learning as well.

In addition, focusing students on improving their work connects directly to creating the supportive community of learners. As Bonstingl says, "Deming encouraged educators to create school environments in which strong relationships of mutual respect and trust replace fear, suspicion, and division" (2001, p. 19). The search for quality based on supportive relationships makes school more enjoyable and helps to motivate students because

> Students enjoy coming to school when teachers focus on ways of enabling every student to succeed. Students get more involved in their work, not only for the grade, but for the intrinsic satisfaction they get from doing good work and building new competencies on what they already do well. . . . School becomes an exploration, a journey of discovery with their teachers as guides and mentors helping them toward greater and greater success. (p. x)

Unfortunately, the Americanized world beyond school often tends to focus on efficiency instead of quality. That is why students seem to be interested in getting an assignment done and turned in, rather than getting it done well and learning anything in the process. To focus students on doing quality work, a teacher must first open the conversation about quality in the classroom (see Box 1.10). Once this discussion is begun, it must become an ongoing theme, a topic of continuing focus, to make a real impact on student work habits.

Box 1.10

Open and Continue the Discussion on Quality by

- Using cartoons, quotes, examples, and statistics to prompt student discussion
- Having groups determine components of quality
- Having groups list barriers to quality and then set goals to work to overcome the barriers
- Illustrating the elements of quality work with models and rubrics

Traditionally, school has not really encouraged quality work either. We often rush students to finish assignments, and we push on once a unit is done, whether or not students did quality work and really know the material. We accept poor work, sometimes gladly, just to get it in and graded so we can move on. Therefore, the longer students have been in school, the more they understand how the system has worked and the more ingrained their habits will be. Because of this, teachers in middle and high school will have to work harder than elementary teachers to shift how students think about doing quality work in school.

Creating a Vision of Quality

A teacher should begin the conversation by helping students create a vision of what quality is. Many students may not have really thought about quality or seen people model quality work in their lives outside school. The first step, then, is helping them verbalize the components of quality so the class will have some criteria to work with as they discuss what quality work on specific assignments will look like. The following exercise is a very effective one for involving all students in the discussion of quality and creating a generic description of what a quality product or performance is.

First, ask students to think of a quality product or performance they have seen outside school. It is important to specify "outside school" since many students have not really done quality work in school and will simply say that an A is quality. It is also important that they have an emotional connection to the item or experience they discuss, and many don't have any positive experiences concerning quality in school. Students will probably need for the teacher to give them some idea of what is being asked, so the teacher should think of a quality product and performance from his or her own life outside school to share with students as examples. As the teacher gives examples, she should give at least two reasons that each one was quality to her. Students should write their responses without talking about them. (See Resources, Sample 9, for quality worksheet.) Primary students would do this as a class, and the teacher could write the responses on the board. They may also need the teacher to supply some physical samples of quality products for them to discuss.

Once students have written responses, students should share their quality products or performances and reasons in groups of three or four. They should listen to each other with the idea that they are looking for what the student examples might have in common. Again, the teacher may need to give them a sample of what is meant here. The teacher can use his own quality product and performance to give something they might have in common. For example, if my product was a car and my performance was Michael Jordan's last slam dunk, they both required that someone take time to prepare in order to get the quality result. So quality requires taking the time to make it happen. The lists of components that groups get will not be long. A normal list will most likely have 5 to 10 components.

When each student has shared, and the small group has created a list, they should share their components of quality with the class as the teacher writes them on the board. Each group will share only one item to start; then add components until all of them are listed. In a self-contained classroom, the teacher now has a description of quality to place on the wall as a guide for student work. If a teacher has more than one class, the lists will be very similar and the teacher can compile a master list of quality components to present to each class for approval. If everyone agrees that this list represents his view of quality, all students should sign the poster and the poster should hang in the classroom (see Box 1.11).

Box 1.11

Student List of Components of Quality

- Meets and goes beyond requirements
- Leaves a good impression—is memorable
- Has no controllable mistakes
- Is your best effort at the time
- Is original—gives a new perspective
- Has value to the creator and others
- Takes and reflects time and effort
- Is inspirational
- Gives you goose bumps!

SOURCE: Adapted from B. Benson's work with 11th- and 12th-grade students at Watauga High School, Boone, NC.

After students have created a vision of quality by listing its components, the teacher should ask them to write their own definition of quality. These can be shared and then the teacher can give students some professional definitions, like Dr. Deming's, for them to compare and discuss.

Continuing the Discussion on Quality: The Quality Cycle

The initial discussion about quality won't be enough to make the changes needed in student work, so teachers must plan many ways to continue to bring up quality in class. For quality to be a focus for the year, teachers must think of it as an evangelical mission and realize that students will backslide into sorry work habits even if they can give a wonderful list of quality components and definitions that are right on target. Teachers will have to plan for revival sessions throughout the year. They can periodically put up an appropriate cartoon or quote for students to discuss or write about. (See Resources, Sample 10, for quotes about quality.) Teachers should also be talking about quality as they give students rubrics with quality criteria for assignments and ask them to self-assess their work.

Even the youngest students can learn to do this if the teacher makes quality a theme in the classroom. I saw a third-grader come to turn in a paper and the teacher asked her if it was her best work. She immediately said, "No. I was in a hurry." Without the teacher asking her to, she returned to her seat and got busy improving the quality of her paper. Since students will give us what we are willing to take, we must demand quality work from them and give them the time and support to assess the quality of their own work and continually improve it.

Teaching students the process for achieving quality work is another way to continue the discussion on quality. Deming and Shewhart's (Aguayo, 1990) Cycle of Continual Improvement offers a simple process that students can apply to their work in school (see Box 1.12).

Box 1.12

Deming-Shewhart Cycle of Continual Improvement

1. Plan what you want to do.

2. Carry out the plan.

3. "Observe the results."

4. "Study the results and decide what you have learned" and need to do to improve.

5. Repeat the cycle.

SOURCE: Deming-Shewhart Cycle of Continual Improvement. Reprinted from Aguayo, R. (1990). *Dr. Deming: The American who taught the Japanese about quality.* Copyright © Rafael Aguayo. Reprinted by permission of Rafael Aguayo.

Since students remember a lot of what they see around them, this is also something that should be hanging in a classroom. It is simple enough to be taught to the youngest children and should be the pattern for everything we do in classrooms. Basically, it involves planning, doing, studying the results, and making a new plan. Athletic coaches have practiced this for years to get improvement on a team. Now we need to make it the process for how teachers and students work.

Once teachers have taught this cycle to students, they must model it, and be very clear about what they are doing. When teachers are giving the objectives for a class, they should say it comes from their plan. After a lesson has gone badly, they can come back and share their thinking and evaluation of the results of the plan with the kids. Then, teachers can let students in on the planning for improvement. Sometimes teachers should even ask students how the teacher might have done it differently to get the result they wanted. Students can help teachers plan for the next step. By modeling Deming and Shewhart's cycle, teachers are giving students a real lesson in a commitment to continuous improvement. Students are seeing the process for learning and quality being modeled by an adult, a professional learner. Many of them have never seen an adult doing quality work and certainly have not been let in on the fact that it doesn't just happen; it is a process that must be learned and practiced.

Barriers to Quality

The first time I had my classes discuss quality, they gave me a great list of components, and I was very impressed that they knew what quality was. We all felt quite noble! On assignments over the next few weeks, however, I got the same kind of sorry work that I had gotten before the quality discussion. This was when I realized that we would have to revisit the concept often and make it part of our regular conversations in class. Two colleagues, Suzi Loya and Jim Phiffer from South Kitsap School District in Washington, shared an idea for dealing with the first real backsliding in regard to quality.

They suggested having students brainstorm all the things that got in the way of their doing quality work. They did not censor the student list—just took it as students gave it, and wrote it up on the board or a chart. (See Box 1.13 for a sample from seventh graders.)

Box 1.13

Barriers to Doing Quality Work in School

- Too rushed
- No second chances
- No time to preview or ask questions
- Family commitments
- Natural disasters
- Illness
- No help from parents
- Lack of materials
- Teacher yells, pressures, nags
- Directions unclear
- Homework unfair
- Teacher talks too much
- No help from teacher

SOURCE: Seventh graders.

Once the list was complete, they asked students to cross out the items that neither teachers nor the students could control in the classroom. Natural disasters and illness are examples of things that should be crossed out. Then, the teacher took one of the items that she thought she could do something about and wrote it on the board in a place where it would stay for a week. Under it, she gave one strategy she was going to try to use to minimize this barrier and improve the quality of student work. For example, if students said that the "teacher yells and nags," the teacher might say that he doesn't realize that he is doing that and he really wants to cut down on it in the coming week. As a strategy, he might ask a student in the classroom to signal when he starts yelling and nagging.

Once the teacher had modeled what he wanted students to do, he gave all of them an index card, and asked them to choose one of the barriers they could work on in the next week. They signed the cards before turning them in and the teacher saved them. A week later, the class took time to review everyone's goals to see if the strategies improved the situation and the quality of the work everyone was doing. Students who did not really try their strategies could decide to keep the same one and work on it for a second week. Students who did try their strategies without results might decide to continue to work on that barrier with a different strategy. As the class reviewed the strategies to measure progress toward quality, teachers were sure to connect what the class was doing to Deming and Shewhart's cycle. This process of planning for improvement, carrying out the plan, reviewing the results, and making a new plan will need to be continued until progress toward quality becomes evident.

Dilemmas in the Search for Quality

Really focusing a class on quality will have some interesting dilemmas and far-reaching effects (see Box 1.14). Since our society is not really set up for quality work, it should not be surprising that the way we run our schools often gets in the way of the people inside doing quality work. Aguayo (1990) says people working in a system "can only produce at the level inherent in the system. They may do worse, but they cannot exceed the capability of the system while working in it" (p. 103). Therefore, if the graduates of our schools are not meeting the standards our communities have for them, the majority of the problems may be in how we are running the system that produces the graduates. If this is true, one would expect that the system would create some major dilemmas for teachers who try to foster a quality focus in their classrooms, and one would be correct.

Box 1.14

Dilemmas in the Search for Quality

- Producing quality work is a process that includes many mistakes.
- Quality takes time.
- Students must understand that quality has substance and looks good.
- Competition sometimes discourages quality.
- Percentages and grades are not always synonymous with quality.

I want to discuss some of the dilemmas that other teachers and I have faced in our classrooms as we tried to focus students on doing higher-quality work. I do not have the final answers to these problems but feel it is important for teachers to know what they might be facing as they struggle to help students raise the quality of their performances. I am also sure that I will only scratch the surface of the difficulties inherent in changing a cultural mindset on how to achieve quality in classrooms; but, again, we must start the discussion if we are ever to raise the quality of our students' performances on learning standards.

Producing Quality Work Is a Process That Includes Many Mistakes

One of the first dilemmas is that getting quality products and performances is a process that involves trial and error and many mistakes. This is a problem for teachers because school doesn't really allow for mistakes from students. Our practice of grading everything a student turns in and averaging those grades to arrive at a final evaluation penalizes risk taking and mistakes as students struggle to understand new content and learn to do new things. This fact explains why high-achieving academic students often won't take risks. Instead, they take the tried-and-true path to doing assignments and often want the teacher to give them very specific information about what is correct. They do not dare to make a mistake, because they know that in the grade-averaging process, one slip-up can ruin their eventual grade. Never taking a risk or trying something new is a guarantee for mediocrity. Any group who discusses the components of quality will agree, because they will no doubt have listed the idea that quality involves something memorable, not mediocre.

A teacher who is really going for quality work from students will need to create ways to allow for mistakes and improvements. For example, some teachers reward students for taking advantage of second chances to improve their work. Teachers do this by changing the first grade to the improved one before it is averaged with other grades. Teachers might also give some credit for student improvement as they determine the final grades for a marking period. Or, even more radical, teachers can refuse to put a grade on work that does not meet acceptable standards. Such work is simply "Not Yet Acceptable" and must be improved to get credit. (See Box 1.15 for a model for grading.)

One important method for helping students understand and do quality work is using quality rubrics that clarify the criteria and standards of performance for a particular assignment or task. Rubrics are guides for students to apply the quality cycle to their own work process, because a rubric gives the criteria by which students should plan the work, do the work, study the results, and plan for improvement on the next assignment. The teacher-made rubric in Figure 1.1 on page 46 is for a weekly assignment called Reading Cards. In this assignment, students read a current event or research article related to the topics being discussed in class and write a brief summary paragraph and a reaction paragraph, which connects the information to the class topics or the student's own experiences. This assignment would be appropriate for Grades 7 through 12 and addresses the standards that require students to read for information, distinguish fact from opinion, analyze, interpret, and evaluate information, document sources correctly, and write clearly, using standard English. It is imperfect but a good first attempt to state criteria for a quality product. I am including it to make the point that having this rubric is certainly better than having no rubric at all because it does give students guidance for improving the quality of their work. I also hope it will encourage teachers who are not using rubrics to learn about them and begin to create and use rubrics in their classes. For those teachers already using rubrics, this is a confirmation that you are on the right track toward better quality student work.

Rubrics can be used for the development and assessment of a process, product, or performance. For example, a good rubric for a research project might have one segment that sets the criteria for the process of research, another segment that clarifies the requirements for the written report or display, and a final segment that covers the presentation the student will make at the end of the project. In a very real sense, rubrics give the student expanded opportunities for correcting errors and doing quality work *before* it is graded, thus improving the quality of the final products. Three

Box 1.15

Sample Grading Model to Encourage Quality Student Work

The focus of this grading system is on what students are learning and how much they are improving, not on the grade they get on any one assignment. Using three levels that are given names instead of point values or letter designations helps to shift the student's attention to the quality of the work instead of the grade. This system works if first attempts are recorded but not necessarily averaged into the final grade. If students improve on the first attempt, their improved version is the one that counts. This system fits well into a classroom where students will be involved in complex performance tasks or creating showcase portfolios for presentation at student-led conferences with adult guests. One of the most positive aspects of a system like this is the use of the term "Not Yet" for unacceptable work. This term implies that there is hope for the student to do better instead of the "not ever" finality that a D or F signifies.

- Use a three-tiered system for assessing student work: Excellent, Acceptable, or Not Yet.
- The system is based on three-tiered rubrics with clear quality criteria and standards for levels of performance (see Figure 1.1).
- Excellent work will eventually be figured in as As.
- Acceptable work will eventually be figured in as Bs or Cs.
- Not-Yet work, meaning the work is not yet of acceptable quality, will eventually be figured in as Fs if it is not corrected and improved in a teacher-determined, reasonable timeframe.
- Ds are not given in this system, because Ds are really unacceptable work, and students will have time and opportunity to improve not-yet assignments that are to be included in the final grading scheme.

Cautions

- Translating the three-tiered rubrics to numerical grades is difficult but can be done as long as the method is simple and fair. Sometimes this can be simplified by creating a four-tiered system, inserting a level such as *Highly Competent* for Bs and making Acceptable equivalent to Cs.
- The method must be clearly explained to parents, students, and administrators before it is used.
- Rubrics to clarify criteria and standards for work must be of good quality.
- Since switching from a traditional grading system to one like this may be difficult, teachers can begin by using the words, Excellent, Acceptable, and Not-Yet instead of grades on small, daily assignments such as class or homework. This way they are giving students feedback on the quality of their work and getting used to assessing student work in a more quality-focused way.
- All Not-Yet work does not have to be corrected and improved. A teacher should determine which assignments are essential to prove the student has learned the major standards or concepts being taught. These are the ones that must be done to an acceptable level.

Figure 1.1   Directions and Rubric for Reading Cards

Benson/English   Directions and Rubric for Reading Cards

Directions: Read an article on the assigned topic. Use a 4"x 6" index card to write your summary and reaction to the article. You may write on both sides of the card but may not use more than one card. Refer to Writing Research Papers for the proper bibliography form for your source.

Rubric

Criteria	Excellent	Acceptable	Not yet
Bibliography	Correct format, accurate, and complete info	Same as excellent	Errors in format or incomplete
Summary Paragraph	First sent. clearly states main idea of reading, rest of paragraph supports topic sent., with quotes and specifics from the reading, and ends with a clear conclusion.	First sent. states main idea of reading paragraph, supports topic with specific examples.	First sent. is not topic sent., and paragraph has no clear proof for topic sent. or does not summarize article. Topic article not one assigned.
Reaction Paragraph	Personal reaction to article's content or style, reaction is substantiated with specific examples and related to class and other learning.	Clear reaction to article's content or style, reaction is explained, supported, and connected to other learning.	Superficial response to article. Reaction not explained, supported, or connected to other learning or class.
Format	In ink, grammatically correct, neatly done—no cross-outs or write-overs.	In ink, no more than three grammatical errors, no more than three cross-outs or write-overs.	In pencil, numerous grammatical errors, messy.

excellent resources for examples of quality-scoring rubrics that are aligned with standards are Arter and McTighe (2001); Marzano, Pickering, and McTighe (1993); and Rogers and Graham (2000). There are also numerous Web sites with rubric examples and templates.

However a teacher deals with the fact that the search for quality means making mistakes, the approach must communicate to students that it is okay to make mistakes if they are trying to do quality work and that they will have chances to improve work that doesn't meet quality standards. One possibility is to give students Quality Coupons they can attach to a piece of work they are afraid won't meet the acceptable criteria. (See Resources, Sample 11, for Quality Coupons.) When they do this, the teacher can give them a second chance to improve the work, or not put a grade on it until it is finished. In this way, students can take risks like trying a difficult writing topic or project, or they can turn in an assignment on time to avoid a late penalty even if the work isn't quite finished, and they want to work on it some more to improve it. The teacher can decide how to let students use these coupons and how much extra time to give for students to improve their work. This is just one idea that can encourage students to self-assess and take responsibility for their work while at the same time acknowledging that they may need to correct errors or revise the work to improve it later.

Percentages and Grades Are
Not Always Synonymous With Quality

In discussing the fact that quality requires risk taking, it becomes obvious that the current grading system used in schools is a real problem in the search for quality. All teachers have sensed this as they attempt to average grades at report card time. A student who has worked very hard and made a lot of progress still may not have the numerical average to pass the class or receive the type of grade that would engender pride in the effort to improve. We often realize that this hard-working, struggling student is, in many ways, a better example of a quality worker than the student who habitually gets the top grades without expending any effort or by cheating that we can't document. So numbers do not automatically certify that the work done was quality or that the person doing it is a quality worker.

Unfortunately, the numerical system for communicating about a student's level of performance gives the false idea that making a 70% is acceptable. In reality, it is very difficult to quantify quality. The great writer often breaks the rules of good writing but is successful in communicating major human truths and touching us deeply. The master painter—think of Monet, Picasso, or Van Gogh—breaks the rules and would never get an A in art because he would not adhere to the items that the teacher would be giving point credits. In an effort to fit what we are teaching and seeing in student work into a 100-point grading system, we count what is easy to count and dismiss what may be more important because we cannot count it (see Box 1.16). Writing teachers, for example, are often forced to count the number of spelling errors, grammar mistakes, and missed punctuation to determine a grade for a writing sample, because quantifying good writing is so difficult.

Box 1.16

100 Points Are Not Enough!

A grading system based on 100 points is perfect for grading content knowledge and facts but inadequate for evaluating progress toward mastery of complex, ongoing processes such as researching, critical thinking, producing quality products, and communicating well.

Barbara Benson

Once a class begins to work toward quality, they can discuss the fact that quality is hard to quantify and may not always correspond to a certain percentage. When my first class of students developed their components of quality (listed in Box 1.11), one example of a quality performance that they mentioned was the young man who fell down on the track during the 1996 Olympic Games. As he got up and struggled to finish the race, his father came out of the stands to help him across the finish line. My students said that this was an example of a quality performance from the runner and his father. When I pointed out to them that he did not win and, in fact, had been disqualified because no one was allowed to help an athlete complete a race, they said that didn't matter. It was still a quality performance. I asked them if that meant that it didn't always have to be an A to be quality work, and suddenly the grade conscious among them, the competitive advanced placement (AP) students, looked at each other as if to say, "Oh my! What have we just said?"

They were now struggling with one paradox in achieving quality: Quality and numerical grades may not be synonymous.

Adding to this problem of finding a way to indicate what is quality work is the fact that the learning standards now in place demand that students make progress on process skills as well as learn factual information. Verbs such as analyzing, questioning, communicating, decision making, and problem solving—the types of verbs listed in state learning standards—cannot be reported effectively with a 100-point grading system. They are ongoing processes that will take years or a lifetime to master. One does not become an effective communicator by the end of third grade or eighth grade or even by graduation from high school. Successful adults who are working in communication fields such as broadcasting, writing, and teaching will tell you that they are still working on their communication skills.

Since this is true, we will need additional means of letting students know how they are doing as they work to meet standards, and we will need additional means for reporting to parents on their children's progress. The system of awarding As, Bs, Cs, Ds, and Fs based on a numerical average would still work for reporting knowledge of a set number of facts or concepts. Reporting on progress toward competencies and becoming a quality worker, however, will require a supplemental method. For more discussion of grading and reporting systems that do reflect the new requirements in the state learning standards, see Guskey and Bailey (2001), Marzano (2000), and Stiggins (2006).

Quality Rubrics Can Help With the Grading Dilemma

Quality rubrics that are aligned with standards and describe the levels of performance expected of students are one means of reporting progress toward the competencies that state learning standards require. For example, using the rubric in Figure 1.2 would give students feedback on their progress toward meeting informational-processing standards. They would not need a numerical grade to determine how well they had demonstrated effective interpretation and synthesis of information, because they have the descriptors for the four levels of performance. Unfortunately, this type of rubric is not prevalent in most classrooms, and even if it is present, teachers, students, and parents often still struggle with a need to convert the information on the rubric into a grade.

Portfolios and Student-Led Conferences as Tools to Report Progress on Standards

Another method used to give the additional information about progress toward the skills demanded in the standards is student-led conferencing using showcase portfolios. Students still receive report cards with traditional grade information, but they also invite their parents or an

Figure 1.2   Effective Communication Standards

Rubric for Self-Assessing Effective Communication Standards

A. I communicate ideas clearly.

4. I communicate ideas by making sure I have a strong main idea or topic and carefully organized details that explain or support the idea or topic. I make sure the details help make the bigger ideas useful and interesting.

3. I communicate ideas by making sure I have a clear main idea or topic and enough details to explain or support the idea or topic.

2. I communicate some important information, but I do not organize it well around a main idea or topic.

1. I communicate information in unorganized pieces.

B. I communicate well with different audiences.

4. I present information to various audiences in a way that makes the most of their specific knowledge and interests.

3. I present information to various audiences in a way that suits their specific knowledge and interests.

2. I present information to various audiences in a way that does not completely suit their knowledge and interests.

1. I present information to various audiences in a way that conflicts with their knowledge and interests.

C. I communicate well using a variety of media.

4. I use many methods of communication and I follow the correct process and use the accepted standards of those mediums. I also use the mediums in new and different ways.

3. I communicate using two mediums and follow the correct process and use the accepted standards for both of those mediums.

2. I try to communicate using two mediums, but I make errors in the processes and misunderstand the accepted standards of the mediums I am using.

1. I do not even try to communicate in more than one medium.

D. I communicate well for different purposes.

4. I clearly explain the purpose of my communication by selecting and using very effective and original methods. My explanation goes beyond just stating the purpose; it adds meaning to the information I am communicating.

3. I clearly explain the purpose of my communication by selecting and using effective methods.

2. I try to explain the purpose of my communication, but I make errors in the explanation or leave out information that would make it clear.

1. I do not try to explain the purpose of my communication or I don't really have a clear purpose.

SOURCE: Marzano, Pickering, & McTighe (1993), pp. 123–124. Used with permission.

adult who cares about them to school for a conference. The students lead the conferences, sharing and discussing the work and reflections they have collected in their portfolios and discussing their learning, progress, goals, and strategies for improvement. In this way, they are reporting on their learning of facts and demonstrating their progress toward the competencies represented by the active verbs in the standards documents. For example, they are illustrating their communication skills and their ability to demonstrate and explain content concepts by conducting this conference about their learning. If the requirements for the work that goes into the portfolios are aligned with the standards through student learning targets, students will also be discussing and proving their achievement of the content expectations at their grade level. For more information on student-led conferencing, see Benson and Barnett (2005).

Quality Takes Time

In many ways, this may be one of the most difficult of the dilemmas related to the search for quality in schools. The reality is that school is driven by time constraints: the length of the day, the length of time devoted to a particular subject or course, the length of a marking period, and, finally, the length of the school year. There are always deadlines that students and teachers must meet, and they are not usually negotiable.

The issue of limited time to cover curriculum and meet standards while preparing for any high-stakes tests that may be required by the district or state is in opposition to the reality that doing quality work does take time. A master craftsperson, a prima ballerina, a musical performer, and a star athlete took many years to reach the level of quality at which they perform, and yet we expect students to do quality work in a hurry, because grades are due or we have to move along since there is so much to cover this year.

One reasonable suggestion for dealing with the issue of time is to use the standards documents in respective states to determine what is essential—the concepts and facts that students must know and the skills they must be working on at any grade level to satisfy the demands. Most of the state and national content area standards do identify limited, essential concepts, because they take a broad view of a particular discipline and often list objectives for benchmark years rather than for every year. Initially, many educators were uncomfortable with this, because these standards did not neatly match the textbooks used in schools or tell them what to teach at each grade. Instead of listing many discrete content facts or objectives, the standards tend to state broader strands of understanding in a content area. If we do want to encourage quality teaching and learning, this broad view of what students should know and be able to do will help us pare down the amount of material we teach so that we can devote enough time to essential knowledge and skills for students to learn well and do quality work. One step a district can take to give students and teachers the time to do quality work is therefore to clarify what is essential knowledge at each grade and be sure that these lists are short. They should give what really is essential, not everything that teachers have always taught, not everything they just love to teach, and not everything that appears in the textbooks in the building.

Recognizing that quality takes time and finding a way to give students the time they need to learn well and produce quality evidence of their learning will be key to meeting state standards. It won't be easy, and we may need the type of reminder I had the first year I really took up the struggle to get students focusing on quality. That year, I was often frustrated, and I am sure it was apparent to my students that I was conflicted at many points by the need to give them time and the need to cover all the books demanded by my department's curriculum—one that had not been pared down to fit the state standards. One young lady did me a great service by saying quietly, so only I could hear, as she walked by me on the way out the door at the end of many classes, "Remember, Ms. Benson, quality takes time!"

Quality Has Substance and Looks Good

A quality product or performance has at least two main attributes that must be in place: appropriate substance and appearance. If I plan to purchase a new, quality automobile, I want it to have an engine, because I want it to take me places. It also has to look good—no ugly paint or scratches down the side. I need both of these things, substance and appearance, to feel confident that I have purchased a quality car. The same is true with student assignments and presentations. They should include the necessary content information and look neat, professional, and complete.

Students often think that having one or the other is enough to get a good grade: that if the paper is written in ink or computer generated and turned in on time, it should get an A even if it doesn't follow the directions or include the required information; or, for the brilliant, divergent thinkers who do not see the need for following the conventions of format, that if it has wonderful ideas and all the information requested, it should get an A even if it is impossible to read, dirty, and on a partial page ripped out of a spiral notebook. In the world beyond school, people willing to pay for quality expect the product or performance to have substance and look good. It will be important in the ongoing discussion about quality in the classroom that teachers help students understand this fact.

Doing a very visual demonstration of the two attributes of a quality product or performance will help students understand and remember that a quality product or performance has both substance and good looks. Following is one method a teacher could use to achieve this:

- Bring some food and a large magazine or poster photo advertisement of the same food to class. For example, you could bring a large hamburger, doughnut, or chocolate chip cookie and a photo of the same product.
- Ask students to look at the food and tell you if it looks like a quality product. If they say yes, get them to tell you what in it makes it quality. You are trying to get them to talk about the attributes of the hamburger—its smell, meat, bun, lettuce, tomato, cheese—or the aroma, icing, flour, flavoring of the doughnut.
- Once they have said why they think this item is quality, take a bite out of it. Now, ask if it is quality, if they would buy and eat it. Be aware that some students will say they'd eat it anyway, especially if you teach adolescent boys!
- If they tell you that it is no longer quality, ask why. Probably, they will say because it has a bite out of it, and it doesn't look right now.
- If they don't get the point that a quality product must look good, throw the food on the floor and step on it. Now ask if it is quality, if they would buy and eat it. Point out that it still has all the things they said makes it quality—the aroma, meat, bun, lettuce, tomato—but it no longer looks as it should.
- To make the point that quality also has to have substance, hold up the photo of the food and ask if it is quality. Ask if they would eat this. If they say yes, give it to one of the students and say, "Go ahead." If the student balks, ask, "What is the problem?" Students will see that, even though it looks good, it is not really a quality product because it does not have the appropriate substance.

This exercise can be done in kindergarten through high school classes and will help all students remember that their work must have substance and must look good if it is to be considered quality.

Competition Sometimes Discourages Quality

In Dr. Deming's (Aguayo, 1990) work with improving the quality of products in industry, he found that competition within a company got in the way of achieving quality. He said, "In a well organized system all the components work together to support each other. In a system that is well led and managed, everybody wins. . . . If by bad management the components become competitive, the system is destroyed. Everybody loses" (p. vii). Systems that rank people and offer rewards and punishments to motivate them do not work well because they force everyone into a competitive state in which cooperating with others undermines an individual's chances of getting the rewards. In a classroom, this means that students will cheat for the rewards or, if they feel that they stand no chance to be rewarded by good grades, will simply give up. In either case, there is no real improvement in student learning or the quality of the work produced.

If one thinks of the school or classroom as a system, Deming's theory favoring cooperation over competition offers a new way to achieve quality. It also presents a real problem, because the current education system is based on fostering competition. Students compete against each other for grades. Teachers compete against each other for recognition. And now, in the era of public accountability, schools compete against each other for monetary rewards and prestige in the states where most improved schools get money to distribute to employees, and test scores and improvement rankings are published in local newspapers.

In our highly competitive society, we will not eliminate competition, but we can change its nature to enhance the learning community within classrooms and schools. We can look to sports for a good model of productive competition. In running, swimming, and other sports in which individuals are always trying to beat their own time or weight, athletes are competing against themselves and their own records. In a classroom, if students competed against their own last best effort, improvement would become a goal for everyone, and everyone would be willing to cooperate with others to improve their performances as well. If we are all improving, the success of my classmate does not diminish my success. Creating this type of competition would, in fact, actualize Dr. Deming's quality definition because everyone would be committed to continuous individual improvement, and we would improve as a group as well.

Considering the difficulties involved, it is obvious that focusing on quality in a classroom or school will require a strong and visionary leader (see Box 1.17). A teacher can certainly be the leader in a classroom and change the attitudes of students about their work and themselves as quality learners. A principal or superintendent can have the same impact on the adults in a school or system and, therefore, influence a lot of students. In the current climate of standards, accountability, and rising expectations for everyone in schools, we will have to figure out ways to solve the paradoxes involved in pursuing quality so that we can create quality classrooms, schools, and school systems. Only then will we be able to graduate the type of students the standards demand.

A Quality Leader's Job Is to

- "Be the primary agent for improvement"
- "Build trust"
- "Cooperate with those in the steps ahead of and following" her or him in the system
- Determine which people are in need of special help and make sure they get it, not to judge or to differentiate the above average from the below average
- Actively work to determine the real causes of problems and work to eliminate them
- Foster cooperation by eliminating barriers to cooperation and barriers to enjoyment of work
- "Work to create an environment where the workers can experience pride"
- Foster continual development of all those who work for her or him
- Allow each worker "to perform his or her job to the utmost while experiencing joy in his or her work and performing in a manner consistent with the aims of the organization"

SOURCE: Reprinted from R. Aguayo (1990). *Dr. Deming: The American who taught the Japanese about quality.* Copyright © Rafael Aguayo. Reprinted by permission of Rafael Aguayo.

THE COMMUNITY OF LEARNERS, A FINAL VIEW ■

Obviously, creating the community of learners necessary for all students to stand the best chance of meeting standards will not be easy. Many components are involved in building the environment most conducive to learning. The good news is that a lot of help and expertise is already available in education today. We know a lot about how to help students learn, and we are finding out more all the time as the research on learning and how the brain works accelerates. Now what we must do is weave this knowledge together in such a way that it fits the students we have and the learning standards they must meet. It is possible to have such a learning community in a classroom, and, best of all, when the students become self-directed, interactive, and focused on quality, they will be motivated to learn, and we, their teachers, will enjoy helping them do so.

IDEAS FOR TEACHERS ■

- Think about how you run your class. How self-directed are your students? How much student interaction do you plan for? Do you train your students to work well in groups? Are students actively striving to improve the quality of their work?

- If you are not satisfied with the answers to the previous questions, try some strategies suggested in this chapter to improve the sense of community in your classroom.
- If you determine that you need to improve all four of these areas, start with one, and work on it first. Don't try to work on all four at once. Remember, if you are learning how to do this along with your students, it is fine to start small and work slowly toward the type of classroom you will need.
- Start collecting strategies for helping students become self-directed, for increasing interaction, for teaching and practicing cooperative behaviors, and for improving quality in your classroom.
- In order to make students feel that your class is a supportive community, you might begin your class in a circle and conduct a meeting to greet and involve everyone in the opening activities. Some resources for this type of class structure are *The Morning Meeting Book* (2002) by Roxann Kriete (for elementary and middle school), Expeditionary Learning Schools' materials on CREW (for middle and high school), and Tribes materials (2006) by Jeanne Gibbs (for middle school).
- If you are not familiar with current research on the brain, find sources to read, attend workshops, and get a study-discussion group together at your school to learn more about how this research can help you teach students better.
- If you must submit a professional development plan to your administrator, be sure to include what you are learning in the areas related to creating the community of learners and how you are using your new knowledge to impact student learning.
- If you would like to find out just how much creating a community of learners improves your students' learning and performance, design an action research project to document what you are doing and how it is impacting students.

■ IDEAS FOR ADMINISTRATORS

Your role in helping the teachers in your school to create a community of learners in their classrooms is crucial. Many of the suggestions in this chapter will require that teachers run their classrooms differently, and if they believe that the administrator who will be evaluating them does not understand or approve of the changes, they will find it almost impossible to make them. You will need to communicate your approval and support in any way you can if you wish to have classrooms that can really make a difference in student performance.

- Assess the needs and strengths of your school. Are the classrooms in your building true communities of learners? If not, why not? What evidence do you have? Is your whole school a community that fosters learning? Will staff members cooperate with each other when they must work together? Are your teachers self-directed learners? Is there a focus on quality in your school?

- If you have real strengths as a school in these areas, congratulate everyone.
- If you have areas that need work, begin that work.
- Ask your faculty to take part in a survey to determine what they are doing now to foster a sense of community and what they might do to enhance that learners' community in your school.
- Look at the ideas in this chapter for creating a community of learners in a classroom, and consider how they could be adapted to create a stronger community of learners among the adults in your building. Your teachers will need a strong supportive community to make changes in their classrooms, especially if the faculty members do not work well together at the present time. There are numerous resources for developing a professional learning community that can help with this effort.
- Collect and model strategies for teachers that will enhance students' self-direction, interactions, ability to work together, and desire to do quality work, or share these with teachers through memos and meetings.
- If you share specific strategies, ask that teachers try them and report on how they went. Expect to see these strategies or evidence that teachers are applying their learning with students when you visit classrooms.
- Find articles or other resources that discuss ways of fostering community in classrooms, and distribute these to your staff. Have group discussions on these materials and the issues involved in them.
- Make the community of learners or quality a theme or goal for your school year. Ask teachers to collect strategies and make opportunities for them to share these ideas with each other.
- Offer or require targeted staff development on interactive classroom strategies, cooperative learning, quality, and brain research and its application to the classroom.
- Begin a regular school newsletter for teachers and parents that discusses and shares classroom strategies for each of the components of the standards-based classroom. (For an example on Community of Learners from Dansville Central Schools in Dansville, NY, see Resources, Sample 29.)
- Be sure to mentor and train your new teachers in methods that will enhance their ability to create a community of learners in their classrooms.

2

Making Reflection Routine

The second major component of a standards-based classroom, after creating a community of learners, is making reflection a routine for the teacher and the students. Reflection is the process of looking back and learning from our experiences and looking forward to plan ways to improve performance. It is a crucial step in any effort to improve student learning—something we must all do in this era of accountability. Reflection has personal value as well because it allows us to pause and take stock of our progress. As Costa and Kallick (2000), respected educators and consultants, state, "Building in frequent opportunities for faculty and students to reflect on their teaching and learning enriches education for all" (p. 60).

Reflection connects to the process for getting quality because it is a major part of the Deming-Shewhart Cycle of Continual Improvement (see Box 1.12). This cycle requires that, if we wish to improve processes or products, we first plan for action, and, after we have acted, we observe and study the results so that we can make a better plan for future action (Aguayo, 1990). Athletic coaches know this process well. They make a plan for the game, play the game, watch the films to study the results, and determine what needs to be done differently as they prepare for the next game. Now they have a plan to play a better game next week. In industry and sports, leaders agree that if we never reflect on what we have done, we will simply continue to do the same things over and over again, never getting any better. Reflection is necessary for improvement in education also.

Another benefit of reflection is that it helps us to process new experiences and new information so that we retain what we learn and can use it later. This is good for teachers, allowing them to develop new, more effective ways to implement standards and teach students well. It is also necessary for students in remembering what they have learned in their classes and succeeding on any mandated, high-stakes tests. Our brains enjoy the process of reflecting and actually need it to move new knowledge to long-term memory. If done properly, both teacher and student reflection can be a delightful exercise. As one workshop participant expressed it in one of her reflections several years ago, reflecting, or "lingering over learning" is pleasant. She said:

> I like the way the words roll around inside my mouth, and I like the taste they leave behind. We usually only linger over those things that we find enjoyable . . . hot cocoa with whipped cream, a good meal, a table whose seats are occupied by really good friends, a movie we don't want to end, poetry that keeps speaking even after the reading is done. . . . It saddens me that we have generally lost the belief that learning is something we can enjoy, something we linger over and something from which we receive satisfaction. Our hectic, hurry-up-and-get-it-done world needs to reincorporate time for lingering.

TEACHER REFLECTION   ■

Before teachers can help students learn to reflect effectively, they must be comfortable reflecting about their own learning, processes, and products. Thankfully, many schools of education are recognizing this fact and requiring that novice teachers reflect on a regular basis as part of their courses and student teaching. Some schools are also requiring that students create portfolios documenting their learning and student-teaching experiences. Such requirements are wonderful preparation for new certification tests such as the Praxis for Reading Certification, which asks teachers to select specific strategies for certain students or classroom situations and explain why they use them. Building the habit of reflection in young educators is also excellent training for the type of professionals needed for the future (see Box 2.1).

Box 2.1

Reflective Practice

The reflective practitioner assumes a dual stance, being, on one hand, the actor in a drama and, on the other hand, the critic who sits in the audience watching and analyzing the entire performance.

SOURCE: K. F. Osterman & R. B. Kottkamp. (1993). *Reflective practice for educators*. Thousand Oaks, CA: Corwin Press. Used with permission.

Induction programs for new hires in school systems are also requiring reflection as part of the process for becoming eligible for tenure. As the North Carolina Department of Public Instruction (2000) explains to the novice educator,

> Through reflection, you begin the ongoing process of blending the art and science of good teaching. Reflection requires you to report and analyze your teaching practice, philosophy, and experience. It also requires you to understand why a lesson was productive or nonproductive. This understanding is a necessary step in your progression from novice to master teacher. (p. 7)

Reflection is also necessary as we progress from the traditional classroom to the new type of student-centered classroom that standards now require. Even though new teachers may be coming into the field with some experience with professional reflection, many veteran teachers were trained before the value of reflection was known. They do not have the habit of formally examining what they are doing in the classroom with the idea of improving it next time. As evidence of this, experienced teachers who go through the process for achieving National Board Certification usually say that the extensive reflection required for the portfolio is the most difficult part. They are used to reflecting in an informal way but have not done the type of deep reflection about their planning, teaching, and assessment methods required for Board Certification.

The fact that teachers are not doing formal reflection on a regular basis, however, does not mean that they do not reflect. All teachers ask three important reflective questions, especially when they have taught something new in class. When the class is over, they think about

- What worked?
- What didn't work?
- What's next?

These three questions are the bare bones of reflection, since they do look back to what happened and forward to next time, but the questions need to be more focused and the answers more detailed if the reflection is to have a serious effect on teaching practice.

Reflection as Part of the Planning Process

Teacher reflection should begin in the planning phase of the lesson. Before teachers can make valid plans to teach students, they must think about many things. The following questions are examples of what teachers must consider as they prepare to teach class.

- What is the essential learning in this lesson?
- How will this lesson fit into what we have already done and what we will be doing next?
- Who are my students?
- What do they already know?
- What would interest them about this content?

- How can I engage the students in this lesson?
- What special needs or situations involving my students should I consider?
- When this lesson is over, what do I want students to know and be able to do?
- How will I know they got it?
- What resources do I have available for this lesson?

These questions focus on key issues in planning lessons but are certainly not the only ones teachers might be considering as they plan. To reflect seriously after teaching or assessing students, teachers must have clear goals for the lessons taught. We can't know whether we've arrived at our destination if we never gave any thought to what that destination was and how we might get there. Reflection before teaching specific material involves goal setting and strategic planning, and it is necessary as the basis for quality reflecting after a lesson and planning for future improvement.

Reflecting After Teaching

Teachers should also reflect when the lesson, unit, marking period, and year are over (see Resources, Sample 12, for a lesson reflection form). They need to look back to consider whether or not they met their targets for student learning. If the lesson was successful, teachers should consider what made it so. In that way they begin to accumulate techniques that work and can be used in future lessons. If the lesson was not successful, the teacher needs to consider what should be changed and how to use the previous experience to improve plans for future lessons. Following are some of the questions teachers could use to reflect on a lesson.

- What did I want to happen during this lesson?
- Did it happen? If so, what went well? If not, where did the lesson stray?
- What could I have done differently to meet the goals I had for the lesson?
- Did the students get the essential learning from the lesson?
- What proof do I have that they understood what I was teaching?
- Were students engaged in the lesson? How do I know?
- What do I need to do when I meet these students again to ensure that they learn essential content that is unclear to them now?
- What did I learn about my class or individual students while teaching this lesson?

Reflecting during and after a lesson is the first step toward planning the next lesson and is the only way that individual teachers will change current practices to meet the new demands of the standards.

Other Times for Reflecting

There are other things that teachers might be reflecting on besides the lesson structure and implementation. They might be looking at how particular students are reacting to the assignments, and are or are not becoming involved in the class activities. Reflecting on student work is also important because it allows us to see how well students are understanding essential concepts or are mastering required skills. In all these ways, reflecting becomes an invaluable instructional tool. It helps the teacher know what to do next with a class or an individual student.

Another type of teacher reflection involves dealing with specific incidences from the classroom. Two educators working together have developed processes for teacher reflection on classroom occurrences. Hole and McEntee (1999)—a fourth-grade teacher in Rhode Island and the cofounder of Educators Writing for Change—offer two guided protocols for teacher reflection (see Box 2.2). The first process is for individual reflections, which may or may not be shared with other teachers. The second protocol is intended for a group of teachers to use to share and discuss things that are happening in their classes. With both of these protocols, the goal is for a teacher to gain perspective on his or her practice in order to improve it.

Finally, teachers need to reflect on what they are learning and how it is impacting their students' learning. When teachers attend professional development activities, do professional reading, take postgraduate classes, engage in study or discussion groups in school, or change their instruction or assessment strategies, they should be reflecting on how these activities change their own thinking. They should also be recording what changes they will make in their classrooms as a result of their learning and then observe how these changes impact student learning. If a professional development session does not ask teachers to reflect on the new information and how it might affect their practice, a teacher needs to make time for that reflection. Otherwise the new learning will probably not impact the teacher's classroom. (See Resources, Sample 4, for a sample reflection form to be used after professional workshops or conferences.)

How to Become a Reflective Teacher

There are numerous ways to make reflection part of your routine as a teacher. For example, if professional portfolios are part of the teachers' evaluation process in your school, reflection becomes a natural accompaniment to the documentation that goes into the portfolio. If portfolios are not required for certified staff, you may decide that you would like to keep a portfolio to document your own learning and practice during a year. This is a great idea, especially if you are changing your instruction and assessment practices. It will document what you did as well as how it impacted your students' success.

Another way to start reflecting is to fill out a reflection form after a lesson that has been observed by an administrator (see Resources, Sample 12, for a sample form). A school might require these forms, or, again, you could decide to do them on your own. In the postobservation conference, this reflection should be part of the discussion, because it will give some insight into your planning and self-assessment process. As a teacher, I know this type of reflection enhances my ability to discuss the observed lesson, and I would definitely use it.

However you begin, do make reflection part of your routine practice. You will need to do this to understand that reflection is more than just what happened. It is a process of understanding why it happened and thinking about what will be necessary to improve the situation or repeat

Box 2.2

Reflection Protocols

Guided-Reflection Protocol (for Individual Reflection)

1. *Collect stories.* Some educators find that keeping a set of index cards or a steno book close at hand provides a way to jot down stories as they occur. Others prefer to wait until the end of the day and write in a journal.

2. *What happened?* Choose a story that strikes you as particularly interesting. Write it succinctly.

3. *Why did it happen?* Fill in enough of the context to give the story meaning. Answer the question in a way that makes sense to you.

4. *What might it mean?* Recognizing that there is no one answer is an important step. Explore possible meanings rather than determine the meaning.

5. *What are the implications for practice?* Consider how your practice might change given any new understandings that have emerged from earlier steps.

Critical-Incidents Protocol (for Shared Reflection)

1. *Write stories.* Each group member writes briefly in response to the question, What happened? (10 minutes)

2. *Choose a story.* The group decides which story to use. (5 minutes)

3. *What happened?* The presenter reads the written account of what happened and sets it within the context of professional goals. (10 minutes)

4. *Why did it happen?* Colleagues ask clarifying questions. (5 minutes)

5. *What might it mean?* The group raises questions about the incident in the context of the presenter's work. They discuss it as professional, caring colleagues while the presenter listens. (15 minutes)

6. *What are the implications for practice?* The presenter responds, then the group engages in conversation about the implications for the presenter's practice and for the participants' own practice. A useful question at this stage might be, What new insights occurred? (15 minutes)

7. *Debrief the group.* The group talks about what just happened. How did the process work? (10 minutes)

SOURCE: S. Hole & G. H. McEntee. (1999, May). Reflection is at the heart of practice. *Educational Leadership, 56*(8), 36–37. Reprinted with permission from ASCD.

an action that was successful. It seems we do obsess on what went wrong more than on what went right, but I believe that good teaching means analyzing the successful lessons as well as the ones that bomb.

In *Becoming a Reflective Educator,* Brubaker, Case, and Reagan (1994) assert that three of the benefits of reflection are that "reflective practice helps to free teachers from impulsive, routine behavior; reflective practice allows teachers to act in a deliberate, intentional manner; and reflective practice distinguishes teachers as educated human being since it is one of the hallmarks of intelligent action" (p. 25). I believe that these benefits are some of the things that give us satisfaction in our work as well as allow us to improve on it each and every year.

This really came home to me at the end of a very successful year with at-risk students. As we were in the middle of the learning, and racing to finish a video project at the end of the year, I was too busy to marvel at the wonderful things that were happening. When several students returned to my room the week after graduation to finish the video that still needed the sound track, my colleagues pointed out that this was not normal behavior from seniors who have graduated. I agreed and began to look back at the year to determine what had happened. I was thrilled to see the success my students had achieved, and I wanted to do it again the next year. Taking this time to reflect on the positive things the students and I had done changed my teaching and made the next year even better. The experience made me realize the value of reflection and made it easier for me to help my students learn to reflect.

■ STUDENT REFLECTION

Reflection is one of the tools for getting students to become more self-directed, responsible, motivated, and concerned about improving their own work. Reflection is also one means of helping students process the content they are learning so that it becomes part of their long-term memory and will be accessible when they must take mandated tests. As Caine and Caine (1994), educators and international consultants on applying brain research to classroom practice, state in their discussion of the necessity for active processing for learning, "active processing is the consolidation and internalization of information, by the learner, in a way that is personally meaningful and conceptually coherent. It is the path to understanding, rather than simply to memory. . . . The pervasive objective is to focus on the process of our learning and extract and articulate what has been explored and what it means. In effect, the learner asks in as many ways as possible, 'What did I do?' 'Why did I do it?' and 'What did I learn?'" (pp. 156–157).

Just as for teachers, there are multiple ways for students to reflect and many times in the learning process when reflection is beneficial.

Reflecting Before Beginning New Learning

Having students reflect on what they already know about a topic before they begin new learning is extremely useful for teachers, because it can often help with the planning process. If we know what students know, or think they know, we can begin a new unit or class in the right place for the learners. If they already know a lot about the topic we wish to discuss, we can quickly review the basics they should know and move quickly to new information. This would make it easier to avoid needless repetition of content segments and give teachers more time to teach the more sophisticated content they are expected to get to in the standards.

A teacher who has students reflect on what they know before starting on new information also might discover that they have gaps or misinformation in what they should know at this point in their education. In other words, they do not know enough to proceed, or what they think they know is wrong—a problem that is particularly prevalent in science, because children tend to come to their own "scientific" theories about how the world works long before they even enter school. These personal theories are hardwired into their brains and often difficult to correct. As a teacher, I really need to know what they think they know to know how to proceed effectively.

There are many ways to have students reflect at the beginning of learning. The K-W-L strategy (see Box 2.3), which asks them to list what they know about a topic and what they want to know, can be used with a whole class or could be done individually so that all the children have their own K-W-L sheet. Once students have filled out "What do I know about rain forests?" for example, the teacher could collect the sheets to assess where the class is in their prior knowledge. A teacher who does take up this sheet must be careful to use it for information only, not to grade the responses. If necessary, the teacher could give the students credit for doing the work seriously and completely but should never assign a grade for the quality of the responses. First, giving a grade for the responses would be blatantly unfair since the teacher has not taught students any information yet. Even if they were supposed to have learned something about the topic in another grade or course, grading the responses is unfair, and will effectively stop any honest student reflection. Instead of reflecting, they will simply try to figure out what the teacher wants to hear and say that.

Another strategy for tapping into prior knowledge is Into-Through-and-Beyond (see Box 2.4) and, just as in K-W-L, students might do this as a group or have their own sheets that a teacher could collect and use to plan appropriate lessons. Teachers can also use Think Pads (Box 2.5) for quick reflections. For example, students can jot down any knowledge about an upcoming topic on their pads and give these to the teacher as they exit the room. If they don't know anything about the topic, they should respond by writing a question concerning something they would like to know.

Using a Web of Knowledge (see Resources, Sample 14) is another way to reflect before beginning new learning. In this activity, students draw a circle on a sheet of paper and write the new topic in the middle. Then they write anything they know or want to know on lines radiating out from the center circle. As they continue through the new material, they may correct anything they wrote initially that they learn is incorrect, and they should add information about the topic. At times, students can compare their Web with others as an opportunity to discuss the content they are working on and to correct or add to their individual Webs of Knowledge.

Whatever strategy a teacher uses, having students reflect before learning new information is good for the teacher and the student. For students, thinking about something they will be learning, and remembering what they might already know, helps them connect the content to their own experiences. If students can relate to what they are learning, we know that they will be more motivated and more likely to remember the new information. Therefore, reflecting at the beginning of new learning, although it may seem to be taking class time away from learning, should be viewed as an instructional activity to engage students in the content. It is not a waste of time. It may, in fact, be the thing that sparks the interest of apathetic students and makes them want to pay attention and, consequently, learn the content.

Reflecting During Learning

Just as finding out what students know before starting a new unit is useful, finding out what they are understanding as they go through the new material is essential. As a teacher, I knew what I had taught, but I was often totally ignorant of what my students understood until they took the test at the end of the unit. If I had been sure to have some student reflection going on along the way, I would have known if they were hearing what I thought I was saying!

If students started an Into-Through-and-Beyond (Box 1.4) sheet or a Web of Knowledge (Resources, Sample 14) at the beginning of a learning segment, they could stop at times and correct misconceptions, add new learning or questions, and compare their learning to that of others in the class for the purpose of clarifying concepts and adding more to their sheets. At times, the teacher can take these up to see if students are getting the essential content being taught.

Tickets Out or In the Door

Students can be asked to do Tickets Out the Door or Tickets In the Door (High Success Network, 1994). The directions for these are in Box 2.3, and Figure 2.1 shows a sample ticket from a second-grade student. This strategy is intended to have students do a quick reflection on their learning. It should take no more than 5 to 10 minutes, depending on the type of questions asked. There should never be more than three questions on a ticket, and the questions should vary so students don't get in the habit of giving generic answers to set questions. You can use Think Pad (Box 1.5) paper for these or create small tickets for students.

Looking at the sample ticket in Figure 2.1 on page 66, I can see that the student has been studying the Pilgrims and has remembered some important information. I was impressed with the fact that this second grader remembered a date, and that it was correct. My high school and college students often got the dates wrong if they used them at all in their writing. A reflection like this would not be graded (remember, it is not a quiz of any kind), but I would want to keep it as evidence of this student's learning. If we were using student portfolios, this might be one of the artifacts that we would include to show learning. In just this brief reflection, this student has let the teacher know that the content being taught is being learned and has supplied some documentation to prove it.

What If I Didn't Learn Anything Today?

If, when the teacher asks, "What did you learn today?" for a ticket out, students say that they haven't learned anything, the teacher should ask,

Box 2.3

Tickets

Ticket Out the Door

1. Give students small pieces of paper—about the size of a small index card—to use as tickets.

2. Ask them to respond to one to three simple questions that do not have a specific right answer but require students to reflect on their own learning and understanding. For example, "List one or two important things you learned in class today and any questions you have about what we were working on."

3. Give students time to respond.

4. Ask them to put their names and the date on the tickets and give them to you as you stand at the classroom door to collect them.

Ticket In the Door

1. This is a good strategy for a Monday, for after a vacation that interrupted a segment of new learning, or for the day after the students have had a substitute teacher.

2. Give each student a small piece of paper to use as a ticket—about the size of a small index card—as they enter class.

3. Ask them to put their names on the paper and to respond to one to three questions that require them to reflect on their learning or questions. For example, questions like, What is the most important thing you learned last time we were in class? and What questions do you have about the homework you had to do last night? are useful.

4. Collect these reflections or ask students to use them to participate in a class discussion about the last class or to share with a learning partner. If students listed a lot of questions, these could be put on the board so students could answer them or look for the answers during the following classes. In this way, students will be focused because they are looking for the answers to their own questions.

5. If the tickets had questions on them, students could write answers they got in class and turn their tickets in at the end of class as evidence of their participation that day.

Reminder: Do not grade the quality of responses on in/out-the-door tickets. Give credit for students taking the assignment seriously and answering all questions!

SOURCE: Adapted from High Success Network (1994, April). Prompt Cards. *The High Success Connection, 2,* 5–6.

"Why?" Students should be expected to write the reasons they are not learning. Getting this information is crucial if teachers really want to address the needs of all their students. If a student reports not learning

Figure 2.1   Sample Student Ticket

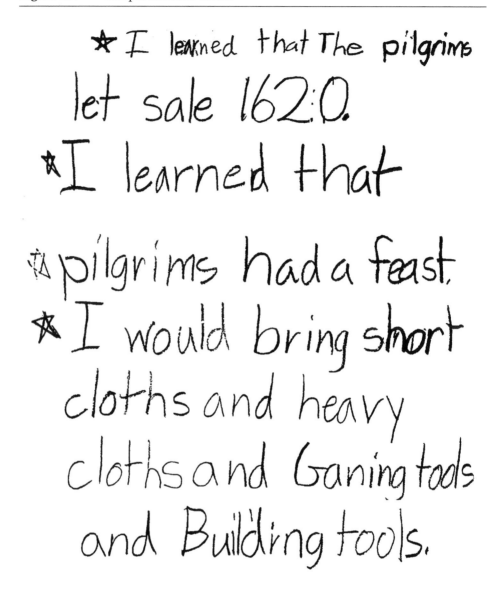

because "Pat is sitting behind me and poking me with a pencil all of class," that is something a teacher can address. If a student isn't getting any sleep because of fighting parents, the teacher can't help the situation but can certainly deal with the student in a sensitive way and, perhaps, increase the student's ability to learn in the class. If a student says, as one of mine did, that "I didn't learn anything in class today because I didn't do my homework and I don't have a clue what you are talking about!" at least the student is taking responsibility for the situation. Certainly, a response like this should be dated and kept for any future meetings with parents.

Student reflection, whether it is on Tickets Out the Door or in other forms, is one way we can get to know our students well so we know how to teach them better. Like teacher reflection, student reflection helps the teacher plan for future classes and is an important step in improving learning.

What If I Can't Write a Ticket Out?

Young students who do not write well can tell what they have learned as their ticket out. Susy Barnett's (personal communication, September, 1993) kindergarten class at Mabel School in Zionville, NC, ended every day with a circle on the floor where all students were to share one or two things they had learned during the day. She always started the sharing with something she had learned, but Ms. Barnett reports that when she first started this practice, few students could think of anything. If one did come up with an idea, others just responded, "What Bobby said!" Once they got used to the practice, however, they were able to report on their own learning. They still needed to be prompted to talk about what they had learned, not just what they had done, during the day. For example, if one reported playing at the sand table, Ms. Barnett might ask, "Doing what?" If the child said "We counted blocks and trucks," Ms. Barnett could agree and say "We were doing math, learning to count and combine." This way, the students connect what they were doing with the content they were learning. Another benefit of this practice is that when their mamas asked what the children learned in school that day, every one of her students had something of substance to share. Ms. Barnett says the parents thought she was "better than sliced bread" because their children were learning so much and were able to talk about it.

In addition to helping students remember what they are learning, and helping teachers know how to work with individual students, reflections like Ticket Out the Door also send a powerful message to students. They make it clear that students are expected to learn something each day they come to school. School should not be an empty exercise, and students should be taking some responsibility for their own learning. One way we know that this type of reflection does, in fact, send this message is that in Ms. Barnett's class, students who could not say what they were learning at the beginning were soon coming to her throughout the day saying "Guess what I'm learning now?" and sharing their new knowledge. If we could imprint this message that each child should be learning every day into all the 5-year-old minds and reinforce it every year, think how wonderful school would be for all of us and what empowered learners we would be graduating each June!

Reflecting on Assignments

Students can also do reflection on assignments. This can be especially useful on homework papers. Students could be asked to reflect before turning in work. On the back of their paper, they could write any questions or confusions they had in doing the work. They could also explain what they want the teacher to notice when evaluating the work. This is a very interesting question that might get responses like "I want you to notice that I finished this time!" or "I want you to notice that I stopped after problem 11 because I got so confused." Such responses give teachers appropriate ways to deal with students and respond to their assignments (see Resources, Sample 16, for a list of questions for student reflection).

Double Windows

A strategy called Double Windows can also be used to have students reflect as they are learning (see Resources, Sample 17, for a Double windows form). The title of this activity comes from the idea of having students stop and step outside of the learning activities they have been engaged in to think about them from two different perspectives—new learning and ways to apply the learning beyond the classroom.

In this activity, students have a page to keep in their notebooks. At times during a week, month, or unit of study, they are asked to take a few minutes to record on the left side of the page what they have learned and, on the right, what they might be able to do with their new knowledge. The types of things they might list on the left are new information, new connections—the "Ah Ha!" experience of suddenly understanding things you knew before but didn't connect in a meaningful way—and new questions the new information might have generated. On the right side, they can list ways they might use what they are learning. Everything listed on the left may not have a corresponding item on the right, because we often learn something new before we can see how we will apply it. An example might be that a third grader has learned to multiply by 3, but it may be awhile before he realizes that he could use this to see how many pieces of silverware to put on the table for a family gathering. Hopefully, students will begin to fill up the right side as they understand the relevance of the content they are learning. Teachers, if you use this strategy with students, you will want to collect these pages at times to see what students are learning so you can plan accordingly.

Keep in mind that reflections along the way, just like reflections at the *beginning* of learning, should not be graded for the quality or correctness of the content information. Reflection is only valuable if it is honest and concerns the students' personal reactions and self-assessment more than it asks for content facts. If students insist on asking "Are you grading this?," tell them they will get credit for taking the reflection seriously and answering all the questions you pose. Usually students will stop asking about how reflection will be graded once they understand its purpose and begin to realize that reflecting on their own work is helping them to improve work when it is going to be graded.

Reflecting at the End

Although there really shouldn't be an end to learning, there are points in the school year when we are done, for the time being, with a particular lesson, concept, or unit. It is essential that students reflect on what they have learned, how they are going to use it, and what they can do to improve their performance on the next assignment. This type of reflection is important because it allows students to review essential learning, helps them clearly verbalize what they have learned, helps with goal setting for improvement, and sets the stage for the next learning.

As with reflection at other points in the learning, there are many ways to reflect at the end. If students have begun a graphic organizer of their learning, such as K-W-L, Into-Through-and-Beyond, or a Web of Knowledge, they can complete these as a means of reflecting on content. Into-Through-and-Beyond is particularly good for this because the Beyond step asks students to think about how they will use the things they have learned in the future. Students who keep journals could be required to reflect on the ending of a unit, and students who are creating showcase portfolios will be doing reflection on individual pieces of work as well as culminating reflections on units, grading periods, and the year as a whole. Students can be asked to reflect on specific content area skills at the end of marking periods (see Resources, Sample 18, for a math form). For example, students learning to write could be asked how they see themselves as writers, how they have improved, what they need to do next, and how the teacher might help them. If they are participating in health and physical education classes, they could be asked to assess their physical fitness level and set goals for improvement. These reflections could reference the goals that students set earlier in the year, to see how they are doing in meeting their targets. Whatever subject is concerned, the reflection should deal with the students' learning process, not the content facts. Teachers should have ample evidence of the content knowledge from other assessments like class assignments and tests. Remember, reflection is about the student and the student's learning processes, not the subject information.

If students are writing this type of reflection, the questions they are asked to respond to should vary so that they don't just reflect on automatic pilot. If students always write to the same questions, you will start to get generic reflections—they all sound the same and really will have little or no impact on student performance. What you would hope to see, as students get better at reflecting, is that their reflections become very honest and elaborated. Once my students got comfortable writing reflections on a regular basis, the formal reflections they put into their portfolios were often more revealing of what they were learning than the piece of work the reflection accompanied.

Reflecting on a Test

Another reflection at the end can occur after students have taken a test, and the teacher has returned and discussed the areas students need to correct. Students could be asked to turn the paper over and respond to the following four questions:

- What did you do well on this test?
- What was your weakest area on this test?
- What could you do to improve on the next test? List one strategy you could use.
- Were any of the questions unclear? Unfair? If so, how?

This is a short but complete reflection because it asks students to look backward and then ahead with the idea of improving their performance. Students should be able to answer the first two questions easily because the teacher has marked the paper. The third question, however, is the most important one, and students may need to discuss realistic strategies. Once again, it is easy to see that reflection connects directly to improving the quality of students' work.

Having students reflect on their learning and progress toward quality sends the message that students are expected to be able to self-assess and work consistently to become better learners. Eventually, the goal of the reflection strategy in the previous paragraph would be to have students answer the four questions *before* they turn in their work for grading. If the criteria for quality work are clear, students should be able to learn how to look at their own work, see what they have done well and not so well, and plan for future improvement. Of course, they will not be able to do this at the beginning of the year, but if they reflect on a regular basis about their learning, their processes, their work, and ways to improve, they should develop the ability to self-assess accurately.

Reflecting on a Big Assignment

Before students turn in a big project or research paper, teachers could ask them to write responses to one or more of the following:

- What did you learn about your topic?
- Did you learn anything interesting that you were not able to include in the paper or other work? If so, what is it?
- What did you learn about the process of researching, experimenting, creating a display, or writing a large piece?
- What are you especially pleased about in your final product?
- If you could do this project again, what would you do differently and why?
- What will you do next time you have an assignment like this to improve the quality of your work?

What a Teacher Can Learn From Student Reflection

To illustrate once again how valuable student reflection can be for helping teachers plan and deal with individual student needs, I would like to share a student reflection. The following was written on the day that senior term papers were due in one of my high school classes. I asked students to take a sheet of paper and answer these questions:

1. Tell me one interesting thing you learned about your topic and one thing you learned about the research process.

2. What are you pleased with in your paper?

3. If you could do it again, what would you do differently to improve it?

One student responded in the follow ways. To the first question, she said, "I learned that AIDS (her topic) is continually overlooked because most people feel it could never happen to them. I also learned that using the computers for research is a quick and effective method." From her first response, I can tell that she is beginning to understand one role technology can play in her education, as an effective tool for research. In some systems, this recognition is part of technology literacy requirements, and if I needed to document that she had met this requirement, I could save this reflection. I also learned that she got one of the major truths about young people and AIDS, which is that they don't think they will get it.

Her second response about what she liked in her paper gave me invaluable information about how to respond to her work. She said, "I'm pleased with my organization of the entire paper; I feel as though it was well thought out." As the person who is going to grade her paper, I gained from this honest answer a lot of insight into how to help her improve her writing. If she has done a good job of organizing her paper, I need to be sure to say so. All English teachers know that at times we get so pressed to finish a set of papers that we only comment on the errors, not the successes. Novice writers need to hear about what they are doing well to give them confidence for trying to do even better, so I need to say "Good job!" whenever I can.

If, however, her paper is not well organized, I need to be very careful in how I let her know. If I did not know that she thinks she has organized well, I might rip into that paper with my red pen and give her permanent writing anxiety. She could end up feeling really stupid—so stupid that she doesn't even know when she is off base! Knowing that she believes she has been successful at organizing this piece, I can weigh how I respond so that I do not destroy her emerging confidence in her writing. I can point out what is organized well or how it has improved from her last assignment before I show her where and how she needs to do even better. She has given me a real key to responding to her work and helping her continue to improve as a writer.

Her response to the third question is also revealing. She said, "I would try to type this paper a little sooner than I did to ensure the final product would be ready on time." In fact, she did not have her paper ready to turn in on the day it was due, even though she did turn in the reflection. Saying that she would start typing sooner is not an excuse but is a realization she has come to since she could not get it done on time. She has accepted responsibility for the late paper and, if it were ever needed, I would have a dated reflection from her to explain any grade penalty that she might get for the late work.

This one little reflection, which took less than 10 minutes of class time, has given me a wealth of information about my student and how to respond to her. It will make me a better teacher as we work on the writing standards the student has to meet and will increase her probability of success. It was not time taken away from my content; it was about the content standards of research and writing, and well worth the time it took.

Reflecting and Sharing

An additional method of reflection at the end of a learning segment is having students brainstorm what they have learned in each subject over a week and then write a letter to their parents to inform them about the week's learning. This is a great strategy for involving parents in the students' learning as well as having students reflect on a regular basis. The brainstorming can be done individually, in small groups, or as a whole class. Most teachers would like to know what students are reporting that they have learned, so there is an opportunity for corrections if kids are confused about something. Therefore, even if students do the brainstorming alone, it is a good idea to have them report to the class or add to a class-brainstorming list.

If letter writing is part of the curriculum at the grade level where students are doing this, it can be covered in this activity as well. This is also an excellent activity for students who will be conducting student-led conferencing with adults at some point in the school year because it gets them into the habit of reflecting on and discussing their learning with adults who care about them. This strategy is appropriate for students who can write, but is particularly successful with Grades 3 to 8.

Figure 2.2   Model Student Reflection Letter

Dear Mom and Dad

   This week I have learned alot of things, like in math we learned about fractions, bell ringer math, and played wheel of fractions. We also did some hard word problems every day.
   In S.S. we learned about farming in the 1800's. It was hard work!
   In reading, I have made my goal and finished <u>farmer boy</u>.
   In science we learned alot of things. We took apart machines to find leavers and pullys.
   I am doing well on math. Plaes write coments.

love,
your son

Look at the student sample letter in Figure 2.2 and consider what you can learn about this student from his reflection. Obviously, his favorite subject is math. He has been setting goals and is proud that he has met his reading goal. He is generally feeling really good about himself as a learner. Many teachers, however, might cringe at the fact that his letter includes numerous errors in standard English and spelling. It is not hard to see that writing is probably one of the areas where this student struggles. With that in mind, consider what would happen if a teacher were to grade this letter for grammar and make him rewrite it to correct the errors. It would destroy his willingness to reflect honestly next time. In fact, this student is smart enough to figure out that if he will have to rewrite until the letter is perfect, he'd better write short.

The purpose of this young man's letter is to communicate with his parents about what he has learned. It is not to write an A letter or even to get a grade on the letter itself. Some parents, however, would be disturbed to get a letter like this with all the errors evident. So if teachers plan to have students share their reflections with their parents, they will need to inform the parents about the purpose of the letters. They can assure the parents that there will be many other graded writing assignments that the child will have to correct, and that the parents should see improvement in their child's writing skills as the year progresses.

The idea of a weekly letter home is such a great way for students to reflect and share their learning that one kindergarten teacher decided to figure out how her nonwriters could do it. Throughout the week as students were working on different parts of their curriculum, she took pictures with a digital camera. On her computer, she put together a one-page newsletter with pictures showing students learning the different content areas that week (see Resources, Sample 19, for a model form). On Friday afternoon, the class looked at the pictures and discussed what they were doing and what they were learning as they worked on the activities shown. Then the students took the newsletter home and shared it with their parents. In this way, students had a chance to verbalize what they had learned, and parents got a view into the classroom. It was a very successful adaptation of the written weekly letter home. It is also a wonderful example of how teachers can and should constantly gather good teaching ideas and adapt them for the learners in their classrooms.

CONCLUDING REFLECTION   ■

Although we have been talking about reflecting at the end of learning, reflection is really an activity that realizes that there is no end to learning. It gives the teacher and the student valuable information with which to move forward into the next learning phase. For teachers, reflection allows them to step back and look at their own practices in the classroom with an eye toward the standards, changes, and improvements they can implement. It also gives them a vehicle for considering how to use their own new knowledge in helping students learn more effectively.

For students, reflection offers a chance to consider what they are learning, a chance to linger over the content and process it in their own minds so that it will become part of their long-term memory, and a chance to communicate with teachers in a nonthreatening, quality-focused way. Teachers often tell me in training follow-up sessions that the one thing they have trouble fitting into class time is reflection. They say they feel so pressured to teach content that there's no time to stop and let students reflect on what they've been learning. Although taking the time for reflection often feels like time off task, it is, in fact, a standards-based activity. Reflection involves many of the process skills that standards demand: analysis, evaluation, self-assessment, goal setting, communication, and acceptance of responsibility for their own learning. It helps students learn the content more effectively because it gives them time to process it and put it into their own words and lives. Reflection also motivates them by giving them an investment in their learning and the belief that they can plan for improvement and do better next time.

In classrooms that must change to meet the demands being made on students by the learning standards, reflection is a necessary tool. It should be part of the planning teachers do, one of the expectations administrators have for teachers and students, and a habit students have. If we are to succeed in raising student achievement, we must all make time for lingering over the learning we've done and planning for the next step.

IDEAS FOR TEACHERS   ■

- Set up a system for your own reflections. For example, you can start your own journal, or you can get a folder and put dated sticky notes in it with brief reflections concerning your students, class, and lessons. If you have a computer in your classroom, you can set up a file for your reflections and take a few minutes at the end of each day to jot down your thoughts before you turn off the computer. Set up a tape recorder and reflect as you drive home in the afternoon. Be sure your give the date of each reflection as you record it.
- You could use a form to reflect on some of your lessons. You can use the one given in Resources, Sample 12, or create your own from the questions listed at the beginning of this chapter.

- Set up an environment in your classroom that is conducive to reflection by providing appropriate wait time when asking questions; using open-ended, problem-solving activities with students and embracing alternative solutions; encouraging students to ask questions and take risks without fear of reprisal; and being sure to have students explain their processes, justify their answers, set goals for improvement, and self-assess their work.
- Develop and use a variety of reflection methods with students. Use some of the ones listed in this and the preceding chapter, like K-W-L, Into-Through-and-Beyond, Think Pads, Web of Knowledge, Ticket In and Out the Door, Double Windows, assessing the test or assignment, or weekly letter home.
- Make reflection time part of your lesson plan. If you don't plan for it, you won't remember to do it in the rush to get the curriculum information to students.
- When you start having students reflect, remember that they really don't know how to do this. You will have to model it. It is also best to start with small reflections that do not take much time.
- Assure students that their reflections will not be graded on the content information, but they will receive credit if they take it seriously and answer the prompt questions completely.

■ IDEAS FOR ADMINISTRATORS

If you want to include reflection in your school as a tool for improvement, you will need to help both teachers and students make reflection a routine. For teachers to make reflection part of their professional practice, they will need to learn how to reflect, have time for reflection, and receive ongoing support to continue the practice. This is where building administrators become invaluable. Principals, you will need to establish reflection as a priority in your buildings (Box 2.4). You will also need to learn to reflect in order to model it for the teachers and help them do it well.

Box 2.4
What Teachers Need to Reflect
Becoming a reflective practitioner requires time, practice, and an environment supportive of the development and organization of the reflection process.
SOURCE: North Carolina State Department of Public Instruction (2000), p. 9.

The first step in having teachers reflect will be making sure that they have a process for reflection. A number of processes could be used as long as they involve looking at past experience and planning for improvement. One that is being taught to young teachers comes from Smyth (1989). It involves a simple cycle with four steps:

- Describing what I am doing now
- Informing by figuring out what my current activity means
- Confronting why I am doing what I do and how I came to this practice
- Reconstructing by thinking about how I might do things differently (pp. 2–9)

Smyth's Cycle of Reflective Practice is very general and intended to focus on all areas of teacher practice. A principal could decide to focus teachers' reflections on lesson planning to meet standards and use Smyth's questions for reflections in planning and analyzing the effectiveness of lessons. These questions could become the process that particular school uses. (See Resources, Sample 12, for a model reflection form for a lesson.)

No matter what process is selected, teachers will need to have the steps clearly explained and have the opportunity to practice as many times as needed to become comfortable with the sequence of reflection questions.

Ideas for other things you can do follow:

- Make reflection a part of what is expected of teachers as they are observed and evaluated.
- Remember that many teachers may never have done formal reflections and will need a definition, a rationale, and some sort of guide for the reflective process you want them to follow. They may also need for you to model what you mean by reflection.
- Find and share good articles on teacher and student reflection with your faculty. If you have shared articles, be sure to allot time for talking about them. This time could be in department meetings, grade-level meetings, study groups, or faculty meetings.
- Schedule time for teachers to share and analyze lessons together. Be sure these sessions are more than just swapping project ideas, but really require that teachers talk about what has worked in their classes, why they think it worked, and what they would caution others about if they decided to try this lesson. These sessions could also involve sharing lessons that didn't work and discussing what might have gone wrong.
- Make your school a place where teachers can take risks without fear of reprisal. Having students do reflection will feel very risky for some teachers, and they will need your support to try it and to continue to do it even if it doesn't go perfectly the first time.
- Assure teachers that reflection is part of teaching to the content standards, which contain both content facts and process skills. For example, in all content areas, students are expected to be able to analyze, synthesize, predict, and write clearly about their learning. When students reflect, they are doing all these competencies and more. Each time they reflect on their learning, they are also reviewing the content they know—one way of helping them remember it.
- If you visit a class and students are reflecting, congratulate that teacher!

3

Teaching Content and Process

As illustrated in the Introduction, the standards have a dimension that was not in former teaching objectives that school systems used. State and national standards now formalize the teaching and assessment of competencies by using process verbs such as communicate, analyze, interpret, organize, explore, question—as well as the content facts and concepts. For example, the Illinois State Board of Education's (1997) learning standards state, "students will be able to understand the roles and interactions of individuals and groups in society" (Benchmark 1SB, p. 58). In the following list, I have italicized action verbs that appear in the Illinois standards to make the point that students are expected to learn content and apply it in complex ways—to think and act like historians.

- At the early-elementary level, this means that students can "*compare* the roles of individuals in group situations (e.g., student committee member, employee/employer)."
- At the middle and junior high school level, one of the ways students will demonstrate this standard is by being able to "*analyze how* individuals and groups interact with and within institutions (e.g., educational, military)."
- And, by late high school social science courses, students will be able to "use methods of social science inquiry (*pose* questions, *collect* and *analyze* data, *make* and *support* conclusions with evidence, *report* findings) to *study* the development and functions of social systems and *report* conclusions to a larger audience." (pp. 58–59)

As is apparent from just this one example, the learning standards require more than memorizing a list of historical facts. The processes of applying content knowledge and communicating findings are now required. The action verbs that specify these processes in the standards are now part of what is mandated for student learning (see Box 3.1). More important, they are the skills students will need to succeed in the world of the 21st century.

Box 3.1

The Learner Actions

Access information

Interpret the information (critical thinking)

Produce evidence of learning

Disseminate learning

Self-assess products, process, and performance for improvement

---

SOURCE: Adapted from H. L. Burz & K. Marshall (1996). *Performance-based curriculum for mathematics: From knowing to showing.* Thousand Oaks, CA: Corwin Press.

Teachers have always taught certain processes like reading and writing, but many teachers do not instruct students in the many processes represented by the action verbs prevalent in the standards. Now we must figure out how to teach students to do these actions well because what students can do with the content is as important as knowing the content itself.

THE LEARNER ACTIONS ■

What do effective learners do when they are learning something new and will have to use it? They go through a cycle of activities or learner actions. This cycle has five steps and contains all the action verbs that are present in the new standards. The learner action cycle requires a learner to

- *Access* the needed information
- *Interpret* the information so that it makes sense
- *Produce* something to demonstrate understanding of the information
- *Disseminate* the understanding clearly to others
- *Self-assess* the processes, products, and performances to improve the next time one must learn something new and apply it (Burz & Marshall, 1996, pp. 7–8)

Explaining the Learner Actions

The first step in learning is always to *access* the information needed. Traditionally, information came solely from the teacher or from the next chapter in a textbook. In today's information age, however, students need to be adept, self-directed learners who can determine what is needed and where to find it in an ever-widening range of sources. Therefore teachers must teach students access processes such as investigating, gathering, observing, reading, interviewing, and collecting, to name a few. Being able to find the information one needs is a critical component of success as a learner in any role in or out of school.

When students have the needed information, they must be able to *interpret* it, make meaning for themselves in order to apply the information effectively. This learner action involves critical thinking, an essential skill for a successful learner. Without the ability to understand content facts or concepts, a student cannot apply the material in any meaningful way; however, this step is often assumed rather than consciously and systematically taught and assessed. Because the student learning standards say that students will be able to do such things as analyze, compare, contrast, categorize, select, and determine, teachers must give students instruction in these interpretive processes. Being able to interpret information well will enable students to deal with the amount of information constantly vying for their time and attention, in classrooms and beyond. It also means they have really learned the content and can apply it on state tests and in real-world, unstructured situations.

Once students acquire the needed information, and they interpret and internalize it, they are ready to *produce* evidence of their learning. Products used to show what students have learned might be posters, books, plays, videos, essays, newspaper articles, letters, and so on. Allowing for products in addition to written work promotes creativity, allows for differing learning styles, and adds interest and authenticity to the tasks, because, in the adult world, learning is often displayed in ways other than writing.

After students create a product to show what they have learned, they need an opportunity to *disseminate* their new understanding. This learner action is crucial because it is when we must tell, share, teach, explain, justify, discuss, publish, present, or perform that we are more likely to retain our learning in a usable form. Having to talk about my learning to an audience also proves that I do know the material. Graduate degree programs recognize this and require that candidates for advance degrees do more than turn in a thesis or dissertation. They must also go through oral exams during which they will discuss their learning and be able to field questions from a knowledgeable audience. K–12 students should also be asked to talk about what they have learned. Their audiences could be classmates, another class, a community expert or group, parents, or the school community. Logistically, giving students the opportunity to disseminate their learning may seem difficult, but it is necessary if we want students to learn more of the required content well so that they can remember more of it when they take state and national tests or graduate into postsecondary schools or careers. In addition, there are many ways to have students talk about their learning. Chapter 1 offers strategies such as discussion appointments that would be very practical for having students talk about their learning on a regular basis.

The final learner action, *self-assessment, is* directly related to student reflection, which is discussed in Chapter 2, and the quality cycle discussed in Chapter 1. Like reflection, self-assessment should be going on throughout the learning process. As previously discussed, a student's ability to reflect and self-assess determines whether or not that student will be an effective learner who feels capable of succeeding and improving on past performances. Self-assessment helps students become more motivated to learn and improve the quality of the work they do. Student reflection on what they have learned and how well they have performed, goal setting, and plans for improvement that include specific strategies are all forms of self-assessment that can and should be used in a classroom.

Teach Students the Learner Action Cycle

Having students actively involved in the learning cycle of accessing, interpreting, producing, disseminating, and self-assessing is the secret to meeting the content standards required by state and national documents. If teachers are going to teach the processes in the standards along with the content, they must take students through this cycle as many times as possible so that the process becomes part of the tape that runs in students' heads. Once this happens, students will have a recipe for success whenever they have to learn something new and use it.

Unfortunately, many students—particularly the ones who feel helpless and hopeless—already have a tape playing in their heads, talking to them every time they face a new learning challenge or assignment. The tape is saying, "I can't do this!" If students believe that they cannot "do school," cannot succeed on the tasks a teacher assigns, we will see various behaviors that are intended to hide that truth. Students put their heads down on their desks, they "forget" to bring materials and work to class, they cut class, they decide to subvert the activities in the class and have some fun, they are surly and aggressive, and, finally, they drop out. The longer students have been failing in school, the more embedded this feeling of helplessness becomes. This is one explanation for the lack of student motivation evident in many secondary classrooms. There is hope, however. Teachers can help motivate students to participate in class and learn. By giving students an effective process for learning, no matter how long they have been in school, we can give them some power over their own learning and, most important, give them hope that they can succeed.

My at-risk 12th graders proved this to me by understanding the significance of the learner action cycle I taught them. Their test on the cycle was to write their own explanation of the cycle, and I was delighted with what they gave to me. Box 3.2 is an example of one group's work, and perhaps the most important line in their explanation is the first one: "You have a new assignment. . . ." The students in that group of three realized that this cycle wasn't just for my class. This cycle was to be used whenever they had to learn something new.

My students were so pleased with using the process that one student asked me to write all their instructions for assignments with the verbs in the order of the cycle so that she would "always know where to start."

Here is a student who felt helpless, who, when given an assignment, was overwhelmed and did not even know where to start. As we all know, if you do not know where to start in completing a task, you tend to procrastinate and hope that it will go away, and this is a sure recipe for disaster in school. Finding out that there was a system for learning and practicing the learner action cycle can get students started on the road to meeting standards.

Box 3.2

Students Using Learner Actions

You have a new assignment so you *access* by listening, observing, reading, and researching, and what you have is a lot of *information.* So, you must *interpret* by selecting, classifying, outlining, sequencing, and comparing, and what you have is your *focus.*

Then you must *produce* something by designing, creating, planning, building, or writing, and now what you have is *a product* and *knowledge* that you have to *disseminate* by teaching, presenting, and explaining to the *audience* for your learning.

All along the way, you must *assess* your performance by reflecting, evaluating, and *planning* for next time, and what you have is *a goal and strategies.*

■ USING THE LEARNER ACTIONS TO MEET STANDARDS

How can we help students learn this cycle so that they know how to begin a new assignment and how to go about learning and improving on their own? First, we need to teach students the learner action cycle. They need to know the process, which activities and verbs are involved in each stage, and how to do those many active verbs that are in the standards. Since the learner action cycle organizes learning and the various competency verbs embedded in state content standards, it is one of the things that should be hanging in classrooms so that students become *very* familiar with it and can look up and use it as a resource when they are beginning any new learning activity.

In one elementary teacher's classroom, she covered one wall in butcher's paper with the learner actions as headings to five columns. As the year progressed, students added verbs to the columns as they did various learning activities. For example, when the teacher gave a new assignment, she asked students how they might go about accessing information for the task or what they might do to produce evidence of their learning. As they came up with ideas, these verbs were added to the wall. By the end of the year, students knew what access, interpret, produce, disseminate, and self-assess meant, and they knew many ways to do these five learner actions. They had created their own learner action wall, and it was full of verbs representing the process skills they could use.

Get the Student Doing the Learner Action Verbs

In addition to teaching students about the learner action cycle, we must give students a lot of practice with the process. As often as possible, we need to guide them through the learner action cycle. One way to do this is to design lessons that get the students doing the cycle as they are learning content. An added bonus is that students will be much more motivated in class if they are active and involved in the lesson. It is much more fun to be doing something interesting with a topic than it is to be watching someone else as they tell you about a topic.

In many classrooms, the only person doing all the learner actions on a regular basis is the teacher. Just think about it. Do you access all the information for the students and then interpret it by organizing it into the lesson, student work sheets, study guides, assignments, and tests? Do you then produce a lesson plan and all the materials needed to go with it? Do you do all the talking about the content by explaining, justifying, and answering questions as you teach the lesson? Finally, when the class is over, do you spend time self-assessing and planning for the next class? If you answered yes to these questions, then you, like most teachers I know, are doing all the work. This is one of the reasons that teachers are so tired at the end of the day and that the students are dancing out of school in the afternoons still full of energy.

Since the teachers are the ones going through the learner actions—doing the verbs—they are also the ones remembering the content. As Wong and Wong (1991) say, "The person who does the work is the *only* one who learns" (p. 204). If you are the one going through the learner action verbs in every class, you are the one doing the work and the learning. So at the end of the year, you are the one who could pass the state tests with flying colors. But it is the students who will be tested, and to get the students to put the content information into their long-term memory, they must be the ones actively involved in the learning activities. They must be the ones doing the verbs in the learner action cycle.

An example of how teachers are still doing much of the work while the students are being passive is found in Stigler, Gonzales, Kawanaka, Knoll, and Serrano (1999). In 236 videotaped eighth-grade mathematics lessons in Japan, Germany, and the United States, they documented that American teachers' lesson plans

> Have two phases: an initial acquisition phase and a subsequent application phase. In the acquisition phase, the teacher demonstrates and/or explains how to solve an example problem. The explanation might be purely procedural (as most often happens in the United States) or may include development of concepts (more often the case in Germany). In the application phase, students practice solving examples on their own while the teacher helps individual students who are experiencing difficulty. (p. 5)

In this lesson model, the teacher gives out the information and then assigns problems for students to work. The work they are doing is not real-world application of the mathematical concepts because the problems are selected for them and are not open-ended, as problems requiring math in the real world tend to be. Therefore, in the typical American eighth-grade math class, the teacher is doing the high-level thinking of organizing the content and selecting the samples, and the students are doing very little.

■ ANALYZING LESSONS TO SEE WHO IS DOING ALL THE WORK

One thing teachers can do to increase the learner activity in their lessons is to design them with the learner actions in mind. This can be done by writing out a lesson sequence and then asking, "How are the students accessing information, interpreting the information, producing evidence of learning, disseminating their understanding, and self-assessing?" Teachers should also be asking, "How can I prove the students are engaged in these actions?" This question of documentation has become increasingly important since districts must have documentation to prove students' achievement of the state standards. So before writing down that students are doing a learner action verb, the teacher should plan to have some tangible evidence that students are engaged in that process. Whatever verbs the students will be doing can be written beside the sequence or highlighted in the lesson. If students are not really engaging in the learner actions, teachers should rethink the lesson and use instructional strategies that will increase student involvement.

The Learner Action Verb List (Table 3.1) is a great tool for looking to see which verbs students are doing in a lesson. The basis for this list was constructed by Burz (Burz & Marshall, 1996) and colleagues to organize the process verbs students needed to succeed in learning. As I worked with the original list over the years, teachers in my workshops and I added verbs to produce the list you see in Table 3.1. Since our amended list is still not comprehensive, there are certainly additional verbs that could be included, so feel free to add to the list if you like. The standards of the states with the largest student populations—New York, California, Illinois, and Texas—do include verbs from all the columns in Table 3.1, illustrating that these learner actions are in fact embedded in the standards. You might like to check your own state standards, highlight the action verbs, and then compare them to Table 3.1. This is one way to see which processes are emphasized in the standards your students must meet.

Looking at this list may remind you of verbs in other contexts, particularly in Bloom's Taxonomy (1956), the first real classification of levels in intellectual behavior. Bloom's six categories—knowledge, comprehension, application, analysis, synthesis, and evaluation—involve levels of thinking and can, in some cases be aligned with the Learner Action Cycle. Learner Action verbs, however, describe the actions a learner would take at each stage as well as the thinking that might be going on in a learner's head.

Looking at standards and at lesson plans, by focusing on what the students are doing, is a shift from the normal analysis of a lesson, which focuses on what the teacher is doing. When teachers assess their lessons by looking at what the learners are doing, many teachers realize that they, not the students, are doing all the work, all the verbs. (See Resources, Sample 20, for a blank Lesson Planner form to use for analyzing a lesson.) Once they see their lessons differently, teachers realize that students are not remembering content because they are not really doing very much with it, and, at this point, teachers begin to look for ways to get the students busy. Analyzing lessons with the learner action cycle can be a first step in changing instructional practice. It also makes teachers realize that they will need a lot more strategies for engaging students in learning,

Table 3.1   Learner Action Verb List

Access	Interpret	Produce	Disseminate	Self-Assess
investigate	analyze	create	publish	review
gather	explain	design	perform	reflect
interview	paraphrase	develop	teach	assess
research	rephrase	draw	present	revisit
listen	identify	write	transmit	compare
observe	compare/contrast	lay out	display	conclude
collect	connect	illustrate	explain	contrast
search	summarize	build	broadcast	generalize
inquire	clarify	draft	telecast	infer
survey	evaluate	invent	speak	interpret
view	translate	model	advertise	predict
discover	prioritize	sketch	disclose	prove
read	synthesize	assemble	send	question
explore	sequence	formulate	illustrate	refute
question	determine	make	sing	support
seek	decide	solve	dance	verify
find	define	compose	participate	test
brainstorm	describe	generate	show	realign
experiment	organize	construct	demonstrate	judge
examine	generalize		engage	plan
ask	prepare		discuss	emphasize
study	predict refine		act	
solicit	infer think		exhibit	
discuss	integrate edit		share	
	critique choose		answer	
	relate assess		respond	
	apply consider		describe	
	plan distinguish		express	
	judge review		narrate	
	realign restate		tell	
	test interpret		interact	
	verify trace		contribute	
	support justify		orient	
	refute select		introduce	
	prove monitor			
	manipulate			
	recognize			

SOURCE: Adapted from H. L. Burz & K. Marshall (1996). *Performance-based curriculum for mathematics: From knowing to showing*. Thousand Oaks, CA: Corwin Press.

and they often start asking for substantive, appropriate staff-development opportunities.

A Sample Analysis of a Lesson

To demonstrate this method of analyzing lessons, let's analyze a typical American eighth-grade math lesson sequence using the learner actions and the question, What are the students doing? In other words, are students watching us work with math instead of struggling to find the information, make sense of it in their own minds, produce evidence that they are learning, explain their processes, and examine their own work to determine what more they need to learn? Figure 3.1 contains a sample of a typical eighth-grade math lesson plan in the United States, as identified by Stigler and colleagues (1999). The sequence that is written on the right of the page is what an observer might script to indicate what happened in that class. On the left side, I have written the learner action verbs that students are engaged in during the lesson. Keep in mind that the verbs do not have to occur in order in a lesson. Accessing, for example, may happen anywhere in the sequence. Also, not every

Figure 3.1   Typical Lesson Plan: Math

LESSON PLAN

Content Area(s): _Math_   **Grade:** _8_   **Teacher:** _Benson_
Essential Learning: _Operations dealing with roots_

Learner Actions	**Lesson Sequence**
How will students	1. Teacher gave answers to homework, asked if there were any questions, answered two, then collected homework
ACCESS: Listen Observe Teacher Read text Question—2 students	
	2. Teacher introduced next section of chapter, giving several examples or problems on the board

INTERPRET:
Compare
  home wordk
  answers to
  correct answers	

	3. Teacher assigned problems 1 through 25 on page 87 for homework, let students start on problems while teacher walked around and answered questions.
PRODUCE: Solve problems Write answers	
DISSEMINATE:	
SELF-ASSESS:	

good lesson has to include the whole learner action cycle. If you would like to look at possible activities students could be doing, you can use the Learner Action Verb List as a reference to see if you would add any student activity to the list I have made.

Even if you look very closely and are really hopeful about what the students are doing, it is easy to see that they are not doing much more than accessing information by listening and observing, and then they are producing solutions to problems by writing them out. There is no evidence of them interpreting, disseminating, or self-assessing during this lesson. For these students to learn the math concepts in the lesson so that they can apply them to problems they have not seen before—the types of problems they will see on the next state test they take—they need to be doing more. They especially need to be doing a lot of the verbs listed in the Interpret column of the Learner Action Verb List. This is the part of the cycle that involves high-level critical thinking, and it is the one most heavily represented in the standards for student learning.

Another learner action that is prevalent in the standards is the disseminate stage in which students are required to verbalize their understanding: to explain, justify, and teach what they know to someone else in a way that allows the listener to comprehend the material. This is very interesting, because the states have not figured out a good way to test this particular step in learning. In fact, if students start disseminating their learning in a standardized test, they will no doubt be told to stop talking and to leave! As schools, districts, and states have realized the emphasis in the standards on this particular stage of learning, many are instituting 8th-grade portfolio panels, 10th-grade passage portfolios with a presentation before a committee, and/or graduation projects, portfolios, and presentations. These practices are part of the Bill and Melinda Gates Foundation small high schools as well as routine in many research-based reform models such as Expeditionary Learning Schools. Later, when students go for advanced degrees, an essential part of that process is being able to defend (to talk about) their research in front of a panel of experts in order to prove that they have learned the material and done their own work. So, as school systems are beginning to expect students to explain verbally what they have learned, having students do this in class on a regular basis is essential both for helping them remember what we are teaching and for determining what they are learning. It also becomes part of the preparation students need to succeed in school and beyond. Obviously, we do need to incorporate this learner action in our lessons.

Ideas for Increasing Student Activity in the Sample Lesson

It would not really be difficult to improve the sample eighth-grade math lesson to more actively engage students in the learning, so that they are doing more verbs. Even incorporating one of the ideas in Box 3.3 would mean that students were more engaged in the learner action cycle, and, therefore, more involved in learning the content for themselves.

> **Box 3.3**
>
> **Ideas for Increasing Student Involvement
> in Sample Math Lesson**
>
> 1. Have students in study groups of two or three go over homework problems to come to consensus on answers and determine questions or clarifications they need. (Teacher circulates to observe, document work, and maintain student focus on task.)
>
> 2. Teacher facilitates discussion on questions homework groups have and has students supply answers and explanations whenever possible.
>
> 3. Teacher introduces new concept by putting up a problem that illustrates it and asking students to analyze it to determine how it is like what they've been doing and what is different about it. They should try to solve the problem, and if they can't, to verbalize why and determine what they need to know.
>
> 4. Students then go to their texts to find the answers to their questions, and they work with a partner to solve another similar problem. If necessary, the teacher can give additional explanation of the new concept to the class or groups who need it.
>
> 5. Students are assigned five problems to solve using the new concept and to write how they did it. Teacher circulates to assist students and to keep them on task. Unfinished problems are to be completed for homework.
>
> 6. Or students could be asked to write a note to someone who was absent today explaining the new concept and creating two sample problems that illustrate the concept.

*Have Students Go Over the Homework
to Uncover the Questions*

Imagine that a teacher has used the first two steps of the lesson sequence in Box 3.3, asking students to go over homework in partners, answer each other's questions, and decide which learner actions students would be doing. Clearly, as students checked their homework, they would be accessing information from each other through discussion; interpreting by analyzing problems, deciding which were correct, and determining what to ask about the problems they did not know how to do; disseminating as they explained their work to each other and then asked their questions of the class and the teacher; and self-assessing as they analyzed their own answers and work process to determine what they needed next to get the work done correctly. This is a vast improvement over the simple accessing they were doing in the original lesson sequence.

Just following these first two ideas, however, would be hard for many math teachers. I have had high school teachers in different workshops tell me that if they tried this, their students would not discuss the math. Instead, they copied each other's answers. In fact, these teachers are probably correct. Currently, many students have decided that all that matters in math class is getting the right answer. Whether or not they understand how to work that type of problem is irrelevant. So in an effort to do what they think is expected, students would copy from each other without hesitation. The purpose of the homework problem analysis suggested in Box 3.3 is, however, not just to get the right answer. Instead, it is to have students analyze their work and process so that if they are confused, they can ask a good question to help them understand how to do the work. The purpose of the activity is learning math, not getting all the answers right.

If teachers wanted to have students really start talking math, they would need to explain the purpose of homework and this way of checking homework. They would also need to be sure students had methods for working together and enough practice doing so that they could be efficient. Finally, the teachers would have to have a way to give students credit for their effort and work that focused on their understanding of the concept being taught. If teachers did these things and were persistent in giving students multiple opportunities to work this way, students would become much more competent and involved in learning math.

Have the Students Discover the New Math Concepts

The third idea in Box 3.3, presenting a new concept by giving the students a problem and having them solve it, is the instructional strategy that was used most often in Japanese classes. Instead of the teacher demonstrating the new concept while students passively absorbed information, students would have to access the necessary information, interpret the sample problem and its new component as well as connect it to previous work, produce a logical solution, and disseminate their strategy to the class. Throughout this learning, they would be self-assessing their own prior knowledge as well as the accuracy of their *thinking* and their work. The third suggestion is very different from the normal approach to teaching a new concept in American math classes. It does, however, involve the students in all five of the learner actions so that they are learning mathematics at a high level. Perhaps that partially explains why Japanese middle and high school students are able to succeed on international tests of math that require retention of concepts and the application of these concepts in unfamiliar problems. Remember, the person doing the verbs is the one doing the learning.

How About Choices for Homework

The homework possibilities listed in Box 3.3, selecting problems to complete and writing how they were done or writing a letter explaining the new concept, would also require students to do higher-level thinking and use their writing skills to communicate about math—something required on many state-level mathematics exams. Actually, students could be offered all three of the homework assignments, including the practice computation assignment in the original lesson. They could choose the one they felt most capable of that day. Or students could be assigned different ones depending on the teacher's assessment of their level of understanding at the time. Giving tiered assignments such as these is one way of differentiating instruction to meet individual student needs. Of course, the issue of how to grade the various products that result from these three assignments will trouble some teachers. If, however, what the teacher wants to know is how well students understood the new concept, that could be determined from the work on any one of the assignments. What is important to evaluate and give students credit for is evidence of understanding, not a certain number of right answers.

Plan for Students to Do the Verbs so They Are Learning the Content

To improve this lesson and get students doing more of the work, a teacher would not have to implement all the ideas in Box 3.3. Just taking one of them would increase the student's engagement with the content. So if you are a teacher who is trying to get more student involvement in learning, you can begin by analyzing your lessons using the learner actions and then selecting a good instructional strategy to improve at least one aspect of the sequence so that the students must do more than they are doing now.

If teachers used all the ideas in Box 3.3 to structure lessons, they would be using the type of hands-on teaching that has been recommended by the National Council of Teachers of Mathematics (NCTM) (2000) standards and is implicit in state learning standards that insist students are able to apply content. Stigler and colleagues (1999) confirm this connection by reporting, "Japanese classes share many features called for by U.S. mathematics reforms, while U.S. classes are less likely to exhibit these features. Although most U.S. math teachers report familiarity with reform recommendations, relatively few apply the key points in their classrooms" (p. 7).

We know that teachers need to become the planners and facilitators of student learning experiences and that students need to be the workers in the classroom. We also know how very hard it is to change ingrained behaviors such as structuring lessons the way they have always been done. No doubt, teachers need a practical way to assess their lessons to see for themselves just how much students are actually doing. Using the learner action cycle offers a quick way to assess lessons and select student activities that can be included in lesson sequences to increase student engagement in learning content.

Looking at Other Content Area Lessons

I have used the math lesson as an example because that particular sequence has been documented as typical of eighth-grade instruction, but all too often teachers are doing the learner actions while students are watching in core academic content areas at all grade levels. For an illustration of this point, analyze the science and world history lessons (Figures 3.2 and 3.3). These lessons represent different content areas and are examples of typical middle school and high school lessons. I know that many teachers do plan lessons for students to become active in the learning process, but, unfortunately, students spend far too much time in school just learning to be passive, because our lessons require too little from them.

If you look over these sample lessons and imagine a student's day that includes the math lesson in Figure 3.1, the science lesson in Figure 3.2, the world history lesson in Figure 3.3, and the language arts lesson in Figure 3.4, you realize the student has spent the majority of the day listening, watching, and reading prescribed and preorganized material and writing

Figure 3.2   Typical Lesson Plan: Science

LESSON PLAN

Content Area(s): *Science*   **Grade:** *MS/HS*   **Teacher:** *Brown*

Essential Learning: *Diversity, Ecology*

Learner Actions	Lesson Sequence
How will students **ACCESS:**	1. Teacher had assigned chapter 5 in the science book for homework. Students were to have read and outlined the major ideas in the chapter.
INTERPRET:	2. Class started with the teacher talking about how species compete for food and living space in the Amazon River basin.
PRODUCE:	3. Then the class watched a video on the Amazon, and students were told to take notes on any new info they got about the competition of species in the jungle. Video ran for 30 minutes.
DISSEMINATE:	4. After the video, the teacher gave the students a quick pop quiz of five questions about the Amazon River and its inhabitants. The quiz questions related to the video's content.
SELF-ASSESS:	5. As class ended, students were assigned the questions at the end of the chapter they had read and outlined the night before and told these questions would be taken up at the beginning of class the next day.

Figure 3.3   Typical Lesson Plan: World History

LESSON PLAN

Content Area(s): *World History*   **Grade:** *10*   **Teacher:** *Evans*

Essential Learning: *Explorers of the New World*

Learner Actions	Lesson Sequence
How will students **ACCESS:**	1. Students were assigned the chapter on exploration for homework. They had been asked to take notes on the explorers in the chapter.
INTERPRET:	2. Teacher asked them to take out their notes and add any new information they got from a lecture on Western European exploration of the New World, focusing on five explorers.
PRODUCE:	3. Teacher lectured for 45 minutes. Teacher gave students a chance to ask questions after the lecture and answered five questions—two asking for correct dates from lecture and three for spelling of terms or explorers' names.
DISSEMINATE: **SELF-ASSESS:**	4. Once the questions were answered, students had class time to write answers to questions # 3, 5, 7, 8, and 10 at the end of the chapter. They could use their notes but not their books to do this. If they did not finish these, they were asked to finish them for homework.

to communicate short, closed responses to low-level questions supplied by texts. It is no wonder that students often blow up by fifth period in middle schools and high schools and end up in the principal's office. They are bored and tired of sitting still doing the same things over and over again. And if they are already failures at school and do not believe they can do any better, they see no reason to continue to participate in what they view as empty, irrelevant, or impossible activities. If we could begin to make the learning process part of learning the content so that the students are actively engaged in something that increases the probability of their success and is interesting, we would surely see a decline in discipline problems. Engaged, motivated students do not cause problems in class because they are enjoying the process of learning.

Just getting kids active, however, is not the goal here. They must be active with a purpose—to learn the essential skills and content. With all good intentions to get students active, teachers sometimes make the mistake of using an activity for activity's sake. Fieldtrips that do not have a focus, and ones for which students are not prepared for and from which they are not expected to come back with substantive information, are just one example of wasted activity. Complex, interdisciplinary projects that focus on things that are not really essential or that never make it clear to students what they are supposed to be learning are a waste of precious time. If a class is studying teddy bears for a week, building a diorama of a Native American village, or having a medieval festival, what are they learning? Is it essential knowledge or a learning process required by the

Figure 3.4   Typical Lesson Plan: Language Arts

LESSON PLAN

Content Area(s): _Language Arts_   **Grade:** _4_   **Teacher:** _Benson_
Essential Learning: _Reading a new story for information_

Learner Actions	Lesson Sequence
How will students **ACCESS:**	1. Teacher introduced story by having a student read the title and another student read the short information about the author.
INTERPRET:	2. Teacher told students to read the story with a buddy and let the teacher know when they were finished.
PRODUCE:	3. When all were finished, teacher asked everyone to look at the questions at the end. She asked one student to read question #1, then asked who could answer it. One student gave the answer, and the teacher moved to the other questions, answering them in the same way.
DISSEMINATE:	4. For homework, students were asked to write a paragraph describing their favorite character.
SELF-ASSESS:	

standards? When it is over, can the students verbalize what they learned and why it is important? Has the teacher documented the important content and processes students have learned or demonstrated? Having activity for activity's sake is not the goal of a standards-based classroom. Instead, we must have students involved in the learning cycle they will need as they leave school and enter a world where being able to learn, unlearn, and relearn have been identified as survival skills for the 21st century. We must produce lifelong learners, not just "A" students who memorized content and quickly forgot it.

Interestingly, in the arts, career and vocational courses, technology classes, physical education classes, many foreign language classes, and specials like student publication courses, students are actively engaged in at least the first four stages of the learner action cycle because all these classes depend on student performance and active demonstrations of learning. These courses are hands-on most of the time. Perhaps that is why students will often work very hard in these classes and be willing to come in extra hours before and after school to practice and prepare for exhibits, concerts, plays, and publication of the school newspaper or yearbook. These courses tend to be interesting to students, and often, by high school, may be some of the courses that keep students in school.

One of my own sons, who was an academically strong student, told me when he was in seventh grade that band "saves my life every day" because it wasn't boring! I believe that his involvement in music did in fact keep him in school long enough to graduate from high school. He was even willing to give up his lunch period his senior year to be in a music production class. For a 17-year-old boy, missing food is a major sacrifice. He would not have done that for one of his academic core courses because he was not involved or active in those classes. He was doing what is evident in the sample lessons described above—sitting quietly, listening, observing, taking notes, and writing canned responses.

For Administrators—Observing and Responding to Lessons by Using the Learner Actions

Administrators can also use the learner actions to analyze lessons when they are observing teachers. The blank form (Resources, Sample 20) can be used to script the lesson that is observed. Then the observer can look at the lesson script using the Learner Action Verb List to determine how much students were really doing. For example, look at the scripted lesson in Figure 3.4. If you had observed this lesson, you could look at your script afterward and ask the question, "What learner actions were the students doing?"

Analyzing the Language Arts Lesson for Student Engagement

During this fourth-grade language arts lesson, it is apparent that students are accessing by listening and reading. The students who answered the questions from the end of the story might have had to disseminate their understanding, but there is no evidence that they had to supply proof from the story of their answers or explain why they answered the way they did, so the level of thinking needed was at the lower end of Bloom's (1956) taxonomy: knowledge and comprehension only. There was no evidence of interpreting, producing, or self-assessing during the class time spent on this lesson.

The homework did require students to interpret by deciding which character they liked and then describing that individual. They would also be producing a written product, a paragraph. Given the fact that state standards are particularly heavy on interpreting verbs, and fourth-grade students often face state tests on writing, it would probably be wiser if the teacher had students doing these activities in class. There, students who really had no clue how to do an assignment like this could be monitored, instructed, and supported. Having this essential interpretive and communication work done as homework turns the teaching of these very important learner actions over to whomever is at home to help the student. As we know, many students have very little or no support at home, so we are setting them up for failure on the homework assignment and on the state tests that will expect them to be able to process information and produce written evidence of their understanding. The learner actions need to be done in class as often as possible so that students who do not know how to do them, the students who are at risk of failure in schoolwork, have the opportunity to learn the skills represented by the verbs as they do the class work.

If, as in this sample lesson, there was not much student involvement during the class time, as the administrative observer, you can target one of the learner action stages and suggest strategies to the teacher that would engage students more. Since this is a reading and writing lesson, many of the strategies that might get the students accessing and interpreting the information at a higher level, and self-assessing and disseminating what they are learning, are research-based methods from good-reading instruction. The ideas listed in Box 3.4 illustrate again that teachers do not need to throw out what they are already doing. They do need to use the best ideas they have at their disposal and organize what they are doing effectively so that students have the best-possible opportunity to meet the demands new standards make.

Conferencing With the Teacher About the Lesson

Administrators, assuming you have observed Ms. Benson teaching this fourth-grade lesson, analyzed the lesson, and found areas that need improvement, what would be most helpful to tell her when you have the postobservation conference? If you hand her the list of suggestions in Box 3.4 and say, "Go forth and do some of these," chances are she will only complain to the next teacher she meets in the hall that you haven't been in a classroom for a long time, and you don't have a clue what these kids are like today.

If she doesn't see the problems with the lesson you observed, you will need to take her where she is in her understanding of the necessity for students to be active learners and try to be very specific about what might help get the students working more. For Ms. Benson, it would be much more useful to select one to three ideas from the list and ask her to try at least one of them. She would probably need ideas that would not involve a great deal of class time or restructuring how she currently runs her class. If she needs support, you could offer to be there when she tries the strategy or have her get back to you on how it goes. After she has tried something, you can suggest other ideas and try to keep her progressing in the right direction with her professional growth and classroom strategies.

Box 3.4

Ideas for Increasing Student Involvement in Sample Language Arts Lesson

- Have students read the title and predict what they think the story is about.
- Ask students if they know anything about the subject of the story or have been in a situation like one a character will face.
- Give students a synopsis of the story or the beginning of the story and ask them to write down any questions they would like to find answers to in the story.
- Give students a vocabulary list from the story and tell them to mark any other words they'd like to talk about as they read.
- Read the beginning of the story out loud and create questions together that need to be answered by finishing the story.
- Read the questions at the back of the story first so students will know what to look for as they read.
- Use a cartoon, anecdote, poem, or references to something else the students have read or know about to introduce the story situation or main idea.
- Have students create some sort of organizer when they have finished the story—for example, a Venn diagram comparing and contrasting two characters, a T chart, a question-answer-response (QAR) sequence of questions, a web. They could do this alone or in a group, and use the information to write about the story.
- Have students share questions they may have created with other students who must find the answers or explain why there is no answer.
- Ask students to create questions for the story once they are finished reading it and exchange these with a buddy or contribute them to a class list to be discussed. They should be prepared to explain why their questions are significant in understanding this story.
- Have students act as TV directors who are making a show of this story and explain how they would like a scene to be played.
- Once students have discussed the story, prepare a reader's theater or radio production to be shared with another class.
- If story generates questions about motive, have students write a letter as the character in question explaining why he or she behaved as he or she did.
- Have students begin keeping a reader response journal with reactions to the story and connections between this story and others they have read or experiences they have had.
- Students could be asked to illustrate a scene in the story for an illustrated edition.
- Others???

Obviously, for administrators to do this type of observation and conferencing with teachers, they will need a wealth of instructional strategies that would fit the five learner actions. In my mind, this type of teacher observation and conversation about ways to increase students' active learning are part of what being an instructional leader means. To be sure students are learning the content and processes in new standards, administrators should be looking at what students are doing and then helping teachers identify strategies to get students doing more. Some good resources for instructional strategies are listed at the end of this chapter in Ideas for Administrators.

Sample Lessons in Which Students Are Doing the Learner Actions

So what would a good, standards-based lesson look like? In Figures 3.5 and 3.6 are two lessons, one for fourth-grade social studies and one that can be adapted for middle school or high school students who are learning how to read poetry. The poetry lesson sample is for 12th-grade British and Western literature, but I have used the sequence successfully with students from fifth grade up. All one must change is the poetry samples used in the lesson so they are appropriate for the age and interests of students.

Students Doing Social Studies

By analyzing the fourth-grade social studies lesson, one can see that students began by accessing information from their prior knowledge, the class, and their small group by brainstorming, listening, and discussing. They produced lists and notes to which they added as the class contributed information. They watched and listened as the teacher modeled the reading and information gathering they would be doing by reading the passage about George Washington. They interpreted information by placing it on an organizer and then disseminated what they had found by sharing with the class. At the end of class, they self-assessed by doing a Ticket Out the Door (see Box 1.5, Think Pads) to record what they had learned about Washington and jobs of the Revolutionary period. In the course of one class, they had been doing a lot of work and had been through all five of the learner action stages.

Critics Reading Poetry

Like the social studies lesson, the poetry lesson includes all five learner actions and various strategies to have students working alone and together to access, interpret, produce, disseminate, and self-assess. Students are accessing by listening, reading, discussing, and researching information that can help interpret the poem they have been given. They interpret by analyzing the poem using the process for reading a poem and the rubric with the criteria for a good critique as organizers for their discussions. They also have to compare the title to the poem in order to decide how the title connects. They have to look at the vocabulary in context and decide on appropriate meanings for the words. They produce a written interpretation for the poem, and they disseminate their understanding by discussing together in their groups. In the next class, they will also be presenting, explaining, and justifying their interpretation to the whole class. They actually did some self-assessment at the beginning of the class as they decided whether or not they liked poetry and why they felt the way they did. They also assessed their interpretation of the poem using

Figure 3.5   Standards-Based Lesson Plan: Social Studies

LESSON PLAN

Content Area(s): *Social Studies*   **Grade:** *4*   **Teacher:** *Barnett*

Essential Learning: *Important Americans and Colonial Life*

Learner Actions	Lesson Sequence
How will students **ACCESS:**	1. Teacher put question from standards on a piece of chart paper and told students they would begin to answer it during the lesson.
	2. Students were divided into groups of three, and each student got a copy of a portrait of George Washington and an organizer.
	3. Students were asked if they knew who the person in the picture was. Several identified him, and then students were given 1 minute to make a list of facts on the left side of their organizer about what they knew about him.
INTERPRET:	4. After 1 minute, students stopped and shared their facts with their group. The group members could add to their list any new ideas they got from their team. [All directions for this activity were written on an overhead so students could refer to them as they worked.]
PRODUCE:	5. Once students had shared in their teams, the teacher quickly called on each group to collect their facts and wrote them on the overhead under the heading, "What We Know About George Washington."
DISSEMINATE:	6. Students were then given a copy of a book entitled Major Washington. The teacher told them that as they read this, they would learn more about George Washington and what people did for a living in colonial America.
SELF-ASSESS:	7. The teacher told them they would be reading it over several days and adding info to their organizers about Washington and jobs at the time. Teacher read two paragraphs aloud to model the technique for filling in the planner, then asked students to read through paragraph 10 and fill in information on their organizers. They shared info on jobs, and teacher wrote these on the chart paper with the question, What jobs did people have in colonial America?
	8. Class ended with a ticket out the door asking students to list one thing they had learned about Washington, one thing about jobs and any questions they had.

Figure 3.6   Standards-Based Lesson Plan: Language Arts (Poetry)

LESSON PLAN

Content Area(s): *Language Arts*   **Grade:** *12*   **Teacher:** *Benson*

Essential Learning: *Teach a process for reading a poem and introduce a unit on WWI British poetry.*

Learner Actions	Lesson Sequence
How will students **ACCESS:**	1. Teacher asked students to think about and share with a partner why people might not like poetry. Then teacher asked them to share with the class and had a volunteer student write the reasons on the board.
	2. Once the student list was complete, teacher said, "How would you like to have a formula to help you when you have to read poems for school?" Students agreed that would be a good idea.
	3. The teacher used a short poem to illustrate the six-step process for reading a poem.
INTERPRET:	4. Then she put them into groups of four, assigned each student a job by having them number off, and gave them a task and a new poem to read and understand using the six-step process.
	5. Before the students started working, the teacher shared and discussed a rubric that gave the criteria for a good discussion of a poem. This was how their presentation to the class would be assessed.
PRODUCE:	6. Since the title of the poem was in Latin, teacher asked if anyone knew what it meant. When they weren't sure, teacher translated it and gave them a little more info on the meaning of the Roman saying it was taken from. Teacher asked students to anticipate what the poem might be about based on this info, thus modeling step one.
	7. Then teacher read the poem aloud, modeling step two. Teacher said she had practiced it and wanted to read it aloud! Students then used the other four steps to discuss the new poem in their groups and prepare their presentations. The teacher circulated, monitoring, asking and answering a few questions with each group.
DISSEMINATE:	8. After about 20 minutes of group work, the teacher asked students to take out their rubric for discussing a poem and to assess their work so far to see how they were doing.
SELF-ASSESS:	9. As class ended, students were told they would have 5 minutes the following day to complete their discussion and prepare, and then they would be giving their interpretations of the poem to the class. If they needed to, they could do additional research on the poem for homework.

the rubric to compare and contrast their interpretation with the quality criteria to be sure they had included all the necessary information.

This lesson is a good example of a teacher planning for student learning experiences and facilitating the student work during the class time. Since the ability to analyze and communicate information is embedded in standards, not only in language arts, students are engaged in purposeful activity that is aligned with important standards for student learning (see Resources, Samples 21 and 22, for the process for reading a poem and a copy of the rubric for discussing a poem; Figure 3.6). As an added bonus, students love this kind of class. Even if they entered the room prepared to sit back and watch the teacher work, they get involved in the discussion right away because the first question the teacher asks about why some people don't like poetry engages them personally. Often the malcontents jump right in to express their own negative opinions, and they are hooked. As one student said with great amazement at the end of class, "This was fun!"

Must All Lessons Have All Five Learner Actions?

When you analyze these two lesson sequences, it becomes apparent that students are engaged in most if not all the learner actions within the confines of one class period. It is not necessary to have students go through the whole cycle in one class, but it is possible. I suggest that teachers plan for students to go through the whole learning cycle at least once a week. If a teacher plans this way, some days may be spent on accessing activities, others doing the interpreting and producing, and so on. As the students move from one action verb to another, the teacher should be telling them what stage of the process they are in by saying things like, "Today we will be interpreting the information you got yesterday by making a Venn diagram," or, "We need to stop and do some self-assessment with the rubric for your product, so you can decide what you need to do next to complete this assignment." In this way, students are getting consistent practice in the learner action process and learning the vocabulary and steps to the process. If they do these things, the chances of the cycle becoming part of how they approach a new task increases greatly.

In addition, students have various ways to approach the content material. They are also working together on open-ended questions, making meaning of the content in their own minds, and working the way professionals in these two content areas, historians and critics, work in the world beyond school. Therefore, they do see some connection between what they are learning and what they call "the real world." This is the type of learner-centered, active learning that should be going on in classrooms K–12. As author and expert on motivating students without grades Kohn (1999) reports, there "is a raft of research demonstrating that the most effective learning takes place when students are able to make choices about what they're doing, when they're about to learn with and from one another, when they're able to plan an active role in making sense of ideas. . . ." (p. 36). This type of class does not just happen. Teachers must plan consciously for students to be engaged purposefully in the learner actions and the essential content for that grade level or course. Since planning lessons using the learner actions and getting the students to do the work is not the traditional way teaching, it will not always be easy for teachers to rethink their lessons and teach differently. Changes like this take time. We must, however, begin.

■ IDEAS FOR TEACHERS

- Become familiar with the five learner actions—access, interpret, produce, disseminate, and self-assess—and the verbs that fit into each stage of the cycle.
- Teach your students the learner action cycle.
- Post in your room the learner actions and some verbs that fit into the five stages.
- Use the Lesson Planner (Resources, Sample 20), and the Learner Action Verb List (Table 3.1) to analyze some of your lesson plans. If the students will not be doing much during the lesson sequence, add some strategies that will get them involved in the learner actions.
- Plan your lessons so that students will go through the whole learner action cycle at least once a week.
- Be sure that if you insert activities into your plans that they are purposeful and will help the students learn the essential content and competencies your standards require.
- To determine which of the learner action verbs are most important for your students to learn at your grade level or in your content area course, look through the standards that apply to your students and highlight the active verbs. Usually there are some that will show up repeatedly. These are the ones you should be sure that your students can do by the end of the year, so you should embed them in your lesson plans regularly.
- Continue to add instructional strategies to your repertoire—your handy card file—and organize them by the learner actions they best address. If you are looking for some books with great strategies, see the resource list at the end of this chapter.
- Be sure that you are not the only one in the class doing the learner actions. Get the students busy doing those verbs!

■ IDEAS FOR ADMINISTRATORS

- Become familiar with the learner actions and the verbs that apply to each stage of the learning cycle.
- Use the learner actions when you observe classes, to help you focus on what the students are doing. (See Resources, Samples 23 and 24, for forms for class observations.) If this proves to be a useful way to observe and discuss teachers' lessons, work with your staff to create your own observation form to document what the learners are doing during a lesson as well as what the teacher is doing.
- As you prepare to meet with teachers for their postobservation conferences, look over their lessons for particular learner actions that students were not doing. Focus the teacher on one or two ideas for improving student engagement in their lesson sequences. Ask to see strategies that would address this area when you go for another observation.
- If teachers have no ideas for improving the student involvement in the learner actions, give them several strategies to try. If you have been modeling strategies in faculty meetings, now is the time to choose one that would fit a particular learner action and suggest that the teacher try it.

- Keep a handy card file of good strategies for involving students in the learner action cycle so you have a wide range of suggestions for teachers as you observe and confer with them. If you see teachers using good ideas, write them down, and add them to your collection. When you go to professional development sessions or conferences, keep your eyes open for ideas you could give teachers.
- Create a lesson plan form that has a space on it for the teacher to indicate which learner actions students will be doing in this lesson. For example, the Sample 20 form in Resources could be used for this purpose.
- Have teachers go through your state standards and ask them to highlight the active verbs they see. Then have them organize those verbs according to the learner actions to see which ones they would need to emphasize in their grade or course. This activity will help teachers see just how many active verbs are in the standards and are expected of students. This realization may help them understand that their lessons need to be planned to get students busy doing all those verbs.
- When you are observing a class where students are busy, ask the students what they are doing, what they are learning, and why it is important. If they cannot answer these questions, or their answers do not correspond to what the teacher intended for them to learn, you will need to talk to the teacher about the fact that it is crucial students know what they are learning and why. Therefore, teachers have to be sure to communicate the purposes for the activities to students, and these purposes need to be connected to the standards students must meet.
- Resources for instructional strategies to help teachers engage students include G. H. Gregory and C. Chapman (2002), *Differentiated Instructional Strategies: One Size Doesn't Fit All,* Thousand Oaks, CA, Corwin Press; E. Jensen (1998), *Teaching With the Brain in Mind,* Alexandria, VA, Association for Supervision & Curriculum Development; R. J. Marzano, D. J. Pickering, and J. E. Pollock (2001), *Classroom Instruction That Works: Research-Based Strategies for Increasing Student Achievement,* Alexandria, VA, Association for Supervision & Curriculum Development; and S. Rogers, J. Ludington, and S. Graham (1997), *Motivation and Learning,* Evergreen, CO, Peak Learning Systems.

4

Developing
More Authentic
Tasks and
Assessments

The fourth component of a standards-based classroom is that students should be doing work that is in line with the dual demands of the standards: that students must learn content and be able to apply their knowledge through many processes in real-world situations. If they are doing this type of complex work, it also follows that we will be assessing their progress and learning in many ways, not only through but including standardized and constructed response tests. Changing the type of work students do and how we assess and evaluate that work is perhaps the most difficult of the four components to implement because of longstanding practices for student work and for evaluating and reporting student progress. In order to create the type of tasks needed, we must build on the other three parts of a standards-based classroom—creating the community of learners, building the habit of reflection, and teaching content and learner action verbs—and we must rethink how we design and assess student learning.

■ WHAT TYPE OF WORK SHOULD STUDENTS BE DOING?

For many reasons, students should be doing work in school that is interesting, challenging, and relevant to their current needs and interests as well as their future success. Our common sense tells us that learners who are more enthusiastic about and engaged in their work will learn more and remember more of the content they study. Research on the brain confirms that students do learn and remember more when they are focused and actively engaged in an activity. Bracey (2001), a research psychologist and writer reporting on findings from the Sloan Study of Youth and Development on what engages students' minds, affirms that, "Instruction that students found relevant to their lives, instruction that was academically challenging, and instruction that made more academic demands . . . increased engagement" (p. 555).

More real-world? More challenging? More academically demanding? Isn't that what the standards are asking for? Absolutely! Looking back at the results of the exercise of taking a big-picture look at standards in the Introduction (see Resources, Samples 1 and 2), it is obvious that the standards are looking for students to apply higher-level content knowledge in more complex and realistic situations, ones like those they will face in their lives after graduation. Therefore, the standards are demanding that we change the type of work students do, and, to do so, we may have to change our thinking about what is appropriate and serious schoolwork.

Reporting on an ongoing study in Chicago, Viadero (November 1999) stated that the more challenging the assignments, the higher the quality of the student work tended to be. The Chicago study had collected 1,400 tasks and accompanying student work samples from Chicago elementary teachers. Teachers designated the tasks they submitted as typical or challenging. Trained teachers from other schools assessed the tasks for challenge using criteria that were based on the level of intellectual rigor needed for students to complete the tasks. "To be considered challenging, for example, an assignment had to require students to 'construct knowledge' by interpreting, analyzing, or synthesizing information and then elaborating on their conclusions. The tasks also had to connect in some way with students' lives beyond school" (p. 10). The quality of student work for each task was also evaluated.

In addition to the positive relationship between the level of challenge in a task and the quality of student work, another important and disturbing finding emerged in this study. Teachers often do not give students challenging assignments even though they believe they are doing so. According to the criteria used to rate the tasks, more than 70% of the tasks submitted by teachers as "challenging" presented students with either "no challenge" or "*minimal* challenge" (p. 10). Therefore, our traditional notions of what is challenging for students does not meet the criteria for what is really challenging and engaging for the learner's brain, tasks that require constructing, interpreting, analyzing, synthesizing, and elaborating in a relevant context.

Making student work more challenging and academically demanding does not mean making the homework assignments longer and the tests harder, as many educators assume when they see the call for higher standards. If the work is also to be more relevant and closer to the work that adults do, it also isn't about covering more chapters in a shorter time, doing more worksheets, having more homework, or taking harder tests. It is fundamentally about doing complex, open-ended, interdisciplinary tasks that give students the chance to learn and demonstrate what they are learning. Creating challenging tasks is also about going through the learner action cycle in the context of complex and real problems that require significant content knowledge. These tasks must be serious and have value for the students and, when possible, for the community at large. Meeting higher standards is about incorporating quality performance tasks into the regular student work in K–12 classrooms.

■ PERFORMANCE TASKS

A performance task is a complex learning and assessment activity during which students must apply content knowledge and competencies to demonstrate what they know. Quality performance tasks insist that the student demonstrate both elements of the standards: the content and the processes (see Figure 4.1). As Darling-Hammond (1997) explains, "Good performance tasks are complex intellectual, physical, and social challenges. They stretch students' thinking and planning abilities and use student aptitudes and interests as springboards for developing competence" (p. 116).

Figure 4.1   Performance Tasks

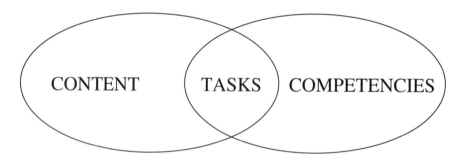

Performance Tasks are the method for having students learn, practice, and demonstrate essential content knowledge and competencies required in new standards.

CONTENT   TASKS   COMPETENCIES

In addition to meeting both aspects of the standards, performance tasks engage students because they are real work, not busy work (see Box 4.1). Whether the scenario is actual or simulated, tasks have students doing what adults do with a particular content. Angelis (2001), associate director of the National Research Center on English Learning and Achievement, in an article about helping middle and high school students learn to read well, reports, "the most effective classrooms engage students in the debates and activities that are central to the field being studied: An effective science lesson has students engage in a scientific inquiry—learning the

---

Box 4.1

A Performance Task Is . . .

- Not a test
- More complex than a traditional assignment
- A way for students to apply content in real-world situations or simulations
- Multifaceted, requiring that students learn and demonstrate essential competencies and content

---

proper methods of exploration and employing the vocabulary and language of the scientist" (p. 51). Quality tasks do the things that Angelis says create an effective classroom because, as McTighe (1996), coauthor of the Association for Supervision and Curriculum Design (ASCD) *Understanding by Design* series, explains, they "call upon students to demonstrate their knowledge and skills in a manner that reflects the world outside the classroom" (p. 8). They give students authentic or simulated roles and scenarios from the adult world. Students take on the job of historian, critic, architect, publisher, filmmaker, or marketer, for example. In the process of completing a task or solving a problem in the context of a particular role, the students begin to learn about the professions and types of situations that will face them as adults in the work world. Connecting the content in school to the lives of students while they are learning motivates them, engages them, puts content facts and concepts in their long-term memory, and, best of all, helps them enjoy school.

A Sample Task

Performance tasks are not tests, although they can be used to get major assessment information and be graded. Because they offer the student a rationale for learning the content *and* doing the work, the task prompt should be given to students as they begin a unit of study that is needed in the task, not as they finish learning the information. A good task will be interesting to the students and will help to motivate them to learn the content they need to complete the task. For example, look at the task prompt "What Did You See?" (Box 4.2).

Box 4.2

"What Did You See?"

You are a witness of an important pre-Revolutionary event, and you have been called to testify before the Continental Congress. You must gather information about the event so that you can describe what happened as you saw it and decide whether you would support going to war for American independence. Draft a speech to be delivered as you testify in front of the members of the Continental Congress.

SOURCE: Tim Kueper (1999), fifth-grade teacher, Elementary School District 20, Hanover Park, IL. Used by permission.

This task sets up a reason for learning about pre-Revolutionary conditions in the American colonies, a topic that, if not approached in a relevant way, does not excite most students. In the context of taking the role of someone who witnessed an event, students must testify before the Continental Congress that is debating whether or not to go to war. The students will be more interested and motivated to find out about that event and think about what it would have been like to have been there than if their assignment was to read the chapter on the causes of the Revolutionary War.

How This Task Was Done With a Class

Students were given the task before the teacher did any teaching about the causes of the Revolutionary War. Students drew a character and event from a hat. To help students see that there was not agreement on going to war with Great Britain, the teacher had made sure that the people in the roles might have different perspectives on the events they saw. For example, one person might be a British sailor on one of the ships in Boston Harbor when the tea was dumped into the bay. Another might be a waitress at the tavern on Lexington Green when the battle took place there. As a class, they brainstormed where they might get information about these events, and then they began research. Guess what source most of them went to first. Yes, the textbook! So in researching, they did read the chapter on the events, but now they did it because they had a personal need to know.

In fact, the teacher did not do any whole-class instruction on the causes of the Revolutionary War until after the Continental Congress (the class) had met, heard the testimonies of the citizens, and voted to go to war. Then, Mr. Kueper asked students what they thought caused the American colonists to fight Great Britain. He reports that they got four of the five causes themselves. All he had to do to review the causes for the chapter test that he normally gave was to discuss the fifth cause with them. He was delighted that every student passed the test, something that had never happened before. They had learned and remembered the essential content that was embedded in the task because they had been actively engaged in the work, and the facts were woven into a personal experience that had meaning for them.

Real-World Connections and Standards in This Task

Although this task was a simulation, it did have an authenticity because, even today, citizens are called before congressional committees to testify about events that can impact laws and governmental actions. As Mr. Kueper introduced the task to the students, he brought in current-events articles that reported on people testifying in Congress about impending legislation. He had several examples of ordinary citizens and of celebrities the students recognized who had been witnesses before committees in recent months. In this way, this historic simulation became immediately connected to modern governmental functioning and, therefore, real.

In carrying out this task, students had to learn and demonstrate their knowledge of social studies facts that are included in the Illinois State

Board of Education's (1997) Learning Standards for Social Sciences such as Benchmark 16B, "Understand the development of significant political events," and Benchmark 16A.2c, "Ask questions and seek answers by collecting and analyzing data from historic documents, images, and other literary and non-literary sources" (p. 50).

Because this task is complex, however, students were also learning other skills that normally come under different content areas. They had to read and research, analyze and synthesize information, write notes on their reading, and plan and deliver a speech. These are traditionally part of language arts curricula and are, in fact, in the Illinois Learning Standards for Language Arts. This illustrates another characteristic of quality performance tasks. They are, by their very nature, interdisciplinary. In the adult world beyond school, very few complex tasks involve only one content area or knowledge base. A scientist's work, for example, involves math as well as science. It will also necessitate that the individual have skills in effective communication—language arts—and knowledge of the past—history—as well as laws that might restrict or protect the work—government. (See Box 4.3 for a science task with other content areas embedded in it.) The real-world aspect of a task's role and scenario will mean that tasks often involve more than one content area. For years, education reformers have proposed interdisciplinary connections to help students relate to and remember content. Using tasks is one way to begin to get those types of connections.

Box 4.3

What Makes It Work? (Fourth-Grade Performance Prompt)

Over the next few days, you and your team of analysts must *gather* information on how simple machines work together to form complex machines.

On Friday, your team will carefully *examine* the inside of a complex machine, and *determine* the types of simple machines most commonly found in your complex machine in order to *develop* a database recording your observations.

Then all teams *will meet* to *share* their research findings, *combine* the information, and *create* a graph comparing the types of simple machines found in various complex machines.

Content standards in this task include:

- Science standards on simple machines and how they make up complex machines, and the scientific method of inquiry
- Mathematics standards on gathering data and representing it in a graph
- Language arts standards on speaking and listening

NOTE: Learner action verbs are italicized to show how students will access, interpret, produce, and disseminate in this task. Self-assessment will take place throughout the task and is not necessarily written into the prompt.

SOURCE: Susy Barnett, Mable Elementary School, Zionville, NC.

The Heart of a Task

When teachers first look at sample task prompts, they, like students, become excited by the interesting possibilities they see in the tasks. They also, however, have some serious reservations about using tasks because they see the potential this type of student work has for chaos. One of the greatest fears of any teacher is losing control of a class. We even have nightmares about it as every new school year approaches.

Teachers are correct that these tasks must have a skeleton to hold them together, to allow the teacher to design them well, and to keep them on track once they get started. No one has time to waste in a classroom in these days of high-stakes testing and newspaper headlines announcing the new school-by-school report cards every year. So tasks must be designed to include essential learning from the state standards and enough important content to make the time spent on the task well worth it. The task must also offer appropriate methods for the teacher to observe and document the student learning.

Lack of planning, substantive content, control, and documentation of student learning are often problems we already have with classroom projects, a type of student work that may seem similar to performance tasks. Well-designed tasks, however, can avoid all the weaknesses of projects and meet the standards at the same time. The secret to a well-designed task is the learner actions: access, interpret, produce, disseminate, and self-assess. Whereas lesson plans need to include the learner actions on a regular basis, performance tasks are built on the learner actions. A good performance task forces students to go through all five learner actions. It is also the learner action cycle that gives the teacher the stages of the task process and the places to document student learning—the content as well as progress on the competency skills. The learner actions are the heart of a task. (See Resources, Sample 25, for a brief, reproducible discussion of learner actions in a task.)

■ DESIGNING TASKS

If you have been waiting for the fun part of creating a standards-based classroom, designing tasks is definitely it. A lot of my work is with groups of teachers who are designing tasks for their own classes or for their districts to use in benchmark assessments of local or state standards, and when we get down to the design process, teachers always get excited. I think that is because these tasks are interesting, offer teachers many creative ways to teach to the standards, and have the potential to really get students involved. All the tasks given in this chapter were designed and used by classroom teachers who reported that they and their students had fun doing the tasks. So even though designing tasks is not easy, the rewards of using them are great.

Designing a task begins with three very important questions:

- What do I want students to learn?
- What will they do to demonstrate they have learned what I intended?
- How will I document their learning?

TASK DESIGN TEMPLATE: The New River   [p.1]

GRADE/LEVEL __8__

EXPECTED TIME TO COMPLETE __4-6 weeks__

COURSE/SUBJECT __Science__

DEVELOPER (S) __B. Benson__

Standards and/or Content Addressed

NC Standard Course of Study, Science

Competency Goal 3: The learner will conduct investigations and utilize appropriate technologies and information systems to build an understanding of the hydrosphere.

Objectives:

3.01 Analyze the unique properties of water including: Universal solvent; Cohesion and adhesion; Polarity; Density and buoyancy; and Specific heat.

3.05 Analyze hydrospheric data over time to predict the health of a water system including: Temperature; Dissolved oxygen; pH; Nitrates; Turbidity; and Bio-indicators.

3.07 Describe how humans affect the quality of water: Point and non-point sources of water pollution in North Carolina; Possible effects of excess nutrients in North Carolina waters; Economic trade-offs; and Local water issues.

3.08 Recognize that the good health of environments and organisms requires: Monitoring of the hydrosphere; Water quality standards; Methods of water treatment; Maintaining safe water quality; and Stewardship.

Retrieved 2/24/08 from http://www.ncpublicschools.org/curriculum/science/scos/2004/21grade8

Student Task Prompt

TASK PURPOSE/FOCUS:

Key Content/Competencies The nature and health of a hydrosphere
OR
Organizing Question/Issue How healthy is our local river?

ROLE: You are a member of a documentary film company that has been hired to make a film about the New River in North Carolina. YOU MUST research the river's history, collect data on current water quality issues
(Accesses   What?)

AND determine what is crucial information
(Interprets   What?)

IN ORDER TO write a script and create a documentary
(Produce   What?)

AND THEN present your film to local conservation groups, schools and local government officials.
(Disseminate   To Whom?)

Throughout this task you will also be reflecting on your work and doing self-assessment.
SOURCE: Adapted from Burz and Marshall (1996).

SOURCE: Adapted from H. L., Burz, & K. Marshall, (1996). *Performance-based curriculum for mathematics: From knowing to showing.* Thousand Oaks, CA: Corwin Press. Task content provided by B. Benson.

A task always begins with the big ideas that I want students to gain. These significant concepts can come from the standards, local issues, or long-term graduation requirements. (See Resources, Sample 27.) For example, if I know that a large part of my eighth-grade science standards deal with the hydrosphere, I must decide how my students could learn that information in a relevant way. If my community has a problem involving the water quality and integrity of a local river, that can be my vehicle to teach the hydrosphere. Now I have the beginning of a task and can go to the task design template to begin to flesh it out.

Page 1 of the template (Form 4.1) gives the overview of the task. Once you have filled in the grade, course, time to complete the task, and your name, you add the standards that you plan to address in the left box of the page. Keep in mind that a complex task may address standards in several content areas, and not all of them may be evident until you have really thought through the task. For example, the science task on hydrosphere will obviously address several of the science standards, but, if students will be reading scientific texts, researching, representing the data they collect in graphs or charts, and presenting these data to a conservation or governmental group in the form of a documentary film, they will also be learning many things that are in the Language Arts and Technology standards. One caution about listing standards the task will address is that you must assess all of the standards listed here in some way to document student learning. If you list every single standard you might touch, you can be totally overwhelmed with the documentation. Be sure to list only the important standards that you really will be assessing as students work through the task.

The Task Prompt

Each performance task needs a prompt in a format similar to the one on the right side of page 1 of the template (Form 4.1). This prompt gives students the scenario of the task and what roles they will play. The prompt also gives them the actions, the verbs, they must do to complete the task and the product or performance they will be doing to demonstrate their learning. Thus, answering in a broad way question 2 of task design, "What will students do to demonstrate their learning?" The first four learner action verbs are always written into the prompt, but self-assessment can happen anywhere in a task and is not in the prompt itself (see Figure 4.2). For example, the prompt for the river task would be:

> You are a member of a documentary film company that has been hired to make a film about the New River in northwest North Carolina. You must *research* the river's history, *collect* data on current water quality issues and *determine* crucial information in order to *write* a script and *create* a documentary to be *presented* to local conservation groups, schools, and county government officials.

In this task, students would need to do self-assessment at all stages to monitor their learning. After research and data collection, for example, they would have to decide if they had enough information to plan a script and filming for their documentary or if they needed to access more information.

Figure 4.2   The Multiple Requirements of the New Standards

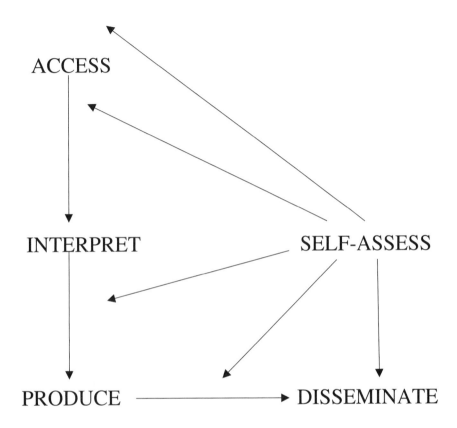

STUDENTS MUST KNOW A GREAT DEAL OF CONTENT AND BE ABLE TO APPLY IT IN COMPLEX, REAL-WORLD PROBLEMS.

ACCESS

INTERPRET

SELF-ASSESS

PRODUCE ⟶ DISSEMINATE

THEY MUST SHOW US WHAT THEY KNOW!

SOURCE: Copyright (1997) by B. Benson, *Teaching in the Changing Classroom.* Adapted from work sessions with the Shenendehowa Central School District, Clifton Park, NY.

What Will the Students Be Doing and How Will You Document It?

Designing tasks, however, involves more than just determining the standards and writing the prompt. It involves thinking through the whole task. On page 2 of the design template (Form 4.2), the teacher must break down the prompt into the learner actions and plan carefully what the students are to do in each phase of the task. These verbs not only guide the student work but also alert the teacher to what actions students need to know how to do to succeed at the task. For example, in The New River task, students will need to be taught how to do water quality testing in

Form 4.2 Task Design Template (page 2)

TASK DESIGN TEMPLATE [p.2]

Breakdown of Task Prompt + Assessment/Evaluation Criteria

Students Will:	Documentation	Quality Indicators
Access By 1) Researching the New River's history and geography. 2) Learn about water quality and collect water samples for testing from various locations at various times. 3) Listen to guest speakers discuss the current issues surrounding the river.	1) Student notes and data 2) Quiz on river history, geography, hydrosphere, and water collection process.	1) Student research notes are accurate and from various reliable sources. 2) Water collection process is correct and data is accurate. 3) 80% score on quiz.
INTERPRET BY 1) Determine what is significant about the river's history, geography, and current situation to create a storyboard for the documentary. 2) Record and analyze the water collection data in appropriate charts and graphs.	1) Student story-boards 2) Student graphs and charts of scientific data	1) Storyboard illustrates important and accurate info about the New River basin, its history, and current issues. 2) Student graphs and charts are accurate, legible and complete.
PRODUCE BY 1) Write the script for the documentary. 2) Film appropriate material and edit to create the completed documentary. [Students will select the part of the process they wish to do, and be working in separate groups on their part of the film.]	1) Student script 2) Finished film	1) Script must be accurate, well written to communicate the information to an audience in an interesting way, and use standard English. 2) Film must meet the rubric requirements for a quality documentary. Students would have helped to create this rubric.
DISSEMINATE BY 1) Presenting the film to a group and leading a discussion of the film and its message after it is shown.	1) Audience response sheets. 2) Teacher observations using presentation rubric.	1) See class Oral Presentation Rubric
SELF-ASSESS WHEN AND HOW? 1) Student River Journal for all of the river activities. 2) Student self-assessment after the presentations.	1) Student River Journals 2) Student reflection after presentations	1) River Journals are complete and legible. 2) Student reflection on presentation are complete.

SOURCE: Adapted from H. L., Burz, & K. Marshall, (1996). *Performance-based curriculum for mathematics: From knowing to showing.* Thousand Oaks, CA: Corwin Press. Task content provided by B. Benson.

order to collect the data they will need to determine the health of the river and where along its flow contaminates are entering the water.

Page 2 of the task design template asks that the teacher list in the left-hand column what activities the students will do and, in the middle column, clarify how these activities will be documented. The accessing, interpreting, producing, dissemination, and self-assessment processes stated in a task prompt and listed along the left side of page 2 indicate where teachers need to document how students are doing so they do not get lost along the way. If, for example, a student has not accessed the proper information about river geography and water testing, it follows that, without teacher intervention at that point, the student will not have any information to interpret and will not be able to produce an acceptable demonstration of learning. Since the task is built on the sequential learner actions, if students miss any stage of the task, they will not be able to complete the task successfully.

The teacher, therefore, should build in some form of check at each learner action stage to see that the students are on track. For documentation, I always ask, "What will I have in my hand to prove what the students have learned?" If the documentation does not show that the students have the content and/or can accomplish the desired skill, the teacher needs to intervene and give those who are struggling the support or shove they need to go on to the next step in the task. In the river task, for example, the teacher might quiz the students on river geographic terms or the process of water collection and analysis. Since students have accessed this basic information, they should do well and be ready to move on to taking river samples and writing up their data.

What Will You Look for in Student Work?

The third column on page 2 of the template, the Quality Indicators, is the beginning of the rubrics teachers will need to develop for the task. Here they will list the criteria they will look for in the student work at each stage of the task. If students are doing research to access information, for example, the quality indicators might include having various types of resources, having at least a certain number of resources, documenting these sources correctly, and so on. This page is a planning page for teachers, so what is listed is not the formal rubric yet. From these planning lists, however, teachers can develop the rubrics that will be necessary for certain stages of the task.

Page 2 is the most difficult part of writing a task because it requires designing backward, a process which moves from the content standards to the assessment of student learning and, finally, to planning to teach what students will need to do the task. This page answers the third question in task design, "How will I document student learning?"

Completing the Task Design

To continue the design process, a teacher would go to page 3 of the Task Design Template (Form 4.3) to list resources that are needed for the task, any interdisciplinary connections that might allow the task to meet standards in more than one content area, and planning notes. Once all

Form 4.3   Task Design Template (page3)

TASK DESIGN TEMPLATE   [p.3]

Possible Interdisciplinary Connections: Language Arts: research, writing, public speaking.

Social Studies: North Carolina history and geography

Math: *Graphing data*

Resources: National Committee for the New River publications and experts

River Keepers' volunteers

Appalachian State University Library's Appalachian History Collection

Appalachian State University Biology and Geology department professors

FAR APPALACHIA by Noah Adams (memoir of a trip down the New River)

Notes to the Teacher:

SOURCE: Adapted from H. L., Burz, & K. Marshall, (1996). *Performance-based curriculum for mathematics: From knowing to showing.* Thousand Oaks, CA: Corwin Press. Task content provided by B. Benson.

three of these pages are complete, the teacher has thought through the whole task and has the information to begin writing lesson plans, rubrics, quizzes, and any other documents that would be needed to start the task with students. The New River task template is now complete, and if you would like to see an additional completed template of a kindergarten science task, please refer to Resources, Sample 28.

Using Existing Tasks

If, instead of creating your own tasks, you decide to use performance tasks designed by others, be sure to check them to see if they include all the learner actions. If not, you will improve the quality of the task if you rewrite it to add the missing actions. For example, the following task does not include the whole learner action cycle:

> Suppose that you want to enclose a 650-[square mile] rectangular plot of land along a river. What can the dimensions of the plot be if you have only 110 [miles] of fencing, and you do not fence the river side? Provide a labeled diagram, and show the method you used to arrive at your answer. If a graphing utility is used, indicate how it was used, and, if applicable, sketch and label curves and any significant points. (Danielson & Marquez, 1998, p. 209)

This task prompt needs to clarify a role for the student who might ask, "Why would I want to do this?" It also needs clear access, interpret, and disseminate verbs. The prompt could be rewritten as follows:

> You are a landowner who wants to create a fenced area on your property for animals. You must *investigate* a plot along a river and *decide* what the dimensions of the plot can be if you have only 110 miles of fencing, and you do not fence the riverside. *Draw* a labeled diagram to show the method you used to arrive at your answer, and *be prepared to explain* it to the workman you have hired to put in the fence.

Now students know why they might need to do something like this, and they have a sequence of verbs to take them through the process. Checking and rewording published performance task prompts so that they include the learner action cycle will enhance the clarity of the prompt for the students and the quality of the work they produce. It will also help students who have difficulty with a multistep task, because now they have a process to follow, and as one of my students said of prompts written this way, "Now I know where to start. I have to get all the information I need before I begin doing anything." Some resources for task ideas and generic rubrics for some of the processes needed in tasks are Marzano, Pickering, and McTighe (1993), and Burz and Marshall (1996, 1997a, 1997b, 1998).

Why Do Tasks?

At the end of a three-day design workshop, one teacher remarked to the group, "When I first saw these tasks, I thought it would be so easy to write one, but it is hard!" After designing my own performance tasks and helping many others do it, I would certainly agree with her. It is hard to be sure that all parts of the task align and that the task does meet learning standards, but the work is worth it, because tasks work with students (see Box 4.4). As Leslie Kenny, an English teacher from Scotia-Glenville High School in Scotia, New York, reported, "It works! I am trying one of the tasks, and the kids are loving it. I have never seen this 10th-grade class so excited. They wanted to give up a free reading day to work on their projects, and they were actually working!" (personal communication, December 13, 2001).

Box 4.4

Why Do Performance Tasks?

- They meet the requirements of standards for students to apply content knowledge.
- They show students how content relates to the world beyond school.
- They require that students become actively involved in learning.
- They motivate students to learn and do quality work.

By following the cycle of learner actions, teachers can plan well, teach students the standards' content and skills they will need to do the task, and document student learning and progress appropriately and at the right times throughout the task. A good, standards-aligned performance task also has the following really important benefits:

- It will meet the standards embedded in it.
- Students will enjoy the task so much that they will remember the content they have learned.
- Students succeed on tasks because they are motivated.
- Teachers will have fun teaching interested students.

The good news is that after designing and implementing the first task, it becomes easier to create new tasks and more and more rewarding to do them with students. Leslie Kenny, quoted earlier, had already designed and was implementing her second task with a different class before the first class was finished with theirs. In the second one, students were "creating advertisements for *The Crucible*" by doing "everything from billboards to radio announcements." She also said they were working so well that all she had to do was "walk around the room" and keep things moving (personal communication, Dec. 13, 2001).

Design Decisions You Will Need to Make

Large or Small Tasks?

Tasks are judged to be large or small based on how much time they take, how many content areas they involve, and the type of need student products might serve (see Table 4.1). For example, the task prompt in Box 4.5 is a

Table 4.1   Tasks May Be . . .

Large	or	Small
Complex multidisciplinary, requiring a lot of time and often providing a needed service to the community		Focused, single discipline, requiring less time and done within the confines of the class

> ### Box 4.5
>
> ### Wee Mart, K-1
>
> You are members of a company that makes products out of recycled items. You must collect items for recycling and **design** and **make** useful products out of your collection so that you can **stock** your Wee Mart store. Then you must **advertise** your store's products and **hold** a sale for students in your elementary school to raise money for a tree and reading bench for the school playground.
>
> SOURCE: Susy Barnett, Mable Elementary School, Zionville, NC.

large task because it will take several weeks and involves science (recycling), math (money), language arts (creating advertising, reading), art (creating posters to advertise), and social studies (community). It is a rich learning experience in which students will be learning and applying science content about recycling, which is required in their standards for early elementary. They will also be involved in an authentic activity to improve their school by setting up a reading area on the playground. In fact, they made enough money from their recycled-items sale that they were able to buy the bench, the tree, and several books for their school library!

The students who did this task also demonstrated the motivation generated by an authentic task. They became so involved in the reality of their Wee Mart that they insisted on having shirts that looked the same because the people who worked at a local retailer did. When the students brought this idea to the teacher on the day before the big sale, as you might expect, she did not have time or the stamina to organize the making of shirts. She said no, and I heard the 6-year-old who brought the idea to her say in a very unperturbed way that the teacher did not have to worry about it because "We are going to do it." The students organized to bring in shirts the next morning, and they painted them to say Wee Mart before the sale began. This is only one example of what happens with a good task that is relevant to students—they are motivated to go above the expectations that the teacher may have had for them. They take ownership of the task and their own learning inside it.

Not all tasks have to be as large and daunting as Wee Mart. Smaller tasks can often be developed from good lesson plans that incorporate the learner actions. For example, the poetry lesson in Chapter 4 can easily be turned into a task because it contains all the necessary elements: a scenario, a student role of critic, and all five learner actions. The prompt would be, "You are a team of literary critics who explore a new process for reading a poem and then read and interpret a new poem using the process, to formulate an interpretation to share with other critics."

For this task, students get the task prompt at the beginning of class so that they know who might actually discuss poems in this way, and they know that they must share their observations with an audience. Both understanding the relevance of class work and being held accountable in a more authentic way motivate students. The teacher could have different groups working with different poems, since the lesson is really about using the process well to read and analyze a sample work from a particular literary genre. In this way, a teacher could have students reading and discussing multiple required poems in one or two classes. They could cover a lot more content in the one- or two-day task than if the teacher had discussed the poems separately over a period of a week or more—another advantage of having students engaged in the learning. This task is small because it would take only one or two class periods and focus on one content area only.

More Small Task Samples

Because of the time it takes to design performance tasks and the challenge of doing something new and different, many teachers prefer to begin with smaller tasks. The task prompts in Box 4.6 are also small tasks because they can be done in either one 90-minute class or two 45- to 50-minute classes. The first task is a focused-reading assignment that could be used in any content area. Even though it is small, it does include a simple role and scenario and all the learner actions. The students become experts in the area they are reading, and they are expected to share their knowledge with someone who has not read the same material. The accessing activities are reading and then listening to others share their expertise. Students will be self-assessing as they decide what of this new assignment they already know and what is new to them. This process of deciding and selecting significant material to share is the interpreting part of the task. Their products will be the marks they make in the reading material. In a short task, one of the things that happens is that the products tend to be less formal and less sophisticated. Often, getting a quality product takes a lot of student time, and that is what makes a task last so long. To disseminate their learning and share what they have read, students will be placed into groups where each student reads something different. This is a form of the cooperative-learning strategy called a Jigsaw, and it is a complete task, because it makes sure the students are doing the whole cycle of learning.

The second small task addresses foreign language standards of being able to converse in the target language and does not require other content areas. Even though this task would be focused on one content area and would not take much class time, it does have a role and scenario that are realistic, and it also takes the students through the whole learner action cycle. They will access by reflecting on personal information and reviewing the target language for expressing this information. They will interpret by selecting what would be important and relevant to the conversation

Box 4.6

Two More Small Tasks

1. Experts Sharing

   You are an expert in *(content topic)* and have been asked to share your information with others. As you *read* the specific material you are assigned, *indicate* things you already know by *making a* check, show what is new to you by *making a* star, and what is unclear or needs to be discussed by *putting in* a question mark. Also, *select* and *underline a* quote you think is significant. Be *prepared* to *share* your information with someone who read a different selection.

2. "Hello, my name is . . ."

   You are a vacationer in a foreign country who will be meeting a native of that country at a restaurant for dinner. You must *reflect* on personal information about your family, your interests, your town, your activities, and your possessions, *select* important and appropriate information, and *translate* it into the native language of your new friend so that you can *carry* on a conversation and *respond* to questions the friend asks about you.

   NOTE: The italicized verbs represent the learner action cycle: access, interpret, produce, disseminate, and self-assess. Remember that the self-assessment will occur at various points in the task and may not be included in the prompt.

they will be having. They will produce a written translation of notes for their meeting, and they will disseminate by having the conversation with a teacher or another student.

This task could actually be used as an exam for level-1 and level-2 students in a target language. The level-1 students would prepare as the tourists, and the level-2 students would be the native speakers expected to prepare questions and conversation for the meeting. Each pair could be taped so that their language proficiency is documented for assessment and evaluation. Teachers often fear performance tasks, because they think they have to be large, complex, and, therefore, very time-consuming. This is far from true. The value of the task for students is not that it is huge but that it allows them to learn content and processes by using the learner action cycle to acquire content knowledge and demonstrate their understanding of it.

Authentic or Simulated Tasks?

Besides size, tasks can also be classified as authentic or simulated. An authentic task would have students involved in a role that is real and work that serves a purpose in the community. The Wee Mart task in Box 4.5 is an authentic task, because it has students doing authentic work of making and selling products to earn money to buy a bench and a tree for their school playground, which, as they had informed their teacher, had no place to sit and be quiet and read. The New River task is also an authentic task because the students are supplying needed information to their community.

Community Planning and History for Fifth Graders

The fifth-grade task in Figure 4.3 has students contributing to their town's collection of oral history by interviewing older residents and participating in the planning for their town's future. This task is also interdisciplinary, including language arts (research, reading, writing, listening, and speaking), social studies (geography, economics, and Texas history), technology (using technology as a tool for research and to produce a presentation), and science because they discovered that their town was located where it was because of the presence of several underground rivers. This discovery led them to investigate geology and landforms. Obviously, this task was a big one because of its complexity and the time that it took. However, it covered a number of standards in social studies and other content areas from the Texas Essential Knowledge and Skills for fifth grade. The teachers, Stone and Steinbruck (personal communication, June 27, 1996), felt it was well worth the time because the students learned, demonstrated, and remembered the essential learning required in those standards.

Figure 4.3   Where Have We Been and Where Are We Going?

You are a member of a research and development team contracted by the Chamber of Commerce to research the growth and development of your town. You must find out why it is where it is, why it is the size it is, and predict what the town will be like in 20 years. You will make a six- to eight-minute video to share with the Chamber of Commerce and other city officials who are making long-range plans for your town.

Texas Essential Knowledge and Skills in "Where Have We Been . . ."

Task

- **History (5.4)** Student understands political, economic, and social changes that occurred in the United States during the 19th century. (A) identify changes in society resulting from the Industrial Revolution and explain how these changes led to conflict among sections of the United States; (B) identify reasons people moved west; (C) identify examples of U.S. territorial expansion.
- **Geography (5.7)** Student understands the concept of regions: describe a variety of regions in the United States such as political, population, and economic regions that result from patterns of human activity.
- **Geography (5.8)** Student understands the location and patterns of human settlement and the geographic factors that influence where people live.
- **Geography (5.9)** Student understands how people adapt to and modify their environment.
- **Economics (5.12)** Student understands the characteristics and benefits of the free enterprise system in the United States.
- **Economics (5.14)** Student understands patterns of work and economic activities in the United States.
- **Citizenship (5.19)** Student understands the importance of individual participation in the democratic process.
- **Citizenship (5.20)** Student understands the importance of effective leadership in a democratic society.
- **Citizenship (5.23)** Student understands the contributions of people of various racial, ethnic, and religious groups to the United States.
- **Science, Technology, and Society (5.24)** Student understands the impact of science and technology on the life in the United States.
- **Social Studies Skills (5.25)** Student applies critical-thinking skills to organize and use information acquired from a variety of sources including electronic technology.

SOURCES: Task adapted from task designed by Susan Stone and Linda Steinbruck (1998), Uvalde, Texas; Texas Education Agency (1998), *Texas Essential Knowledge and Skills* (TEKS), Austin, TX: Author.

An Authentic Literacy Task

Box 4.7 contains a double authentic task involving high school students and their first-grader reading partners. The purpose of this task was to focus on the issue of literacy and improve the skills of both sets of students by giving young students some individual attention and reading practice and training older students to read to children in hopes they would read to their own children, thus helping to prepare the next generation for success in school. The high school students are serving a need in their community for volunteers to take time to read with young students. The first graders are helping their older reading buddies by showing them the impact that being read to can have on a child's ability to learn to read.

Box 4.7

Reading-Partner Tasks

12th-Grade Students' Task

You are a reading volunteer who wants to help young readers learn to read better. You must research literacy and gather information about reading to young children in order to select appropriate books and plan lessons to read and discuss with your reading partner throughout the school year.

First-Grade Students' Task

You are a young reader who wants to learn to read well. You will listen and observe your reading partner reading a variety of books with you. You will decide what strategies good readers use when they read so that you can create a list of strategies, practice reading, and select an appropriate book that you can read to your reading partner.

This two-part task was complex, involving many steps. It also lasted through an entire school year and, even though it did not include different content areas, it did cover the majority of the language arts standards in both first grade and twelfth grade. Students were reading, writing, listening, and speaking in various situations to various audiences. The older students wrote about their experiences and wrote and illustrated gift books for their reading partners at Christmas that year. The young students started the year by drawing pictures to reflect on their visits with their reading partners but were soon writing reflections and letters to their partners. They wrote and illustrated books as graduation gifts for their reading partners. This was an authentic learning experience for all the students. One of my students said it best when he remarked, "This is bigger than a grade. This is real life!"

Simulated Tasks Are Okay, Too

Doing authentic tasks is not always easy or practical. Many excellent tasks are simulations that connect to the real world through a hypothetical scenario that can be almost as captivating for students as real situations. In Box 4.8 are several tasks that are simulations. Like the authentic tasks, they have a role, a scenario, and the learner action cycle. All three of these tasks also teach and have students demonstrating essential content from their particular state or provincial standards documents. It may seem artificial or superfluous to adults to be sure the tasks have roles and scenarios, but to students of all ages, these are the things that give relevance to the content they are learning, because appropriate roles and scenarios make it clear who uses this content in the world beyond school.

Box 4.8

Sample Simulated Tasks

Poetry in Cherries, Grade 3

You are an illustrator who must view Japanese cherry blossoms, observe the flowers, stems, and leaves, and analyze the feeling or mood the Japanese experience when they create art in order to create a border of Japanese cherry blossoms for students' haiku. Then, you must display the finished illustrated haiku and discuss your painting process.

Debbie Friedson, Niskaycna, NY

The Seventh-Grade Stock Exchange

You are a group of three stockbrokers who are forming a new investment firm. You must research how stock exchanges and brokerage firms work, determine a name and logo for your firm in order to produce business cards, and advertisements, and plan marketing and investment strategies. Then you will open your business and take part in the Seventh-Grade Stock Exchange Day.

Lin Dickson, Ottawa, Ontario

Lots of Land, High School Mathematics

You are a contractor friend of someone about to purchase a home. Your friend has asked you to help determine if the acreage on the deed is correct. You must gather information about the lot from the lot description on the deed and analyze the description to verify the lengths of the property lines and calculate the acreage in order to design a clear drawing of the parcel illustrating your calculations and findings. Then you must present the description to your friend confirming and/or disputing the figures in the deed.

Task developed by teachers from Shenendehowa Central Schools, Clifton Park, NY

SOURCE: Created in work sessions facilitated by B. Benson in the school districts.

ASSESSMENT AND EVALUATION   ■

Assessment and *evaluation,* although they are often used to mean the same thing, are two very different words, requiring two very different activities. To align classroom practice with the standards for students and the demand for school accountability, teachers and administrators need to have a clear understanding of what these words mean and what doing them would look like in a classroom.

Clarifying "Assessment"

The term assessment is being used in education for *everything,* and the word authentic tends to get attached if a particular test is not traditional pen and paper. Current use of these two terms is often in error, however, because much of what is called assessment and authentic is neither. The term authentic assessment would be appropriate only for those times when student learning is being applied in a complex, real-world situation, and assessment is more than an event for a grade—it is a complex and long-term process.

Assessment comes from a Latin word, *assidere,* which means "to sit beside." Assessment is not an event that happens on test day but is an ongoing conversation about learning and improvement between an expert and a novice. According to the National Center for Fair and Open Testing (1995), "The primary purpose of assessment is to improve student learning" (Principle 1). Similarly, Tomlinson (1999), a specialist in differentiated instruction, says, "Assessment always has more to do with helping students grow than with cataloging their mistakes" (p. 11). I would agree that teachers who are doing assessment are watching, questioning, listening, and collecting information about where students are in their learning so that they can move the students forward. Teachers should be doing this all the time, whether or not there is a grade for the student's work. It is not the grade that is most important; what is really important is the information the teacher and student get about what students have learned and what they still need to learn (Benson, 2001).

Traditionally, what I am calling assessment was referred to as *formative assessment.* Stiggins (2006) calls these ongoing conversations "assessment *for* learning" because they "are the assessments that we conduct throughout teaching and learning to diagnose student needs, plan our next steps in instruction, provide students with feedback they can use to improve the quality of their work, and help students see and feel in control of their journey to success" (p. 31). He asserts, and I agree, that this type of assessment motivates students to work for success because it encourages them and gives them the information they need to succeed on short- and long-term targets.

Assessment is an ongoing dialogue between the student and teacher, not a singular event. This is far from the present state "assessments" that occur on a set date and do not get results back to teachers until the students have finished the school year. In these situations, there is no real ongoing conversation between the teacher and student based on the information they may have gotten from the test event. The difference between an assessment and a test, as one high school student explained very vividly, is that if assessment is "sit beside" then a test is "stand over."

And What Is Evaluation?

Evaluation, also called summative assessment or "assessment *of* learning" (Stiggins,2006, p. 31), is not an ongoing conversation, but an event intended to see how a student is doing at a particular moment. Anything that is given a grade is really an evaluation of that student's work measured against criteria for that assignment. The biggest problem with evaluations is that parents and students have come to believe these grades are the reason students come to school. They are missing the point that one comes to learn and make progress, not just to get a number or letter grade that can signify many things other than learning. Focusing on the reward rather than the learning also causes various undesirable behaviors from adults and children. Viadero (February 1999) reports that, when the reward becomes more important than the learning, a number of things begin to happen. For example, high school students will forgo a tough high school class to preserve a high grade point average, or third graders will look for the shortest, easiest books to read for a school contest that awards prizes for the most books read (p. 24). We have also seen that students who want to get the highest grades, and even teachers and principals faced with the pressure to raise test scores for their schools, will cheat to achieve the desired grade or scores (Kleiner & Lord, 1999, p. 54).

An evaluation such as a test, rather than being the be-all and end-all, is intended to give information about how a student is doing at a certain checkpoint in the school year, and many people need to know how students are doing so they can make plans to help them do even better. Student performance tasks and portfolios can also be used to gain information for assessment and evaluation, but teachers need to be clear about when they are gathering information and giving students feedback and when they are taking grades that will be recorded and reported. The assessment process should be happening all along the way as students and teachers are working together. Evaluation should happen at benchmarks and at stages of the process, to report student learning and progress toward goals and expectations. And, most important, the evaluation is not the end of the cycle. It supplies information for what the next steps should be in the process of learning and improving performance. In the cycle of continual improvement discussed in Chapter 1 the evaluation, the grade a student gets, is the result of the student's action, and the student should reflect on that work to make a new plan to do better next time. The evaluation is not the end of the road. Instead, it is one piece of information in the ongoing assessment conversation the student and teacher are having.

Important Assessment Questions

In carrying out the larger process of authentic assessment, we should be asking students the following questions regularly:

1. How are you doing now?
2. What do you need to work on to improve?
3. What strategies could you use to improve?
4. What have you learned, and how can you use it beyond the classroom?

These four questions demonstrate the process that all of us go through in learning situations. We take stock of what we know; we decide what we need to know or do next to improve our performance; we plan strategies to improve; and we decide how we will use the information and skills we have acquired. If a written test is the only evaluation of student learning, the process of assessment never formally goes beyond the first question. Only those students who are already motivated because they see some relevance to the learning activities in the class will ever go on to questions 2 through 4. Most of our students are not able to apply this process to our classes. Consequently, we must help them internalize this process by practicing it through the way we assess their learning.

ASSESSING AND EVALUATING PERFORMANCE TASKS

It should be obvious from looking at the sample performance tasks in this chapter that this type of student work will have to be assessed, documented, and evaluated differently from traditional homework, class work, and tests. When a student works on a small task, one that takes a class or two and is not very complex, the work can be graded by looking at the product the task requires. On a bigger, more complex, and interdisciplinary task, however, the student's work should be assessed and documented at every learner action stage, because the processes represented by the verbs are as important in a larger task as the content, since they are an equally important part of student learning standards.

To assess and document student progress through a task, the teacher will need many methods. Taking grades on parts of the task like written assignments, and even tests or quizzes that may be given at different stages of the work, is fine, but tests should not be the only type of documentation. In addition, grading only the finished product of a task that is multifaceted and takes weeks in class is inappropriate, because it ignores the important learning that should be recorded throughout the task.

Assessing, Documenting, and Evaluating Student Learning in a Task

So how should teachers give students feedback on their work in a big task? Let's walk through the New River (Forms 4.1, 4.2, and 4.3) task and see where and how the teacher would assess, document, and evaluate the student work and progress toward the standards. At the beginning of the task, students would be given the task prompt as written on the first template page.

In this task, the first learner action of accessing will begin by having students research the history and geography of the New River. Students could do this by listening to a teacher or guest lecture, by reading their texts or other primary or secondary sources, by watching videos, and by visiting a local cultural museum that has period photos and maps of the river basin. It is the teacher's choice what methods students might use, and when they have their information, the teacher could plan a quiz to document that they understand the historical and geographical facts. Or the teacher could check their information by looking at the notes students took from their sources. Either of these activities could be used for a grade at this point in the task if the teacher chose to do that.

The second learner action, interpret, could be documented through a graphic organizer that shows the students' thinking as they begin to determine what information would be useful in their documentary. Since another part of the accessing of information was to gather water samples at different times and from different locations on the river, the graphs or charts the students use to record their findings can be the teacher documentation of learning. The teacher might have the students turn any of these work samples in or walk around and check them as students are doing them.

For the next part of the task, the production of the film, students will be working in teams to complete different parts of the production process. Each student can be responsible for documenting his or her work on a record sheet. Each part of the production company would also have products that would be needed to create the finished film. For example, students working on the script would have it approved before it was read into the film. Each of these component parts of the finished product would be assessed and would become documentation of student learning. Students would also be working to meet the requirements of a quality documentary film that they would have determined by looking at various films and discussing what makes a good professional documentary. The teacher would take the criteria they identified and create a rubric to evaluate the finished product. (See Box 4.9 for processes to create rubrics.)

Box 4.9

Processes for Creating Rubrics

PROCESS FOR CREATING AND USING A TEACHER DESIGNED RUBRIC

- Select an assignment.
- Write the directions.
- Visualize and describe completed work at different levels of performance.
- List basic criteria of performance.
- Write rubric in selected format. To decide format, answer "Who will use the rubric?" and "What is the purpose of the rubric—to supply information for improvement, to get a grade, or both?"
- Give students the assignment and rubric.
- Model finished assignment.
- Allow students to do assignment.
- Assess assignment processes/products/performances using the rubric.
- Evaluate the quality of the rubric and make notes for improvement before next use.

PROCESS FOR CREATING A RUBRIC WITH A GROUP

- Look at models of finished work.
- Generate lists of criteria and descriptions of levels of quality in products and/or performances (Excellent, Acceptable, and Not Yet).
- Decide on a format for the rubric.
- Create the rubric, and try it out with the task.
- Get reflection/feedback on how well the rubric worked.
- Revise the rubric to improve it.
- Use it again.

One Format for Rubrics

DIRECTIONS:

Criteria	Excellent	Acceptable	Not Yet

In a complex task like this one, just having an answer sheet or counting the number of items included is not really sufficient for getting a good report on student learning. Rubrics are one of the invaluable tools for evaluating student work on complex tasks because they clearly spell out the quality criteria and levels of performance for students and teachers. Rubrics can be created by the teacher or with the help of students. If the students help to define the criteria of quality work, they will understand the rubric better and be more likely to use it to self-assess as they do the work. Therefore, they will produce better products and begin to internalize the process and components of a quality product and/or performance. They will also be able to offer substantive ideas for improvement for their peers when they critique each other's work.

To complete the task, students disseminate their learning by presenting their film and leading a discussion of it with local conservation organizations, school groups, and government officials who are dealing with issues that impact the river. These presentations would be guided by a class rubric for oral presentations. (See Resources, Sample 32, for an example of a generic presentation rubric.) Different students could take the lead in presenting the film as they shared it with different groups, thus showing their understanding of the content and processes in their work. These presentations could be documented with video, photos, audience response sheets (see Resources, Sample 31), and student reflections.

In terms of proving that the students had learned the significant content and processes in this task, the teacher would have multiple documents and numerous ways to show student progress. No test could give as rich a view of what students had learned as the multifaceted assessments in a quality performance task.

■ TASKS AND ASSESSMENT: FINAL THOUGHTS

Having students work on performance tasks is an important tool for meeting higher content standards, because quality tasks require that students learn and use content in real-world contexts. Using performance tasks will change the nature of classroom assessment and evaluation, because the skills and work required in performance tasks are different from the more traditional memorize-and-repeat model of demonstrating learning. We will need to assess student learning more along the way, since they are learning processes such as critical thinking that must be practiced over and over again before they become second nature. We will need a lot of evidence of student work and progress, but, perhaps, not so many daily or weekly grades, since we want students to focus on learning, not on the grades they get for every little thing they do. We must get to know our students. We must make sure that the work we give them to do is worth doing and will teach them the essential content and competencies of whatever standards our system has for them. We must give them substantive feedback on how they are progressing, and do it often. Finally, we must help them see that learning and improving the quality of their work is more important than any grade they might get. Instead of filling them full of facts that they do not know how to use, our obligation is to light students' fires for learning by teaching them how to be self-directed learners and giving them every opportunity to practice learning on their own.

IDEAS FOR TEACHERS ■

- Learn how to design good performance tasks using the learner actions. Be sure your tasks are teaching the essential content and competencies your system requires so that the time spent on the tasks will be worth it.
- Be sure to give students the task prompt and any rubrics at the beginning of the learning they will be doing relative to a task. That way, they will know why they are learning specific content. The task prompt, if it is engaging enough, will give them the motivation to learn the content because they can see that they need it to do the task.
- Make certain that women and men are equally represented in tasks and role plays.
- When you give students a task prompt, ask them what they need to know to do this task. If the role they have is an archeologist, and they are third graders, the first thing they may want to know is, "What is an archaeologist?" This would be a great place to begin, and it moves students right into the access phase of the task. If they have other questions, be sure to list them, because these questions can guide the progress of the task. Better yet, the students want to know these things, so they will be following their own curiosity. Now the task is under way and students are already on a search for information that is relevant to it. Often, starting this way will also help you know what content and skills students will need to be taught to succeed on the task.
- The important stages of a task need to be done in class so that you can teach needed skills, support kids as they work, ensure all students have the resources they need, and document the students' progress on the learner action cycle.
- If a task will need a rubric, make one yourself, but consider having the students help create the one that will be used. The one you made can help you focus the student discussion on what is important in doing quality work on this task. Having them help set up the rubric, however, gives students ownership of the process and a better understanding of what the descriptors on the rubric mean.
- If you do not know how to create and use rubrics, learn. You can do this by working with teachers who know how to design quality rubrics, by reading professional resources on the topic, and by attending workshops on rubrics. Two good resources on rubrics are Arter and McTighe (2001) and Rogers and Graham (2000).
- When your class is doing a performance task, be sure to post the prompt and the standards this task meets on the wall in your room so that anyone who comes in and asks about what is going on can see that the students' activities are aligned with the standards.
- As the class works on a task, invite your administrators to come and see what is going on. That way, you are helping them to understand what a standards-based classroom might look like when the students are doing performance assessments.
- Consider using student portfolios and student-led conferencing as a method of assessing student learning and reporting to parents about the complex tasks and learning students must do to meet standards. These two strategies together form a performance task. The prompt for this task would be:

You are a portfolio designer who wants to create a showcase portfolio to document your learning. You must gather and analyze work samples for evidence of learning in order to select appropriate ones to be included as you design and develop a showcase portfolio. You will be presenting this portfolio to your parents or invited adult guests in a student-led conference at the end of the semester.

For information on how to implement these two performance assessment strategies, see Benson and Barnett, 1999.

- Start asking students self-assessment questions such as, "What did you do well on this assignment?" "What didn't you do well?" "What is one strategy you could use next time to do a better job?" "How could you use what you are learning somewhere beyond this class?"

■ IDEAS FOR ADMINISTRATORS

- Encourage teachers to learn how to design and use performance tasks as part of their regular classroom assessments. If your teachers are not familiar with the process for designing and using tasks, seek staff development opportunities for them to learn, or schedule time for inhouse study and discussions.
- Ask teachers who are using performance tasks to post the standards that are being addressed in the specific tasks in their rooms, and be sure that they can clearly explain the connection. This is important as part of our efforts to inform parents about the type of work students must do to meet the standards.
- When a teacher is using a task with students, visit the classroom to see how tasks work and to talk to students about what they are doing and learning.
- Be sure your teachers know how to create and use quality rubrics. If they do not, find ways for them to learn how, so that they can clarify criteria for students as they are doing assignments and give students better feedback on the quality of their work on complex learning tasks.
- Help schedule time for groups of teachers to work together to create tasks and rubrics and to discuss how the tasks worked in their classes. Grade level or content area groups can work on tasks that they all might be able to use, thus saving time for individual teachers who would not have to design all the tasks they might need.
- If a number of teachers in the school or district are designing and using tasks, begin to create a task bank on the school or district computer network so that teachers can easily access and use good tasks designed by others. If you do this, you should have some teachers acting as a quality control team to screen tasks before they went into the task bank. All tasks would need to deal with the essential content and competencies in the standards, and all tasks should include the learner action cycle.
- If teachers are using tasks, be careful not to set a requirement that they use a specific number of tasks in a year unless you know the size and complexity of the tasks they are using. Doing more than two big tasks a year is not practical.

- Consider having a team of teachers create tasks that can be used in content areas or at grade levels where there is not already a state- or local-mandated assessment of student learning. The documentation from tasks can be used to chart student progress on content and learner action verb skills to supplement the data gathered from tests. Having performance assessments each year can also give schools useful information as to how their students are progressing toward state benchmarks and test years.
- Don't set policies that require teachers to grade every piece of work that students turn in. Facilitate discussions and professional development activities about the difference between assessing student learning and evaluating student work. Encourage your teachers to assess more and document how students are doing but grade less.
- Offer to be part of the audience for student products and performances that result from the tasks. Teachers will need people from outside their classrooms to see and appreciate student work and to allow students to talk about what they are learning.

Conclusion

*Implementing the Four Practices
in a High-Stakes Test Environment*

As I have described the four components of the standards-based classroom, I hope that you, teachers and administrators, have begun to see what a great learning place this classroom would be and become excited about the possibilities for your students. I believe the new standards have been a positive factor for public education. I agree with Bezy (1999), a building administrator at Franklin Count High School in Rocky Mount, Virginia, when he says, "Instead of viewing state standards as a threat or intrusion, schools should use them as an impetus for improvement" (p. 5). We can take the best practices we already have and put them into the structure of

- Building a community of learners
- Making reflection for teachers and students a routine
- Teaching content and the processes in the standards
- Developing more authentic tasks for students and assessment of student learning

Using this structure for thinking about what we need to do in our classrooms to help all students succeed in meeting the higher expectations everyone has for them does not require massive expenditures or mountains of new books and materials. What it requires is the will to collaborate across grade levels and disciplines for the good of students and to learn a new way to think about what a classroom should look like.

In this chapter, I want to discuss briefly the issue of the high-stakes tests being used to measure student progress toward state standards. As I said in my opening chapter, this book bases the classroom model on the requirements of the standards, not the content or format of a particular state's required tests. I did this because the standards are the statements about what we feel students need to know and know how to do and are amazingly consistent across states and provinces. I believe they have come from concern that our students are able to succeed in their own communities and within the global economic community that will be their workplace. The tests, however, are not always the best means of measuring student learning, even if the students are meeting the standards. Also, the test quality and content vary from state to state and it is impossible to address all of those variations in this book.

WHAT ABOUT THE TESTS?   ■

We all know what tests we mean here—the high-stakes tests that students are being required to take to measure their progress as well as a teacher's teaching and the school's quality. Well, first, let me say something that I know most educators have sensed. The tests don't always match the standards! The push for standards has come from our whole society—from industry, higher education, government, and parents—and the laws governing creation and use of tests to match the standards have sometimes caught state testing divisions off guard. It takes a long time to create a test that one can ensure is as unbiased and valid as possible. The test creators and state administration organizations haven't always had time to get that done before mandated deadlines for state tests to go online. Therefore, many states are still using tests that they used before the current standards came into being, or they are purchasing tests from venders. These tests do not always match a particular state's standards or are so generic that they really don't test some of the more complex concepts and skills in the standards documents.

In all honesty, it would be very difficult, if not impossible, to create a test for use with large numbers of students that would in fact test the type of application activities that are in the standards. How, for example, could one test a student's ability to solve open-ended problems with a team on a timed, selected-response test? Despite the difficulties, states are trying to figure out how to assess their students' progress toward the benchmarks set in standards, and they are moving closer to higher-level processes students must master. For example, the Texas Assessment of Academic Skills II (TAAS) tests in Texas schools do require students to demonstrate deeper understanding of content concepts. North Carolina's revisions of its state tests are attempting to do the same thing, and New York's regents exams are now more interdisciplinary and require more complex processing of content information. Even so, they still can't really document whether or not students have reached proficiency on all facets of the standards as they are written in these three states.

IF TESTS DON'T ALWAYS MATCH THE   ■
STANDARDS, WHY DO WE HAVE THEM?

Acknowledging that the tests don't always match the standards and that there are valid reasons to believe they never quite will, we still have to deal with the tests. Remember, the people who make the decisions about testing and about how to hold students, teachers, administrators, and schools accountable are themselves products of the traditional American classroom model. In this model, if you wanted to find out whether someone knew something, you gave a pen and paper test. So the only way they know to hold us accountable is to give us more tests.

This mentality is recognized by Stiggins (1999), author and founder of the Assessment Training Institute in Portland, Oregon, who asserts that the effort to use assessment to help improve schools has "focused almost totally on the use of standardized tests," and "that those efforts have been shortsighted because they have been founded on a set of naive assumptions about the relationship between assessment and student and teacher motivation" (pp. 191–192). One of the main assumptions Stiggins refers to is the belief that if students have to take a high-stakes test, they will be more motivated to learn. Researcher Ryan (as cited in Viadero, February 1999), psychology professor at the University of Rochester, New York, echoes my feelings when he says, "Every time I hear some politician in the news talking about higher standards, I wince because what they're talking about is more testing," and he has shown that more testing just "takes away teacher enthusiasm, and kids are more turned off than ever" (p. 24). Despite the fact that many agree that the tests are inadequate to assess student learning and to motivate all of us to create better quality education, the chance that the tests will go away is slim to none. The best we can do is to lobby for rational, humane testing policies and tests that are much better than the ones many of our students have to deal with now.

■ TEACH PAST THE TESTS TO THE STANDARDS

In the meantime, teachers and administrators have a dilemma. Do we teach to the tests or do we teach to the standards? I would say, "Teach to the standards!" The standards are built on what we, as a local, state, or national community feel is important for our children to know and be able to do if they are to succeed in the future. Because of this, the standards are a much bigger picture than the tests, and they require much more complex and sophisticated learning—the type of learning that will be remembered for a lifetime. So don't just teach to the tests: Teach past the tests to the essential content and competencies in the standards.

To illustrate what I mean by teaching past the tests, and to make the point that doing so will make the tests easier, I'd like to use something from Asian martial arts training. When novices are being trained to focus energy to complete a task like breaking wooden blocks with their hands, they are told to focus not on the blocks but on the floor below them. The reason for this is that if they focus on the wooden blocks, subconsciously they will start to pull up as they approach the blocks. This lessens the power of the stroke of the hand. If, however, novices focus on the floor beyond the surface of the block, they will strike the block at full force. The block will then be easy to break.

The blocks are like our high-stakes tests, a barrier to be gotten through, and the floor is the larger target of the standards. Focusing only on the tests, students stop learning when the test skills are mastered, and they think they are done when the tests are over. If you want evidence of this, just visit a school after the state testing is complete, and you will see students who have quit for the year, frustrating their teachers who are still trying to teach. If, however, we focus on the standards, the tests become benchmarks along the *way*, not the end of the road. The other benefit is that if students are learning all the content and skills in the standards, demonstrating their knowledge and ability on the tests is much easier. They don't "pull up" as they approach the tests. They breeze right through.

DON'T IGNORE THE TESTS,   ■
BUT DON'T OBSESS OVER THEM

Teaching to the standards does not mean ignoring the tests or failing to inform students of what the test format will look like. We do have to be aware that the tests are a reality and prepare our students for them in rational ways. Students who will be facing a state-mandated test at the end of a year or course need to know about it from the beginning. But, they don't need to be browbeaten with it, and it should not be the justification for all the assignments they have to do along the way. If they have never seen a test like the one they will take, they need information about the type of questions they will be expected to answer and some, but not constant, practice working in that format. This kind of test preparation does not need to take much time, however. If students get information about an upcoming test at the beginning of the year or course, some practice along the way with the kind of questions they will be expected to answer, and some quick review just before the test, they should be well prepared.

Of course, the type of test preparation recommended here assumes that the teacher has examined the test format and content and made sure that the content covered in the class includes what will be tested. Many states publish test analysis documents that give information about the concepts to be tested and the percentage of questions devoted to each concept. Often, these documents include samples of test questions and examples of student work. Teachers need to use these documents and plan their units and lessons to take into consideration what information students will be expected to know. Analyzing the tests does not have to be a time-consuming activity for teachers either. Most tests are not long, and analyzing them for content focus is not too difficult. To save even more time, a grade-level group or a content area department can do test analysis and planning for including the test concepts in lessons. An added benefit of group discussion about what the tests include is that it helps teachers ensure that all students are exposed to the needed information.

Even as teachers analyze the tests, they need to be clear about the fact that the standards are the bigger picture, and the tests are a step along the way. Focusing only on tests in fourth, eighth, or tenth grade, for example, means I, the student, can quit once that step is done. It also means that I, the student, am learning content in little segments aimed at passing one test, and I have no idea how it all fits together. We know that the brain likes to see the big picture and connect new learning to prior knowledge in order to file new information into long-term memory. So teaching just to the test is probably going to ensure that students will not retain much content information over the long haul. Teaching exclusively to the tests also leads to doing what some schools have begun: giving students practice tests every six weeks from the time they are in second grade! No wonder students are burned out on tests before they ever get to middle school. No wonder many just fill in the scan sheet circles without taking the real tests seriously. For a number of reasons, teaching to the tests will not get us the long-term results we want, even if it does get an initial bump in test scores the first time we focus on success on tests.

Using the tests wisely by alerting students to the impending tests and the format to expect, as well as being sure that the class content will include the key information that will be tested, does not mean being driven by the tests alone. Instead, it is an intelligent way to use the tests to help students succeed.

■ TEACHING THE LEARNER ACTION VERBS IN THE STANDARDS IS TEST PREPARATION

Again, don't just teach to the tests; teach past them to the essential content and competencies in the standards, and, by doing this, you will be helping students to succeed on the tests. If we look beyond the tests to the standards, if our students learn content by being active in the learner action verbs embedded in the standards, they remember content because they did something with it. They have become learners who can access and interpret information, skills one needs to be a good test taker. They know how to produce quality writing samples in various formats to communicate their understanding of content, something they will be asked to do on state tests.

Training students in the learner action cycle is a way to prepare them for high-stakes tests. If they know that they should *access* and *interpret* information before they try to solve a test's math problem, they will read all the directions and the whole problem first. Then they will select the information that is useful and omit what is extraneous before they begin to work on a solution. If they are taking a test that requires a written response, students will read all the directions, the prompt, and any reading samples or documents in the question before they begin writing. They will also know they need to interpret the information by planning before they begin to write. Learning these test-taking skills in the context of how their classes worked all year, students would be more successful on the state-mandated tests.

Tasks as Test Preparation

As an example of how focusing on the standards' essential content and competencies will lead to test success, let's look at a small performance task and what it involves (see Explorers' Networking Box). Think for a moment, if students successfully completed the performance task in this box, how

---

Explorers' Networking

You are an explorer who needs to promote your business. You must review your achievements and design a business card emphasizing your strengths. Create six copies of your card to be distributed as you meet other explorers at the Explorers' Networking Social on Friday.

SOURCE: From Nancy Feeley, Uvalde Jr. High School, Uvalde, TX. Used with permission.

relatively easy a few multiple-choice questions on the state test about explorers of the Western Hemisphere would be. The students would most definitely remember the basic facts about five of the explorers that might be on the test. They would remember because they made a card for one and can associate the other four with real faces of classmates. They had the visuals on the cards and the research they did on their explorer to help them remember as well. Their brains have multiple ways to file the information. They also learned or practiced some communication and interpersonal skills and, if they decided to make their cards on a computer, some technology skills.

If this social studies class did this type of class learning and assessment throughout the year, students would have a rich memory of the content and would have practiced their learner actions many times. Assuming the content facts taught in the class were the ones required by the standards for that course, students would have met the content and competencies in the Texas Essential Knowledge and Skills, the standards document in the state where this task was first used. And these students would be ready to take the TAAS test in social studies for that year and succeed.

Allowing students to get involved in the process of learning, and giving them some voice in what they are to do as well as how the work is to be assessed, are two powerful ways to help them understand the content they are learning. Martin (cited in Edmond, 2001), a middle school special education teacher in Dansville, New York, supports this notion with her own classroom experience. She reports, "When I ask students what I can do to help them understand things better, they always ask if they can make something that demonstrates what they have learned, and it helps them to understand better if they can work through it and produce something" (p. 1). Performance tasks allow students to do this type of learning so that when it is test time, they really understand the content they have studied and are more likely to be able to use it to answer questions they have not seen before.

What we teach, how we teach, and how we assess in our classrooms on a regular basis will have the biggest impact on how our students will do on meeting standards and passing required tests. According to Black and Wiliam (1998), professors of education and educational assessment at King's College, London, "Standards are raised only by changes which are put into direct effect by teachers and pupils in classrooms. There is a body of firm evidence that formative assessment is an essential feature of classroom work and that development of it can raise standards" (p. 148). Formative assessment, assessment for learning, is what teachers should be doing all the time in their classrooms. It is the type of assessment that teaches while it allows students to demonstrate what they are learning. It helps teachers know where students are and what they need in order to reach targeted learning. It is the type of student-teacher communications recommended throughout this book. It means using strategies like reflection, rubrics, and performance tasks. As Moloney (cited in Edmond, 2001), an elementary teacher in Danville, New York, reports, "I love reflection activities. They help get kids ready for the state tests in that they are asked to explain what they think or feel about the content they've learned in their reflections" (p. 1). Her experience confirms that the type of instruction and assessment suggested in this book will help students succeed on the tests, on meeting the standards, and on being ready for whatever is next for them.

■ FINAL THOUGHTS

I know that it is a leap of faith to weigh the tests that our society seems to put so much emphasis on, and the standards that often seem so lofty and sometimes vague, and choose the standards as the guide for teaching students. But I would bring you back to the vision of the standards-based classroom and tell you from personal experience, it is a place where students stand the best chance for success, no matter what we demand that they learn. It is also a wonderful place for teachers. It is full of energy and enthusiasm for learning. It is an environment that fosters trust and faith in everyone's ability to learn, take risks, learn from mistakes, and *succeed*.

The standards that are set for our students are our best effort to prepare them for the futures they will face. It is our responsibility as educators to find ways to help all our students learn and succeed, in our classrooms and schools and in the world they will find beyond school. Since these standards are really about students' future needs, and they will change as the world and what it takes to survive in it change, we will constantly be on a learning curve. We will have to teach and assess differently from the ways we were taught and assessed. And, as people who became educators because they loved learning, we should be excited by being constantly involved in learning. Implementing these standards will mean that "we must develop the same kind of learning environment for adult learners that we advocate for students in the classroom—an environment in which learners willingly take the lead. This strategy is affordable, effective, and essential if we seek to create effective schools" (Stiggins, 1999, p. 198).

Building standards-based classrooms and schools using the four components discussed here does not have to cost a lot of extra money, but it will take a strong belief in the ability of our students to learn and take responsibility. It will take a great deal of collaboration and energy on the part of the adults in schools and communities, and, perhaps most difficult of all, it will mean that those of us who have spent our lives in school will have to run our classrooms in new ways. We already have many of the tools to do this well. The standards have given us a golden opportunity to rethink school and move into this new century with a bright vision for our students. I agree wholeheartedly with Meier (1995), someone who succeeded in creating a new model for high school at Central Park East Secondary School in New York City. She tells of the struggles to rethink how high schools operate and to make this school succeed; she comes to the conclusion that "The real question is not: 'Is it possible to educate all children well?' but 'Do we want to do it badly enough?'"(p. 4). I would respond to her question by saying we can educate all students well, and we *must* decide that it is worth the effort. Our students are depending on us wanting to do it badly enough to make it happen.

Resources

Reproducible Forms

Sample 1   Instructions for Facilitating a Big-Picture Look at Standards

---

1. Divide the participants into groups of four or five. If they are teachers, mix content areas or grade levels in the small groups.

2. Have the group members number off, and assign a job to each number: for example, #1, Liaison (will contact you and let you know if the group needs clarification and when they are finished with their work), #2, Supply Officer (will get needed materials and post results if asked), #3, Recorder (will record the group's responses on chart paper), #4, Reporter (will report responses to the larger group when asked), and #5, Bouncer and Morale Officer (will keep the group on task and pleasant).

3. Give each group a sample of six student-learning standards required in your school system. Be sure that these samples come from six different content areas and state what the students should be able to do when they exit a grade or content area.

4. Have the Supply Officer get the needed paper and markers and give these to the Recorder.

5. Ask the Recorder to fold the paper into three segments, titling the segments Demands, Differences, and Implications.

6. Tell the group members to look over the sample standards and discuss what these statements demand of students. The Recorder should write their ideas in that column on the chart paper. This is a brainstorming activity, so the group needs to list all demands that they see in the standards; they should not be looking for content-specific information, however, but at demands that seem to cross content areas.

7. Once the demands are listed, the groups should look at these demands and list ways that they are different from what was demanded of them when they were in school.

8. Then, looking at the demands and differences on their charts, the group members should discuss and record any implications they see for the classroom. For example, if the standards demand oral communication

skills and this is different from the quiet classroom the adults remember when they were in school, then an implication might be that students will have to have more chances to talk about the content in class. Each demand in the first column does not have to be followed through in the other two columns because some of the demands will get lumped together once the group starts talking about how these are different from what was demanded of them in school.

9. When the groups are finished, the Liaison should signal the facilitator, and each group should then go back to their lists to select and highlight the most significant item in each of their three columns.

10. At this point, the groups will need to share their information in some way. They could post the charts, and everyone could do a gallery walk to view what others observed in the standards. If you do this, have the Reporters stand next to their group's chart to clarify information if necessary. Or the Reporters could stand and share the items that their groups felt were most significant. Then the charts could be posted.

11. Be sure to keep the charts, especially if the group will be meeting again to discuss implementation of standards. When they do meet again, post the charts to remind them what they said was going to be needed in the classroom and why.

Sample 2   Taking a Big-Picture Look at Standards

TAKING A "BIG-PICTURE" LOOK AT STANDARDS

1. Examine the sample standards, and list what these statements demand of students.

2. Look at the demands you listed, and list ways these are different from what was expected of you when you were a student.

3. What implications do the differences between the current demands on students and the ones of the past have on classroom practice? What will need to change to adjust to these differences?

Sample 3   Staff Development Survey for Standards-Based Classroom
Components

Directions: Check the concepts below that were the focus of a staff
development program you have attended or studied in the last 5 years.
Then put a star next to the ones you use on a regular basis in your
classroom.

Building a Community of Learners

- Cooperative learning
- Quality classroom
- *Discipline With Dignity* (Curwin & Mendler, 1999)
- Student-centered classroom
- Multicultural, inclusive classroom
- Multiage classroom
- Looping, vertical teaming
- Multiple intelligences
- Brain-compatible instruction
- Differentiated instruction

Making Reflection a Routine

- Brain-compatible instruction
- Quality classroom
- Student self-assessment
- Reflective educator
- Writing workshop
- Reggio Emilia approach to early childhood education (Educational
  Resources Information Center Clearinghouse on Elementary and
  Early Childhood Education, n.d.)
- Outdoor adventure experiences
- Higher Order Thinking Skills (HOTS; n.d.)

Teaching Process and Content

- Brain-compatible instruction
- Process writing
- Problem-based learning
- Interdisciplinary, thematic teaching
- School to work
- Paideia Seminar (Adler, 1984)
- Inquiry-based science
- Technology
- Curriculum mapping
- *Dimensions of Learning* (Marzano, 1992)

Moving Toward More Authentic Tasks and Assessment

- Developing performance tasks
- Service learning
- Problem-based learning
- School to work
- Technology in the classroom
- Portfolios with student-led conferencing
- Standards-based instruction
- Developing effective grading and reporting practices
- *Understanding by Design* (Wiggins & McTighe, 1998)

Sample 4 Professional Development Forms

Professional Development Request Form

Name: _____ School: _____

Date: _____ Location: _____ Expected Cost: _____

Title of Professional Development Activity/Conference: _____

How does this activity relate to the school or district improvement plans?

_____
_____
_____
_____
_____
_____

How does this activity relate to your professional development plan?

_____
_____
_____
_____
_____
_____

What do you expect to gain from this professional development activity?

_____
_____
_____
_____
_____
_____

How will you use this knowledge in your class to improve student learning?

_____
_____
_____
_____
_____
_____

How will you share what you learn with colleagues?

_____
_____
_____
_____
_____
_____

Sample Professional Development Reflection Form

Name: _____ School: _____

Date: _____ Location: _____ Expected Cost: _____

Title of Professional Development Conference: _____

Titles of Individual Sessions Attended at Conference:

_____

_____

_____

How would you rate this professional development activity?

_____

_____

_____

Would you recommend it to others? Would it help your district and school meet improvement goals? Explain.

_____

_____

_____

What did you gain from this professional development activity?

_____

_____

_____

Give at least one idea or strategy that you can use or adapt for your classroom or share with a colleague.

_____

_____

_____

How do you plan to use your learning to improve your students' learning?

_____

_____

_____

How do you plan to share with colleagues what you learned?

_____

_____

_____

Sample 5 Idea Rolodex

- Teachers need a place to keep good classroom strategies so that they can get to them quickly. If teachers had a large Rolodex on their desks, they could put one strategy per card and organize these cards any way they liked. For example, they could put them in order by the type of activity they would produce, such as cooperative groups, assessment, student reflection, or discussion partners.
- An idea Rolodex is a great gift for new teachers.
- If all the teachers in a school have an idea Rolodex, they can have sharing days. Teachers would bring new strategies on cards to share with others.
- The principal can give everyone a new strategy on cards each month of the school year.
- When teachers go to staff development sessions, they can take their cards with them to jot down good ideas. That way, ideas can be quickly filed in the teachers' Rolodexes, and the chances of the new ideas being used will increase because they are handy when the teacher needs a new strategy to try.

Sample 6 Goal Card

GOAL CARD

Please write down who you are
and why you are here

What are your goals for this class, and what strategies can
you use to ensure that you meet them?

Sample 7   Discussion Appointments in Space

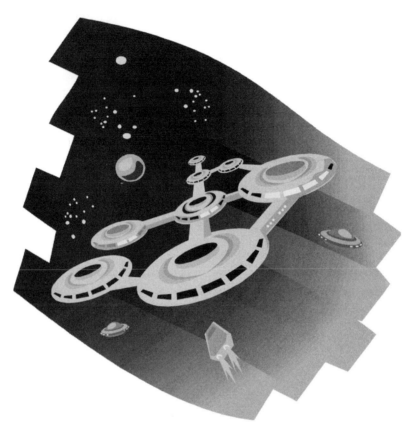

DISCUSSION APPOINTMENTS IN SPACE:

On the Sun with

On Mars with

On a comet with

In the asteroid belt with

On Neptune with

Sample 8   Group Task Sheet

Group Task Sheet

Group Name:

Task:

Jobs: Liaison:
       Bouncer:
       Recorder:
       Reporter:
       Supply & Morale Officer:

Three things we did well as a group:

Something we could improve on next time:

Signatures of all members of the group to indicate agreement with answers and group assessment:

Sample 9 Quality: Opening the Discussion

Think of a quality product or performance, and write it down with two reasons you think it is quality.

_____

_____

_____

_____

_____

_____

_____

_____

Share your quality product or performance with your team, and list common components of quality.

_____

_____

_____

_____

_____

_____

_____

_____

_____

Now write your definition of _quality_.

_____

_____

_____

_____

_____

_____

_____

_____

Other thoughts . . .

_____

_____

_____

_____

_____

_____

_____

_____

_____

Sample 10 Sample Quotes for Discussions on Quality

"If you're not improving, you're getting worse!"

Ron O'Brien, Olympic diving coach

"I've missed more than 9,000 shots in my career. I've lost more than 300 games. Twenty-six times I've been trusted to take the game-winning shot—and missed. I've failed over and over and over again in my life, and that is why I succeed."

Michael Jordan, basketball player

"If you have made mistakes, there is always another chance for you. You may have a fresh start any moment you choose, for this thing we call failure is not the falling down, but the staying down."

Mary Pickford, actress

"Failure is success if we learn from it."

Malcolm S. Forbes, financier

"Not everything that counts can be counted, and not everything that can be counted counts."

Albert Einstein, mathematician

"Success is not a doorway, it's a staircase."

Dorothy Walters

"Yesterday, shoving and backbiting as people climbed up the corporate ladder was normal. Today, that should be punishable behavior."

Larry Bossidy, CEO Allied Signal Co.

"Success is not measured by what you do, compared to someone else. Success is what you do, compared to what you are capable of doing."

Zig Zigler, motivational speaker

"The credit belongs to the man who is actually in the arena; whose face is marred by dust and sweat and blood; who strives valiantly; who errs and who comes up short again and again; who knows the great enthusiasm, the great devotions, and spends himself in a worthy cause; who at the best knows in the end the triumph of high achievement; and who at the worst, if he fails, at the least fails while daring greatly. . . ."

Theodore Roosevelt, President of the United States

Sample 11   Quality Coupons

It's okay to make a mistake! This coupon lets you "off the hook" in your quest for **Quality.**

It is okay to make a mistake! This *coupon* lets you "off the hook" in your search for QUALITY.

It is okay to make a mistake! This *coupon* lets you "off the hook" in your search for QUALITY.

It is okay to make a mistake! *This coupon lets you "off the hook" in your search for* QUALITY.

It is okay to make a mistake! This coupon lets you "off the hook" in your search for ZUALITY.

It is okay to make a mistake! This coupon lets you "off the hook" in your search for QUALITY.

Sample 12 Reflecting on a Lesson

Reflecting on a Lesson

Name_____ School _____

Grade Level _____ Subject _____ Date _____

What did I plan for students to learn? What did they learn and how can I document that?

How did I plan for students to be actively involved in the lesson? How did my plans for student engagement work out?

Based on my observations, how might I improve this lesson plan?

Based on my observations of student learning today, what do I need to plan for tomorrow to ensure students reach our learning targets?

Sample 13

Looking ahead to next year

What will I be doing differently? How will my classroom look? What will my students be doing? How will my instruction methods and assessment of student learning change? How will my interactions with parents and/or colleagues change? How will I continue my learning?

Sample 14 Web of Knowledge

Web of Knowledge

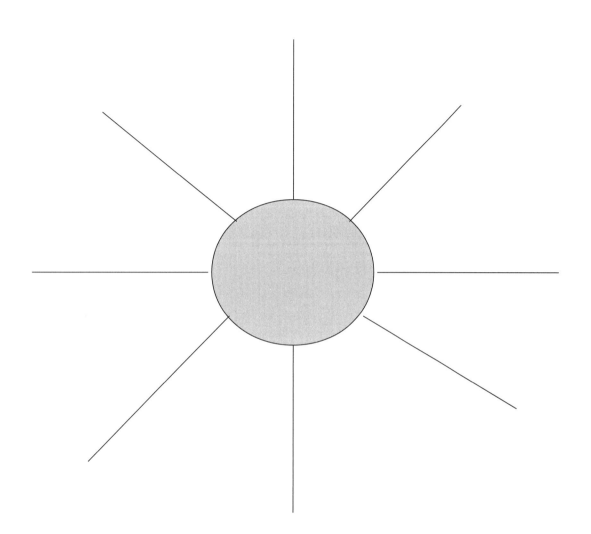

DIRECTIONS: Write the topic in the circle, and write what you already know about it or want to know on the lines, one fact or question per line. You can add more lines as you need them.

Sample 15 For Tickets in or out the Door

Time To Think...

Hold
    That
        Thought!

I
C
A
N

U
S
E

T
H
I
S
!

Key Points to Remember

SOURCE: Created by S. Barnett & B. Benson. © 2000.

Sample 16 Questions That Promote Student Self-Reflection

1. What makes this your best piece of work?

2. How did you go about (writing, solving) it?

3. What problems did you have? How did you solve them?

4. What have you learned, and how does this work sample show that?

5. What goals did you set for yourself? How well did you accomplish them?

6. What questions do you still have about this work, and what help do you need?

7. If you could go back and work some more on this assignment, what would you do to improve it?

8. What was particularly important to you as you worked on this assignment?

9. What do you want me to look for when I evaluate this work?

10. How does this relate to what you have learned before?

11. What grade would you put on this paper? Why?

12. Of the work we've done recently, I feel most confident about . . .

13. I still don't understand . . .

14. I didn't enjoy _____ because . . .

15. I find _____ is most challenging because . . .

16. Why did you decide to do the work the way you did?

17. Is this assignment quality work? If not, why not? If so, why?

Sample 17   Double Windows

DOUBLE WINDOWS
My Learning   My Plans

Sample 18 Math Reflection

As you think about yourself as a mathematician, answer the following questions:

1. You have worked hard this 9-week period in math. As you look back over your work, what are two things you want someone to notice about you as a math student?

2. What strategies have you learned during the current 9 weeks in math?

3. How can you use in the real world what you have learned in math?

4. What do you find most difficult in math? What can I do to help you?

SOURCE: B. Benson and S. Barnett (1999).

Sample 19 Look What We Learned This Week!

WRITING

SOCIAL STUDIES

Look what I did!

SCIENCE

MATH

READING

Sample 20 Lesson Planner

Content Area(s):_____ Grade:_____ Teacher:_____
Essential Learning:_____

LEARNER ACTIONS	LESSON SEQUENCE
How will/did students **ACCESS**:	
INTERPRET:	
PRODUCE:	
DISSEMINATE:	
SELF-ASSESS:	

Sample 21   How to Read a Poem

1. Read the title.

2. Read the poem straight through, aloud if possible.

3. Look up any words you cannot easily define.

4. Read the poem again.

5. Decide what happens in the poem. If you are unsure, repeat step four.

6. Decide what the poem means. Remember, it may mean exactly what it says! If you feel it means more than "what happened," but you aren't sure what, use such tools as background on author and times and others' interpretations—including published critics and your peers—and the poet's use of poetic devices.

Sample 22 Rubric for Discussion of a Poem

EXCELLENT DISCUSSION	ACCEPTABLE DISCUSSION	NOT YET ACCEPTABLE DISCUSSION
Explains the title's relationship and significance to the poem.	Explains the title's relationship to the poem.	Does not explain the title's relationship to the poem.
Defines vocabulary as it is used in the poem.	Defines vocabulary used in the poem.	Does not define vocabulary used in the poem.
Explains what is happening in the poem.	Explains what is happening in the poem.	Does not explain what is happening in the poem.

Explains a logical interpretation of the poem's meaning which is supported by
   - quotes from the poem,
   - examples of poetic devices used for effect in the poem,
   - references to the author's life and other works,
   - references to the time period of the poem,
   - and references to other critical opinions of the poet and the poem.
	Explains a logical interpretation of the poem's meaning which is supported by
	   - quotes from the poem,
	   - examples of poetic devices used for effect in the poem.
		Offers an illogical or unsupported interpretation of the poem's meaning.

Sample 23   Observing a Lesson

Directions: As you watch, take notes on the following items.

What was the essential learning in this lesson? Do you think the students would be able to tell you at the end of the lesson? Why or why not?

Do you see evidence of the four components of a standards-based classroom?

1. A community of learners

2. Reflection

3. The teacher's teaching process and content

4. More authentic student tasks and assessment

What instructional strategies do you see the teacher using?

How successful do you think the lesson was? Why?

Do you have any questions for the teacher or suggestions for improving the lesson?

Sample 24   Classroom Observation #3

NAME: _____   BLDG.: _____

DATE: _____   TIME: _____

I SEE	IDEAS/QUESTIONS/ SUGGESTIONS
ESSENTIAL LEARNING: To review myths students had read according to plot, characterization, setting, theme; to set the stage for writing their own myths, using writing process and FCA's	Students accomplished a lot in a short time; time limits helped them.
ACCESS: Prior knowledge and stories; handouts	It might have been interesting when looking at process, to see what they would have come up with if you had told them they had 7-8 minutes to complete the chart and do quality work. "How might you accomplish this?"
INTEPRET: Determining criticals of characterization, setting, conflict, climax, resolution, theme (what learned) for chart Reviewing charts and deciding which myth was being described Brainstorming potential ideas for own myth	
PRODUCE: "Mystery Myth" Chart	
DISSEMINATE: Students telling each other what the important aspects of a particular myth were	Good use of affirmation web when you told groups they could add info to other charts (webs).
SELF-ASSESS:	
Community of learners: Highly interactive, motivating; requires cooperation, yet each student showed accountability by contributing to them to the task	Brought closure by sharing why they did that particular activity, and, at the same time, you transitioned them into the next task.
Teach content and process: Students very aware of process in all they do, especially when it comes to writing, and they take ownership of that writing, knowing the "means will justify the end."	Good idea to have students write in the due dates
Move toward more authentic tasks and assessments: Students become more cognizant of genre through writing (in this instance, they were asked to write their own myths)	Adding 3 FCA's let students take accountability for their own growth.
Make reflection a routine: The addition of 3 personal FCA's	Thank you for your interest in the standards-based training. You already have a phenomenal skill set and expertise, yet, you are willing to continue to grow and share. (That's part of the fun...).

Sample 25 Learner Actions: The Heart of a Task

A good performance task is built on the cycle that any learner goes through to learn new information and apply it in an authentic situation. This cycle has five steps, or learner actions: access, interpret, produce, disseminate, and self-assess. To complete a performance task successfully, a learner must go through all five. The way that a prompt is written and the way that page two of the design template is organized require that teachers guide students through the learner actions. Teachers should also observe and document how well students are learning these processes as well as the content being taught.

Each performance task begins with a prompt that gives the student a role and a task to complete. The first step in carrying out the task is always to access the information needed for the job. Traditionally, information came solely from the teacher or from the next chapter in a textbook. In today's information age, however, students need to be adept, self-directed learners who can determine what is needed and where to find it in an ever-widening range of sources. These are skills that must be taught. Therefore, the performance tasks require that teachers teach access processes such as investigating, gathering, observing, reading, interviewing, and collecting, to name a few. The tasks also ask teachers to document how well students collected the required information. Accessing is an important first step to completing a performance task successfully and a critical component of success as a learner in any role in or outside of school.

When students have the needed information, they must interpret it in order to decide what is useful for the particular task and then apply it effectively. This phase of the task involves critical thinking, an essential skill for a successful learner. Without the ability to understand content knowledge, a student cannot apply it in any meaningful way; however, this step is often assumed rather than consciously and systematically taught and assessed. In performance tasks, teachers are asked to interpret processes for critical reasoning, problem finding and solving, and decision making. Therefore students are asked to do such things as analyze, compare, contrast, categorize, select, and determine. Being able to interpret information well will enable students to deal with the amount of information constantly vying for their time and attention in classrooms and beyond.

Once students acquire the needed information and they internalize and understand it, they are ready to produce evidence of their learning. Products used to show what students have learned might be posters, books, plays, videos, essays, newspaper articles, letters, and so on. Allowing for products in addition to written work promotes creativity, allows for differing learning styles, and adds interest and authenticity to the tasks, because in the adult word, learning is often displayed in ways other than writing.

After students create a product to show what they have learned, they need an audience so that they can disseminate this information. This audience is crucial, because it is only when we must tell, share, teach, explain, justify, discuss, publish, present, or perform that we retain our learning in a usable form. One need only ask teachers when they really learned what they teach to have evidence of the significance of an audience. We did not learn our content in school; we learned it when we had to disseminate it to a class! So each performance task has a disseminate phase where students are asked to convey what they have learned to an audience. This audience may be classmates, another class, a community expert or group, parents, or the school community. Logistically, this phase of the task may seem difficult to complete, but it is necessary if we want students to learn more of the required content well so that they can remember more of it when they take state and national tests or graduate into postsecondary schools and careers.

The final learner action, self-assessment, is not given a specific spot on the task design template because it should be going on all through the task. A student's ability to self-assess determines whether or not that student will be an effective learner who feels capable of succeeding and improving on past performances. Research on learning, brain function, and quality work has proven the importance of self-assessment for helping students become more motivated, learn more, and improve the quality of the work they do. Student reflection on what they have learned and how well they have performed, goal setting, and stating strategies for improving are all forms of self-assessment and may appear throughout the tasks as a means of assessing student progress and documenting student learning.

Knowing that the learner actions are the heart of a task, teachers should look for the key verbs that state what students are to do in any phase of the task. These verbs will guide not only the student work but what the teacher needs to be sure students know how to do in order to succeed at the task. The access, interpret, produce, disseminate, and self-assessment processes stated in a task also indicate where teachers need to document how students are doing. If a student has not accessed the proper information, it follows that without teacher intervention at that point, the student will not have anything to interpret, and will not be able to produce an acceptable demonstration of learning. Following the cycle of learner actions, both teachers and students will find tasks to be positive-learning experiences, which not only allow students to succeed in the present but also give them instruction and practice in the learning process they will need to be successful in the increasingly complex world they will enter after graduation.

SOURCE: B. Benson, *Teaching in the Changing Classroom* (1997).

Sample 26 Task Design Template

TASK DESIGN TEMPLATE   [p.1]

GRADE / LEVEL _____   EXPECTED TIME TO COMPLETE_____

COURSE / SUBJECT _____   DEVELOPER (S) _____

Standards and/or Content Addressed	Student Task Prompt
	TASK PURPOSE/FOCUS: Key Content/Competencies _____ OR Organizing Question/Issue _____ ROLE: You are a _____ YOU MUST _____ What?) (Access AND _____ What?) (Interpret IN ORDER TO _____ What?) (Produce AND THEN _____ To Whom?) (Disseminate Throughout this task you will also be reflecting on your work and doing self-assessment.

TASK DESIGN TEMPLATE [p.2]

Breakdown of Task Prompt + Assessment/Evaluation Criteria

Students Will:	Documentation	Quality Indicators
ACCESS BY		
INTERPRET BY		
PRODUCE BY		
DISSEMINATE BY		
SELF-ASSESS WHEN AND HOW?		

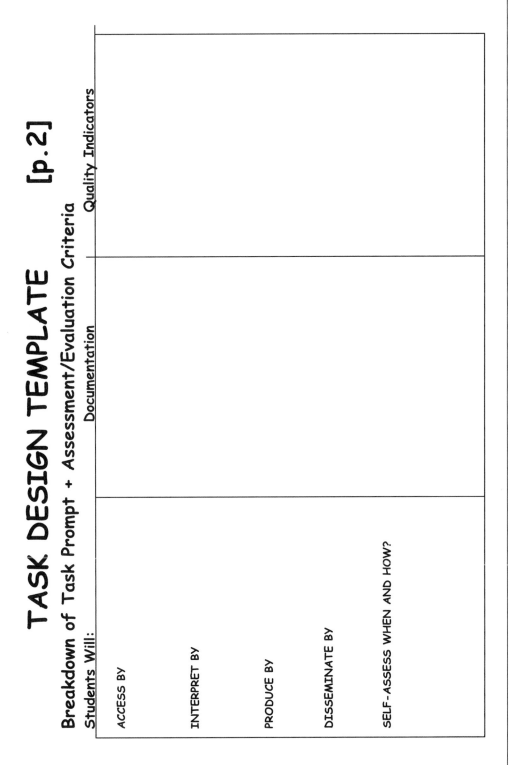

(Continued)

Sample 26   (Continued)

TASK DESIGN TEMPLATE   [p.3]

Possible Interdisciplinary Connections:

Resources:

Notes to the Teacher:

SOURCE: Adapted from H. L. Burz and K. Marshall (1996).

Sample 27 Paths for Designing Student Tasks

SEQUENCE #1	**SEQUENCE #2**	**SEQUENCE #3**

SEQUENCE #1

If you begin with content objectives,

Look at real-world applications of that knowledge/skill—this skill leads to a focus question concerning a big issue.

Create a task prompt.

Break the task into the Learner Actions.

Look for all possible content/competence connections (in curriculum and graduation expectations/standards) with task in order to determine learning emphasis and documentation.

Develop the Quality Criteria by which the student demonstration will be assessed and evaluated.

Develop lesson plans and collect needed resource materials.

SEQUENCE #2

If you begin with a theme, issue, problem, focus question, or unexpected learning opportunity.

Look at curriculum to see content/competence connections.

Create a task prompt.

Break the task into the Learner Actions.

Look for additional content/ competence connections (in curriculum and graduation expectations/standards) with task for determining emphasis and documentation.

Develop the Quality Criteria by which the student demonstration will be assessed and evaluated.

Develop lesson plans and collect needed resource materials.

SEQUENCE #3

If you begin with graduation expectations/standards,

Look at curriculum to see content/competence connections.

Look at real-world applications of the knowledge/skills—this can lead to a focus question concerning a big issue.

Create a task prompt.

Break the task into the Learner Actions.

Look for additional content/ competence connections with task for determining emphasis and documentation.

Develop Quality Criteria by which the student demonstration will be assessed and evaluated.

Develop lesson plans and collect needed resource materials.

Sample 28a   Student Prompt for Kindergarten Science Task

Art Gallery

You are an artist who observes and explores the properties of paper. After discussing your findings with your peers, you will create a sculpture. This sculpture will become part of the classroom Art Gallery. When visitors come to the gallery, you will explain to them the properties of paper.

SOURCE: Task designed by Cathy Bolger, K–1 Teacher. Used by permission of Elementary School District #20, Hanover Park, IL.

Sample 28b   Task Design Template for Kindergarten Science Task

TASK DESIGN TEMPLATE   [p. 1]

GRADE / LEVEL __Kindergarten__   EXPECTED TIME TO COMPLETE   __1 Week__
FUNDAMENTAL LEARNING AREA(S)   __Science__   DEVELOPER(S)   __Cathy Bolger__
__Paper – Matter and Energy__

TARGET CHARACTERISTICS AND STANDARDS

District 20 Graduate Profile Characteristic(s):

Effective Communicators Who: read, write and listen in a variety of contexts.

Illinois Learning Standards and Benchmarks:

Goal 12.C. Know and apply concepts that describe properties of matter and energy and the interactions between them.

PERFORMANCE TASK TITLE: Art Gallery

TASK PURPOSE/FOCUS:
Key Content/Competencies: Matter/energy (paper unit).
and
Essential Question(s): What is matter?

ROLE: You are an artist.

WHO: Observes and explores the properties of paper.
_____ (Accesses _____ What?)

AND: Synthesizes your findings.
_____ (Interprets _____ What?)

IN ORDER TO: Create an exhibit to illustrate properties of paper.
_____ (Produce _____ What?)

AND THEN: Display it in a gallery and explain to visitors the properties of paper.
_____ (Disseminate _____ To Whom?)

Throughout this task, you will also be reflecting on your work and doing self-assessment.

4/2000 Task 1

SOURCE: Task designed by Cathy Bolger, K–1 Teacher. Used by permission of Elementary School District #20, Hanover Park, IL. Template format adapted from H. L. Burz and K. Marshall (1996).

Sample 28c   Task Design Template (Continued)

TASK DESIGN TEMPLATE   [p. 2]

Breakdown of Task Prompt + Assessment / Evaluation Criteria

Students Will:	Documentation	Quality Indicators
ACCESS BY: 1. Searching and collecting paper materials to make an exhibit. 2. Discussing properties of materials.	1. Samples of materials. 2. Class list of properties on chart paper.	1. Variety of class samples showing various properties of paper.
INTERPRET BY: Planning and deciding how to make an exhibit.	Sketch of possible exhibits by whole class.	Complete or incomplete sketch.
PRODUCE BY: Create, build, design exhibit.	Exhibit.	The exhibit displays individual sculptures with written dictation of at least 2 properties of paper.
DISSEMINATE BY: Display and explain exhibit to a visitor on "Exhibit Day".	Photo picture of child with own sculpture. Child has dictated at least 2 properties of paper sculpture.	Child identified at least 2 properties of sculpture in dictated sentence.
SELF-ASSESS WHEN AND HOW? Reflect on display and share with an adult.	Chart paper or tape recorder — ask/list: Tell me 1 thing about your exhibit you're proud of? Tell me 1 thing you would change if you did it again? Tell me 1 thing you learned?	Child can answer 2 out of 3 questions thoughtfully.

SOURCE: Task designed by Cathy Bolger, K–1 Teacher. Used by permission of Elementary School District #20, Hanover Park, IL. Template format by B. Benson, *Teaching in the Changing Classroom* (1997).

Sample 28d   Task Design Template (Continued)

TASK DESIGN TEMPLATE   [p. 3]

RESOURCES/SPECIAL NOTES:

Foss Kit – Paper Unit

Literature for students (enclosed in kit)

Collection of paper samples

<u>Special Notes</u>:

- Read Foss Kit—<u>Getting to Know Paper</u> – all lesson plans, activities, and materials are listed in Foss Teacher Manual. Teacher/Helpful Hint notes are also included in kit.

- <u>Science Vocabulary</u>—development is needed on a daily basis. **Properties, texture, sculpture, art, design should be used** throughout the unit.

- Find space to collect variety of paper samples and have "art gallery".

- Use vocabulary—properties, texture, throughout unit.

- Find space to collect variety of paper samples to offer to kids.

- Chart paper/tape recorder for documentation is needed.

- Gallery can have cards with child's name, and properties,listed on cards.

- "Exhibit Day" in gallery can be for other classrooms, parents, reading buddies, and others.

- Accessing and gathering information can be whole class, small group,or individual, depending on class needs/size.

- Disposable camera and computer can be used for photo and explanation of exhibit.

SOURCE: Task designed by Cathy Bolger, K-1 Teacher. Used by permission of Elementary School District #20, Hanover Park, IL. Template format by B. Benson, *Teaching in the Changing Classroom* (1997). Foss products: retrieved July 18, 2002, from www.lhs.berkeley.edu/FOSS/FOSS.html

Sample 28e   Rubric

1.

Can tell 3 properties of paper exhibit

Can clearly explain how exhibit shows properties

3   ☺

2.

Can give at least 2 properties of paper exhibit

Can explain some connection of properties to exhibit

2   😐

3.

Gives 1 property of paper or none

and

Child can make no connection between
properties of paper and own exhibit.

1   ☹

SOURCE: Task designed by Cathy Bolger, K–1 Teacher. Used by permission of
Elementary School District #20, Hanover Park, IL.

CURRICULUM & INSTRUCTION CORNER

September 7, 2001   Vol. 2, No. 1

CREATING A COMMUNITY OF LEARNERS

A district goal this year, based on "Building Standards-based Classrooms and Schools," is focused on how we can insure every student willingly takes responsibility for his/her and others' learning. We need to take the time to develop a safe, inviting, and motivating learning environment both physically and emotionally.

One step in this process is developing a "Code of Conduct" (or class rules) with your students. When they become part of that decision making process, they feel greater ownership and responsibility for their own behaviors as well as class behavior. Sometimes when brainstorming as a class what might go on the list, a student will throw out an "idea" such as "No Homework" or "Gum Chewing." Write down these ideas/suggestions with all the others. When you begin reviewing the brainstormed list, you have the opportunity to facilitate the discussion and decision-making. "If a code of conduct deals with attitudes and behaviors, is 'no homework' an attitude or behavior? Should we look at 'gum chewing' from a broader perspective? Why do you think teachers frown upon gum chewing? So is there a behavior we are looking for?" Typically if you honor their responses, they will come up with a list similar to the one you would have given them. Because they were actively involved in the process, however, they will believe in them and more willingly abide by them.

Avoid approaching the code of conduct as a negative "don't" list; use positive statements: *Respect all ideas, comments and questions; Listen with your ears, eyes, head and heart; Actively participate, etc."* Make sure the class has discussed what each means in detail. What does "actively participate look like and sound like? What does respect look like and sound like? This conversation clarifies for everyone what the code means.

Keep the list to a minimum, 3 to 6 ideas. Try not to use complete sentences. Instead, the code might look like a series of "headlines" or catchy phrases. Remember, since you discussed what each means as a class, this list can be a quick reference.

Place the "Code of Conduct" in a visible spot in the room. Make sure you use the code throughout the year. For example, if several people are talking at the same time in a whole group setting, and it appears some students are inattentive and/or bothered, it is the perfect time to refer to the code instead of telling them to be quiet. As the teacher, you ask for a time-out and get their attention. Then, referring to the code on the wall, "We said we would listen to one another. Right now it sounds like we are doing more talking than listening. Help me out here. What's going on? Can we get back on track?" Then invite students to use the code in a similar fashion, especially when they are working in smaller groups. Let them practice referring to the code on the wall. (Some students haven't had the opportunity to develop the skills we would like them to have.)

Give them some scenarios to practice: *Tom is dominating the group discussion, telling everyone what to do. People in the group are getting frustrated with his bossiness. A typical response would be for someone to finally shout, "Tom, would you shut up and give someone else a turn?" Now Tom feels angry, embarrassed and threatened. The situation intensifies. Instead, what might you say or do that would enable Tom to take care of his own behavior and allow everyone else the opportunity to participate?* Students come up with good ideas and will learn the code is a safe place to get the group back on track and working productively.

And, finally, let students know that as they practice the skills, it will feel uncomfortable and even contrived, but as Mary Kay says, "Fake it 'til you make it." It's like learning to ride a bike; you have to practice to find your rhythm and feel confident enough to take your hands off the handlebars.

Students need to know what the expectations for behavior are just as well as the expectations for work, and they need to be involved in their development. Your community of learners will be focused on the learning and the tasks when they (your students) believe they are an integral part of the learning environment. The "Code of Conduct" (or whatever you want to call it) is a first step in creating this community.

Remember, if you believe students can do it, they will.

TIDBITS

STANDARDS-BASED TRAINING
61 teachers have participated in Level I Training. (29 teachers & administrators participated in this August's training cycle; a total of 64 participated from all three districts: Dansville, Keshequa, and Way-Coh.)

15 teachers are actively involved with Level II Training.

SUMMER CURRICULUM WORK
ELA→ 15 K-8 teachers
MATH→15 K-12 teachers
ELA/SS→11 HS teachers

SUMMER MINIGRANTS
15 teams/38 teachers

A WAY TO ASSESS YOUR LEARNING ENVIRONMENT
DESCA Scale for Rating a Class: a simple, user-friendly "rubric" that focuses on a class's dignity, energy, self-management, community, and awareness (DESCA). Call Connie Peabody (ext. 3032) at the curriculum office for a copy.

STANDARDS FOR DIVERSE LEARNERS
Five Conditions:
1. Standards are developmental and flexible.
2. Standards require a wide range of assessment tools.
3. Standards allow equitable access to meaningful content.
4. It takes a community to implement standards.
5. Standards are a catalyst for other reforms.

To find out about each of these, read the 3-page article "Standards for Diverse Learners" by Paula Kluth and Diana Straut in September 2001 Educational Leadership. (Call Connie, ext. 3032, for the article.)

BOCES WORKSHOP OFFERINGS:
✓ "Infusing Critical Thinking in the Primary Grades" (12/3-4)
✓ "Implementing the New Physics Core Curriculum" (9/24)
✓ "Differentiating Instruction for the Mixed Ability Classroom" (10/15&26, 11/28)
More information? Call Connie, ext. 3032.

Facts by themselves are nothing...It is through teaching that they become something real, something students can grasp and use to shape their tomorrows. The Master Teacher

Assessing a Performance Task Design

The document is intended for use assessing performance tasks being prepared for use in classrooms. This is a two-tiered guide with the categories of "**Quality Task, Completed and Ready for Use with Students**" and "**Not Yet Ready**," and it is in the form of questions to allow teachers and others to look at task designs to determine when tasks are complete and of sufficient quality to be used with students. Teachers should realize that designing and using a student performance task is a process that will require trial and error, self and peer assessment, reflection, feedback from students, parents and colleagues, and ongoing revision of the task in order to ensure the task does what it is intended to do. With that in mind, teachers are encouraged to use this document to look at their own plans, and ask colleagues to use it to give them responses to their tasks-in-progress.

Before being used in a classroom, a task should be carefully planned, be complete, and be of the highest quality possible. A task that is ready should be written on a completed **Task Design Template** and have some accompanying lesson plans, rubrics, materials, and resource lists.

Q   N Y

TASK PURPOSE AND FOCUS:

• Are the task's purpose and focus clearly stated?

• Is the task's purpose significant enough to justify the time spent?

• Does the task focus on relevant issues to students and community? (This may be in the form of a statement, an issue, or a question.)

• Are key concepts or competencies to be taught clearly stated?

THE PROMPT:

• Is the prompt complete—
  including the role students will play,
  how they will access information and what that
    information will be,
  how they will be expected to interpret that information,
  what they will produce to show their learning, and
  how and to whom they will disseminate that
    information to demonstrate their understanding
    and application of knowledge?

• Do all of the stages of the prompt connect in a logical way and lead to an end consistent with the stated purpose and focus of the task?

• Are the prompt and subsequent directions for students clear?

• Is the role the students will play appropriate to the task and as authentic as possible?

• Is the task developmentally appropriate for students who will do it?

• Is the content required in the task appropriate to course/ grade level of students, built on their prior knowledge, and challenging, but not impossible, for them?

• Will the required product be observable?

• Will the required presentation be in a real-world context and/or to an audience beyond the classroom? [If not, is there a written rationale for context of the task?]

	Q	N Y

CONTENT/STANDARDS ALIGNMENT AND CONNECTIONS:

- Does the task include significant content objectives from TEKS and are these stated on the Task Design Template?
- Does the task have interdisciplinary connections and/or possibilities, and are these stated on the Task Design Template?
- Does the task fit into district's curriculum alignment and/or state frameworks at that grade level?
- Does the task align with and help students achieve district expectations for graduates ?

DETAILED BREAKDOWN OF THE TASK:

- Are all pages of the Design Template complete?
- Do student activities/teacher lessons provide for various learning styles? (NOTE: Student activities and teacher lessons are very briefly indicated on pages 2 + 3 of the Template. More detailed lesson plans should be attached.)
- Do student activities/teacher lessons provide for opportunities for cooperation and collaboration between students and between teachers and students?
- Does the task require and plan for students to use a variety of information sources?
- Are necessary resources to complete this task available to all students?
- Do teacher plans assess student ability to carry out required learner actions and teach the processes students need to complete the task?
- If task offers various roles for students, are all corresponding student actions taught and assessed?
- Do teacher plans indicate that necessary content will be taught?
- Do student activities/teacher lessons provide opportunities for feedback from students on the progress of the work, the assistance they need to complete the work, and the quality and implementation of the task itself?

	Q	N Y

- Do student activities/teacher plans require ongoing student and teacher reflection, self-assessment, and goal setting to improve the quality of student work?
- Do student activities/teacher plans indicate that students may help develop rubrics for parts of the task when feasible?
- Can the task be done well in the allotted time?

QUALITY CRITERIA FOR ASSESSMENT AND EVALUATION:

- Are the essential criteria for quality completion of the stages of the task clearly stated?
- Have rubrics been developed from this criteria? Do they accompany the completed Task Design Template?
- Do rubrics clearly state and separate directions for student activities, criteria necessary, and standards for levels of performance?
- Do rubrics value quality learning and performance over quantity of information?
- Do rubrics help assess, document, and evaluate students' processes, products, and performances?
- Will students be assessed and evaluated both collectively and individually if the task requires collaborative work?
- Will student products and/or presentations be assessed and evaluated by others as well as by the teacher?
- Does the task offer opportunities to use traditional and alternative means of assessing, documenting, and evaluating student learning and progress?

COMMENTS:

Sample 31   Sample Audience Response Sheet Questions

Following are two examples of the questions you can have student audience members answer after a student presentation. The most efficient way to do this is to make three Audience Response slips per page and give students a slip for each presentation they watch. The slips can then be given to the presenters to give them feedback and ideas for improving presentations next time.

Audience Response Sheet #1

Your Name _____   **Presenter/Group** _____

1) What was the best thing about this presentation?

2) List two important things you learned from this presentation.

3) If this were your presentation and you could do an instant replay, what would you do differently to improve the presentation?

Audience Response Sheet #2

Your Name _____   **Presenter/Group** _____

1) I noticed (something positive) . . . .

2) List one or more important things that you learned from the presentation.

3) I wonder (a question about the topic or the presentation that would improve it) . . . . . .

Sample 32   Presentation Rubric

Evaluating Student Presentations					
Adapted from Information Technology Evaluation Services, NC Department of Public Instruction					
	1	**2**	**3**	**4**	Total
Organization	Audience cannot understand presentation because there is no sequence of information.	Audience has difficulty following presentation because student jumps around.	Student presents information in logical sequence that audience can follow.	Student presents information in logical, interesting sequence that audience can follow.	
Subject Knowledge	Student does not have grasp of information; student cannot answer questions about subject.	Student is uncomfortable with information and is able to answer only rudimentary questions.	Student is at ease with expected answers to all questions, but fails to elaborate.	Student demonstrates full knowledge (more than required) by answering all class questions with explanations and elaboration.	
Visuals	Student uses superfluous visuals or no visuals.	Student occasionally uses visuals that rarely support text and presentation.	Student's visuals relate to text and presentation.	Student's visuals explain and reinforce screen text and presentation.	
Mechanics	Student's presentation has four or more spelling errors and/or grammatical errors.	Presentation has three misspellings and/or grammatical errors.	Presentation has no more than two misspellings and/or grammatical errors.	Presentation has no misspellings or grammatical errors.	
Eye Contact	Student reads all of report with no eye contact.	Student occasionally uses eye contact, but still reads most of report.	Student maintains eye contact most of the time but frequently returns to notes.	Student maintains eye contact with audience, seldom returning to notes.	
Elocution	Student mumbles, incorrectly pronounces terms, and speaks too quietly for students in the back of class to hear.	Student's voice is low. Student incorrectly pronounces terms. Audience members have difficulty hearing presentation.	Student's voice is clear. Student pronounces most words correctly. Most audience members can hear presentation.	Student uses a clear voice and correct, precise pronunciation of terms so that all audience members can hear presentation.	
				Total Points:	

References and Further Readings

Adler, M. J. (1984). *The Paideia program: An educational syllabus.* New York: Collier.

Aguayo, R. (1990). *Dr. Deming: The American who taught the Japanese about quality.* New York: Simon & Schuster.

Angelis, J. I. (2001, November 7). What about our older readers? *Education Week, 21,* 48, 51.

Arter, J., & McTighe, J. (2001). *Scoring rubrics in the classroom: Using performance criteria for assessing and improving student performance.* Thousand Oaks, CA: Corwin Press.

Benson, B. (2001). *Classroom assessment, a conversation about learning* (Professional Pamphlet, Series 7, Issue #3). Albany: New York State Middle School Association.

Benson, B., & Barnett, S. (1999). *Student-led conferences using showcase portfolios.* Thousand Oaks, CA: Corwin Press.

Bezy, K. G. (1999, December). State standards fuel innovation and collaboration. *High School Magazine,* pp. 5–7.

Black, P., & Wiliam, D. (1998, October). Inside the black box: Raising standards through classroom assessment. *Phi Delta Kappan, 80,* 139–148.

Bloom, B. S. (Ed.). (1956). *Taxonomy of educational objectives: The classification of educational goals* (Handbook I, Cognitive domain). New York/Toronto: Longmans, Green.

Bonstingl, J. J. (2001). *Schools of quality* (3rd ed.). Thousand Oaks, CA: Corwin Press.

Bracey, G. W. (2001). At the beep, pay attention. *Phi Delta Kappan, 82,* 555.

Brubaker, J. W., Case, C. W., & Reagan, T. G. (1994). *Becoming a reflective educator: How to build a culture of inquiry in the schools.* Thousand Oaks, CA: Corwin Press.

Burz, H. L., & Marshall, K. (1996). *Performance-based curriculum for mathematics: From knowing to showing.* Thousand Oaks, CA: Corwin Press.

Burz, H. L., & Marshall, K. (1997a). *Language arts.* Thousand Oaks, CA: Corwin Press.

Burz, H. L., & Marshall, K. (1997b). *Science.* Thousand Oaks, CA: Corwin Press.

Burz, H. L., & Marshall, K. (1998). *Social studies.* Thousand Oaks, CA: Corwin Press.

Caine, R. N., & Caine, G. (1994). *Making connections: Teaching and the human brain* (rev. ed.). Alexandria, VA: Association for Supervision and Curriculum Development.

California State Board of Education. (2000). *Science content standards for California public schools.* Sacramento: Author. Retrieved February 23, 2008, from http://www.cde.ca.gov/be/st/ss/scinvestigation.asp.

Checkley, K. (2000, March). The contemporary principal. *Education Update, 42,* I.

Costa, A. L., & Kallick, B. (2000). Getting into the habit of reflection. *Educational Leadership, 57*(7), 60–62.

Cousins, E. (1998). *Reflections on design principles.* Dubuque, IA: Kendall/Hunt Publishing Co.

Curwin, R. L., & Mendler, A. N. (1988). *Discipline with dignity.* Alexandria, VA: Association for Supervision and Curriculum Development.

Daggett, W. (1994, July 6–10). *Designing curriculum for today's and tomorrow's labor market demands.* Materials from workshop presented at the Reaching New Heights in Learning Conference, Vail, Colorado.

Danielson, C. (1996). *Enhancing professional practice.* Alexandria, VA: Association for Supervision and Curriculum Development.

Danielson, C., & Marquez, E. (1998). *A collection of performance tasks and rubrics: High school mathematics.* Larchmont, NY: Eye on Education.

Darling-Hammond, L. (1997). *The right to learn: A blueprint for creating schools that work.* San Francisco: Jossey-Bass.

Deming, W. E. (1990). Foreword. In R. Aguayo (ed.), *Dr. Deming: The American who taught the Japanese about quality* (pp. vii–viii). New York: Simon & Schuster.

Edmond, E. (2001, September 28). *Sharing success. Curriculum and instruction corner* (p. 1). Dansville, NY: Dansville Central Schools.

Educational Resources Information Center Clearinghouse on Elementary and Early Childhood Education. (n.d). *Reggio network contacts.* Retrieved July 20, 2002, from www.cmu.edu/cyert-center/reggio.htm.

Education World for state curriculum standards. Retrieved February 23, 2008, from http://www.educationworld.com/standards/state/tx/index.shtml.

Farrell, G. (2000). Introduction. In E. Cousins (ed.), *Roots: From outward bound to expeditionary learning.* Dubuque, IA: Kendall/Hunt Publishing Co.

Farrell, G. (2003). *Expeditionary learning schools core practice benchmarks.* New York: Expeditionary Learning Schools.

Gibbs, J. (2006). *Reaching all by creating tribes learning communities.* Windsor, CA: Center Source Systems.

Gregory, G. H., & Chapman, C. (2002). *Differentiated instructional strategies: One size doesn't fit all.* Thousand Oaks, CA: Corwin Press.

Guskey, T. R., & Bailey, J. M. (2001). *Developing grading and reporting systems for student learning.* Thousand Oaks, CA: Corwin Press.

High Success Network. (1994, April). Prompt Cards. *The High Success Connection, 2,* 5–6.

Higher Order Thinking Skills. (n.d.). Retrieved July 20, 2002, from http://www.hots.org/.

Hole, S., & McEntee, G. H. (1999). Reflection is at the heart of practice. *Educational Leadership, 56*(8), 34–37.

Hord, S. M. (1997). *Professional learning communities: What are they and why are they important?* Available at http://www.sedl.org/change/issues/issues61.html.

Illinois State Board of Education. (1997). *Illinois learning standards.* Springfield: Author. Retrieved February 23, 2008, from http://www.isbe.net/ils/social _science/standards.htm.

Information Technology Evaluation Services, North Carolina Department of Public Instruction. Retrieved February 25, 2008, from http://www.ncsu.edu/midlink/rub.pres.html.

Jensen, E. (1998). *Teaching with the brain in mind.* Alexandria, VA: Association for Supervision and Curriculum Development.

Kane, S. (2007). *Literacy and learning in the content areas,* 2nd edition. Scottsdale, AZ: Holcomb Hathaway.

Kleiner, C., & Lord, M. (1999, November 22). The cheating game: "Everyone's doing it," from grade school to graduate school. *Z.I.S. News & World Report, 127,* 54, 9p, 6c.

Kohn, A. (1999, April 7). Direct drilling: Children as machines to be programmed. *Education Week, 18,* 36.

Kriete, R. (2002). *The morning meeting book.* Turners Falls, MA: Northeast Foundation for Children.

Marzano, R. J. (1992). *A different kind of classroom: Teaching with dimensions of learning.* Alexandria, VA: Association for Supervision and Curriculum Development.

Marzano, R. J. (2000). *Transforming classroom grading.* Alexandria, VA: Association for Supervision and Curriculum Development.

Marzano, R. J., Pickering, D. L., Arredondo, D. E., Blackburn, G. J., Brandt, R. S., & Moffett, C. A. (1992). *Dimensions of learning: Teacher's manual.* Alexandria, VA: Association for Supervision and Curriculum Development.

Marzano, R. J., Pickering, D. L., & McTighe, J. (1993). *Assessing student outcomes: Performance assessment using the dimensions of learning model.* Alexandria, VA: Association for Supervision and Curriculum Development.

Marzano, R. J., Pickering, D. J., & Pollock, J. E. (2001). *Classroom instruction that works: Research-based strategies for increasing student achievement.* Alexandria, VA: Association for Supervision and Curriculum Development.

Massachusetts Department of Education. (1994). *The Massachusetts common core of learning: Working and contributing.* Boston: Author. Retrieved June 19, 1999, from http://www.doe.mass.edu/doedocs/commoncore/working.html.

McREL Institute. (1993). Mid-Continent Research for Education and Learning; 2550 South Parker Road, Suite 500; Aurora, CO 80014. Retrieved May 21, 2002, from http://www.Yncrel.org.

McTighe, J. (1996). What happens between assessments? *Educational Leadership, 54*(4), 6–12.

Meier, D. (1995). *The power of their ideas.* Boston: Beacon Press.

Mizell, H. (2000, September). Standards make the difference. *NSDC Results,* p. 5.

National Center for Fair and Open Testing. (1995). Retrieved July 14, 2002, from http://www.fairtest.org/princind.htm.

National Council of Teachers of Mathematics. (2000). *Principles and standards.* Retrieved July 12, 2002, from http://www.nctm.org/standards/.

New York State Education Department. (2005). *Learning standards for mathematics, science, and technology.* Albany: Author. Retrieved February 23, 2008, from http://www.emsc.nysed.gov/ciai/mst/math.html.

North Carolina Department of Public Instruction. (1999). *Classroom assessment: Linking instruction and assessment.* Raleigh: Author.

North Carolina Department of Public Instruction. (2000). *Performance-based lansure handbook.* Raleigh: Author.

North Carolina Department of Public Instruction. (2004). *English language arts standard course of study.* Raleigh: Author. Retrieved February 23, 2008, from http://www.dpi.state.nc.us/curriculum/languagearts/scos/2004/30english4.

North Carolina Department of Public Instruction. (2004). *Science standard course of study.* Raleigh: Author. Retrieved February 24, 2008, from http://www.ncpublicschools.org/curriculum/science/scos/2004/21grade8.

North Carolina Department of Public Instruction. (2006). *Teacher handbook: Social studies, K–12.* Raleigh: Author.

Ogle, D. M. (1986). K-W-L: A teaching model that develops active reading of expository text. *The Reading Teacher, 39*(6), 564–570.

Olson, L. (1998, May 13). A question of value, *Education Week,* pp. 27, 30–31.

Oregon Department of Education. (1999). *Content standards.* Salem: Author. Retrieved July 5, 2002, from http://www.ode.state.or.us.

Osterman K. F., & Kottkamp, R. B. (1993). *Reflective practice for educators.* Thousand Oaks, CA: Corwin Press.

Richardson, J. (2000, February-March). Teacher research leads to learning, action. *NSDC Tools for Schools,* pp. 1–2.

Richardson, J. (2001, December-January). Support system: School improvement plans work best when staff learning is included. *NSDC Tools for Schools*, pp. 1–2.

Rogers, S., & Graham, S. (2000). *The high performance toolbox.* Evergreen, CO: Peak Learning Systems.

Rogers, S., Ludington, J., & Graham, S. (1997). *Motivation and learning.* Evergreen, CO: Peak Learning Systems.

Sizer, T. R. (1999). No two are quite alike. *Educational Leadership, 57*(1), 6–11.

Smyth, J. (1989). Developing and sustaining critical reflection in teacher education. *Journal of Teacher Education, 40*(2), 2–9.

Sparks, D. (1999, November 2). Using lesson study to improve teaching. *National Staff Development Council Results*, p. 2.

Stiggins, R. J. (1999, November). Assessment, student confidence, and school success. *Phi Delta Kappan, 81*, 191–198.

Stiggins, R.J., et. al. (2006). *Classroom assessment for student learning.* Portland, OR: Educational Testing Service.

Stigler, J. W., Gonzales, P., Kawanaka, T., Knoll, S., & Serrano. A. (1999). *The TIMSS videotape classroom study: Methods and findings from an Exploratory research project on eighth-grade mathematics instruction in Germany, Japan, and the United States.* Washington, DC: U.S. Government Printing Office, U.S. Department of Education, National Center for Education Statistics. Retrieved July 5, 2002, from http://nces.ed.gov/timss.

Sylwester, R. (2000). *A biological brain in a cultural classroom.* Thousand Oaks, CA: Corwin Press.

Texas Education Agency. (1995, revised 2001). *Texas essential knowledge and skills: Algebra I.* Austin, TX: Author. Retrieved July 5, 2002, from http://www.tea .state.tx.us/rules/tac/chapterlll/ch111c.html#111.32.

Texas Education Agency. (1998). *Texas essential knowledge and skills: health education.* Austin, TX: Author. Retrieved February 23, 2008, from http://www.tea.state .tx.us/rules/tac/chapter115/ch115b.html#115.23.

Tomlinson, C. A. (1999). *The differentiated classroom: Responding to the needs of all learners.* Alexandria, VA: Association for Supervision and Curriculum Development.

Viadero, D. (1999, February 10). Lighting the flame. *Education Week, 18,* 24–26.

Viadero, D. (1999, November 3). Chicago Study: Students rise to challenging assignments. *Education Week, 19,* 10.

Wiggins, G., & McTighe, J. (1998). *Understanding by design.* Alexandria, VA: Association for Supervision and Curriculum Design.

Wong, H. K., & Wong, R. T. (1991). *The first days of school.* Sunnyvale, CA: Harry K. Wong Publications.

Index

Accessing information, 77–78, 108, 109
    (figure), 123, 134
Accountability, viii, ix, 1, 11, 23
    quality-focused learning and, 38
    See also High-stakes testing; Standardized
        tests; Standards-based classroom
Action research, 15
Active learning, 8, 16, 23, 62
    See also Authentic tasks/assessments;
        Content-process teaching; Learner
        action cycle; Self-directed learning
Administrators, viii, ix, 23
    authentic tasks/assessments and, 128–129
    lesson analysis, content/process and,
        91–97, 93 (box), 95–96 (figures)
    quality-focused learning and, 54–55
    reflective practices and, 74–75, 75 (box)
    standards-based practices, support of,
        x, 16–20, 18 (figure), 19 (box)
    See also Instructional leadership
Aguayo, R., 38, 41, 43, 52, 53, 56
Angelis, J. I., 102, 103
Annual yearly progress (AYP), 11
Application Taxonomy, 6–7, 7 (box)
Arter, J., 46, 127
Assessment, 1
    clarification of, 121
    differentiated instruction and, 121
    evaluation and, 122
    formative assessment, 121
    portfolios, 48–50, 57, 58, 60
    rubrics for quality-scoring, 44, 46, 46
        (figure), 48, 49 (figure)
    standards-based instruction and, 10–13, 10
        (figure), 12 (table)
    student-led conferences, 48–50
    student self-assessment, 78–79
    See also Authentic tasks/assessments;
        High-stakes testing; Standardized tests
Assessment Training Institute, 131
Assignments. *See* Authentic
    tasks/assessments; Final projects;
    Homework
Association for Supervision and Curriculum
    Design (ASCD), 103
Audience Response Sheet
    Questions Form, 180

Authentic tasks/assessments, 13, 100, 126
    administrator strategies for, 128–129
    assessment for learning and, 121
    assessment questions and, 122–123
    authentic tasks, 117, 118–119, 118 (figure),
        119 (box)
    brain-compatible learning and, 101
    challenging assignments and, 101–102
    evaluation and, 122
    existing tasks, utilization of, 111, 113
    history task, 118, 118 (figure)
    learner action cycle and, 102
    learner activities, documentation of,
        108–109, 109 (figure)
    literacy task, 119, 119 (box)
    performance task assessment/evaluation,
        123–126, 124 (box)
    performance tasks, 102–105, 102 (figure),
        103 (boxes)
    quality-focused tasks, 102, 103
    real-world connections and,
        101, 104–105
    rubrics/quality indicators and, 109, 111,
        123–126, 124 (box)
    sample task, 103–105, 103 (box)
    size of tasks, decisions about, 114–117, 115
        (box, table), 117 (box)
    standards and, 101, 104–105
    student work, preferred types of, 100–102
    task design, 105, 106–113, 107 (form), 110
        (form), 112 (form)
    task performance, rationale for, 113–114,
        114 (box)
    task prompt, 106, 108, 113 (box)
    teacher strategies for, 127–128
    whole-class task performance, 104
    See also Content-process teaching; Quality-
        focused learning

Bailey, J. M., 48
Barnett, S., 50, 113, 115, 128, 154, 157
Benson, B. B., 34, 40, 47, 50, 109, 120, 128,
    138–139, 141, 143–148, 150–163, 165, 169,
    172–173, 179–181
Best practices, 1, 10
Bezy, K. G., 130
Biadero, D., 101

Big Picture View of Standards, 14, 16,
 101, 137–139
  See also Authentic tasks/assessments;
   Standards
Bill and Melinda Gates Foundation, 85
Black, P., 135
Bloom, B. S., 91
Bloom's Taxonomy, 9, 82, 91
Bolger, C., 170, 171, 172, 173, 174
Bonstingl, J. J., 37
Bracey, G. W., 101
Brain-compatible learning, 22, 23
  authentic tasks and, 101
  reflection and, 57, 62
  See also Authentic tasks/assessments
Brubaker, J. W., 62
Burnout, ix
Burz, H. J., 77, 83, 107, 110, 112,
 113, 168, 171

Caine, G., 62
Caine, R. N., 62
California Model Technology
 High School, 36
Case, C. W., 62
Central Park East Secondary School (New
 York City), 33, 136
Challenging tasks, 101–102
Change:
  facilitation of, x, 17–20, 18 (figure), 19 (box)
  past vs. contemporary standards and, 7–8
  school change, rationale/support for, 3
Chapman, C., 99
Checkley, K., 7
Class Observation Forms, 98, 162–163
Classroom environment:
  competition, 52
  emotional safety, learning and,
   22, 23, 24 (box)
  positive student attitudes and, 22, 23 (box)
  quality work and, 39, 52
  student involvement and, 23
  See also Classroom management;
   Instructional strategies; Interactive
   learning; Standards-based classroom;
   Student achievement; Teaching
   practices
Classroom management, 22
Coalition of Essential Schools, 27
Collaborative teaching, 15 (box), 16
Communication skills:
  administrator communication of
   standards, 17
  Into-Through-and-Beyond learning map,
   29, 30–31 (box)
  rubric for assessment, 48, 49 (figure)
  student communication skills, 8
  teacher communication of standards, 14
Communities of learners, 13, 21, 53
  administrator strategies for, 54–55

classroom communities,
   rationale for, 21–22
classroom environment, student learning
   and, 22, 23, 23 (box)
collaborative teaching practice,
   15 (box), 16
cooperative learning and, 35–36, 36 (box)
CREW structure and, 28, 54
discussion appointments and, 33–35, 34
   (boxes)
emotional safety, learning and,
   22, 24 (box)
Expeditionary Learning Schools
   and, 28, 54
group work, strategies for, 36–37, 37 (box)
helpless/hopeless students and, 22–23, 27
K-W-L strategy and, 28, 29 (box)
self-directed learning and, 24–27,
   26 (table)
teacher strategies for, 53–54
Think Pads strategy and, 29,
   31–32, 32 (box)
Tribes materials, 54
See also Classroom environment;
   Interactive learning; Quality-focused
   learning; Reflective practices
Competitive environment, 52
Conferences:
  administrator-teacher conferences,
   92–94, 93 (box)
  reflection form/professional
   conferences, 60
  student-led conferences, 48–50
  See also Communication skills; Parent
   involvement
Content area skills reflection, 69
Content-process teaching, 76
  accessing information and, 77–78
  administrator's lesson analysis, 91–97
  administrator strategies for, 98–99
  discovery-based learning and, 87
  dissemination of new understanding
   and, 78, 85
  history lesson, 88–90, 89 (figure), 94, 95
   (figure)
  homework assignments and, 86–88
  increasing student activity, strategies
   for, 85–91, 86 (box), 89 (figure),
   90 (figure)
  interpretation of information and, 78
  language arts lesson, 88, 90, 90 (figure),
   91–94, 93 (box), 96 (figure)
  learner action cycle and, 77–79, 80 (box),
   85, 91, 97
  Learner Action Verb List and,
   83 (table), 85
  lesson analysis/planning and, 82–97
  lesson model for, 81
  mathematics lesson, 84–88, 84 (figure),
   86 (box)

producing evidence of learning
and, 78, 85
purposeful activity and, 90–91
quality performance tasks and,
102–103, 102 (figure), 103 (box)
sample lesson analysis, 84–85, 84 (figure)
science lesson, 88–90, 89 (figure)
self-assessment processes, 78–79
social studies lesson, 94, 95 (figure)
standards, action vocabulary and, 76–77,
77 (box)
standards-based lessons, learner actions
and, 94–97, 95–96 (figures)
student involvement, planning for, 88,
91–94, 93 (box), 96 (figure)
student responsibility and, 80–81
student self-assessment and, 78–79
teacher strategies for, 98
See also Authentic tasks/assessments
Continuous improvement, 38, 40–41, 41
(box), 126
evaluation and, 122
planning for, 59
See also Quality-focused learning
Cooperative learning, 13, 23, 35–37,
36–37 (boxes), 52
Costa, A. L., 56
Cousins, E., 28
CREW structure, 28, 54
Critical thinking, 6–7, 7 (box), 8, 9–10, 126
Curriculum and Instruction Corner
Form, 175
Cycle of Reflective Practice, 74

Daggett, W., 6, 7
Danielson, C., 111
Dansville Central Schools (Dansville,
NY), 55
Darling-Hammond, L., 35, 102
Data collection, 9, 31, 108
Deming-Shewart Cycle of Continual
Improvement, 41, 41 (box), 43, 56
Deming, W. E., 37, 38, 40, 41, 52
Discovery-based learning, 86 (box), 87
Discussion Appointments Form, 33–35, 34
(boxes), 146
Dissemination of new understanding,
78, 85, 108, 109 (figure), 126, 134
Districts, viii, x
aligned district curriculum, 11
See also Administrators; Principals
Double Windows strategy, 67–68, 74, 156
Durham (NC) public schools, 17

Edmond, E., 135, 175
Edna McConnell Clark Foundation, 2
Educators Writing for Change, 60
Emotional safety, 22, 23, 24 (box)
Engaged students, 1, 8, 11, 16, 23, 99,
134–135

See also Authentic tasks/assessments;
Content-process teaching
Evaluation, 122
Exit standards, 3–5, 4–5 (box), 7, 8, 106
Expectations, x
past vs. contemporary standards and, 7–9
See also Standards; Standards-based
classroom
Expeditionary Learning Schools
K–12, 28, 54, 85

Feeley, N., 134
Final projects, 70
Formative assessment, 121
Forms. *See* Reproducible forms
Franklin Court High School (Virginia), 130

Gates model for high schools, 28
Gibbs, J., 54
Goal Card, 25, 26 (table), 145
Goal setting, 25–27, 26 (table), 59
Gonzales, P., 81, 84, 88
Grading, 92
authentic assessment, 123–126, 124 (box)
improvement, encouragement of,
44, 45 (box)
quality, measure of, 47–48, 47 (box)
rubrics for quality-scoring, 44, 46, 46
(figure), 48, 49 (figure)
See also Authentic tasks/assessments;
Quality-focused learning
Graduation requirements, 3–5, 4–5 (box), 7,
8, 106
Graham, S., 31, 46, 99
Gregory, G. H., 99
Group Task Sheet, 36, 147
Group work, 35–36, 36 (box)
strategies for, 36–37, 37 (box)
See also Communities of learners
Guskey, T. R., 48

Hahn, K., 28
Higher order thinking, 6–7, 7 (box), 8, 81
High-stakes testing, 1, 8, 57, 130
learner action cycle and, 134
rationale for, 131–132
standards and, 131, 132, 133, 136
tasks as preparation, 134–135
teaching past tests and, 132, 134
test preparation and, 133–135
High Success Network, 64, 65
History lesson, 88–90, 89 (figure), 94, 95
(figure), 118, 118 (figure)
Hole, S., 60, 61
Homework assignments, 9, 67, 86–88,
86 (box), 101

Idea Rolodex, 144
Illinois Learning Standards for Social
Science, 4 (box), 104–105

Illinois State Board of Education's learning standards, 4 (box), 76, 104–105
Induction programs, 58
Instructional leadership, x, 17–20, 18 (figure), 19 (box)
  quality-focused learning and, 52, 53 (box)
  See also Administrators; Teaching practices
Instructional strategies, ix
  individualized instruction, 27
  interdisciplinary/integrated instruction, 5–6
  modeling of, x, 20
  questioning strategy and, 8, 9
  standards-based practices, components of, x, 1–2, 10–13, 10 (figure), 12 (table)
  teacher practices, standards-focus of, 13–16, 15 (box)
  See also Authentic tasks/assessments; Content-process teaching; Interactive learning; Quality-focused learning; Reproducible forms; Standards; Standards-based classroom; Student achievement; Teaching practices
Integrated instruction, 5–6, 8
Interactive learning, 13, 23, 27–28
  CREW structure and, 28
  Into-Through-and-Beyond learning map and, 29, 30–31 (box)
  K-W-L strategy and, 28, 29 (box)
  questioning strategy and, 29, 31–32
  remediation/re-teaching and, 32
  student-student interaction, 33
  talking time, discussion appointments and, 33–35, 34 (boxes)
  teacher-student interaction, 28–29
  Think Pads strategy and, 29, 31–32, 32 (box)
  See also Communities of learners
Interdisciplinary instruction, 5–6, 8, 90, 101
Internet resources, 9
  Instructional Strategies on Line, 28
  See also Reproducible forms
Interpretation of information, 78, 108, 109 (figure), 124, 134
Into-Through-and-Beyond learning map, 29, 30–31 (box), 63, 68, 74

Jensen, E., 99

Kallick, B., 56
Kane, S., 29
Kawanaka, T., 81, 84, 88
Kenny, L., 113, 114
Kindergarten Science Task Rubric Form, 174
Kleiner, C., 122
Knoll, S., 81, 84, 88
Kohn, A., 97
Kottkamp, R. B., 57
Kriete, R., 54
Kueper, T., 103, 104

K-W-L (know/want to know/learned) strategy, 28, 29 (box), 63, 68, 74

Language arts lesson, 88, 90, 90 (figure), 91–94, 93 (box), 96 (figure), 119, 119 (box), 120 (box)
Learner action cycle, 77–79, 77 (box), 91
  challenging tasks and, 102
  high-stakes testing and, 134
  standards and, 76–77, 80–81
  standards-based lessons and, 94–97, 95–96 (figures)
  student responsibility in, 80–81
  task design and, 105
  task performance and, 114
  teaching of, 79, 80 (box)
  See also Content-process teaching
Learner Actions: The Heart of a Task Form, 164–165
Learner Actions in Tasks Form, 105
Learner Action Verb List, 82, 83 (table), 85, 91, 98
Learning:
  active involvement in, 8, 16
  brain-compatible learning, 22, 23
  classroom management and, 22
  emotional safety need and, 22, 23, 24 (box)
  ownership of, ix, 1, 8, 16
  personalized learning, 27
  positive student attitudes and, 22, 23 (box)
  standards-based practices and, 11, 13
  See also Authentic tasks/assessments; Communities of learners; Instructional strategies; Interactive learning; Reflective practices; Self-directed learning; Standards; Standards-based classroom; Student achievement
Lesson analysis, 82
  Learner Action Verb List, 82, 83 (table), 85
  sample analysis, 84–85, 84 (figure)
  standards, lesson plans and, 82
  student activities, analysis of, 82
  See also Authentic tasks/assessment; Content-process teaching
Lesson Planner Form, 82, 98, 99, 159
Lesson Reflection Form, 59, 60, 151
Literacy task, 119, 119 (box)
Looking Ahead to Next Year Form, 152
Look What We Learned This Week Form, 158
Lord, M., 122
Loya, S., 42
Ludington, J., 31, 99

Making Middle Grades Matter initiative, 2
Marquez, E., 111
Marshall, K., 77, 83, 107, 110, 112, 113, 168, 171
Marzano, R. J., 46, 48, 49, 99, 113

Mathematics lessons:
increasing student activity, strategies for, 85–88, 86 (box)
sample lesson analysis, 84–85, 84 (figure)
simulated task, 120 (box)
See also Content-process teaching
Math Reflection Form, 157
McEntee, G. H., 60, 61
McTighe, J., 46, 49, 103, 113, 127
Meetings. *See* Conferences; Staff meetings
Meier, D., 136
Memorization, 6, 8, 77, 126
Middle school model, 28
Mitzell, H., 2
Modeling instruction, x, 20, 55
Motivation, 1, 22, 24
prior knowledge, reflection on, 64
supportive relationships and, 38
See also Communities of learners; Content-process teaching; Quality-focused learning; Self-directed learning

National Board Certification, 58
National Center for Fair and Open Testing, 121
National Center for Restructuring Education, Schools, and Teaching, 35
National Council of Teachers of Mathematics (NCTM), 88
National Research Center on English Learning and Achievement, 102
National Staff Development Council, 17
Neier, D., 33
Newsletters, 72
New York State Learning Standards and Core Curriculum in Mathematics, 4 (box)
No Child Left Behind (NCLB) Act of 2001, viii, 11
North Carolina Department of Public Instruction, 29, 31, 58, 75, 131
North Carolina Standard Course of Study in English Language Arts, 5 (box)

Observation. *See* Class Observation Forms
Olson, L., 14
Osterman, K. F., 57
Outward Bound, 28
Ownership of learning, ix, 1, 8, 16

Parent involvement:
classroom visitation, 14
student reflection, sharing strategy and, 71–72, 72 (figure)
student work, understanding of, 14
Performance Task Design Assessment Form, 176–179

Performance tasks, 102–103, 102 (figure), 103 (box)
assessment/evaluation of, 123–126, 124 (box)
authentic tasks, 117, 118–119, 118 (figure), 119 (box)
existing tasks, utilization of, 111, 113
history task, 118, 118(figure)
learner activities, documentation of, 108–109, 109 (figure)
literacy task, 119, 119 (box)
organization of, 105
quality tasks and, 102, 103, 103 (box)
rationale for, 113–114, 114 (box)
real-world connections/standards and, 104–105
rubrics/quality indicators, 109, 111
sample task, 103–105, 103(box)
simulated tasks, 117, 120, 120 (box)
size of tasks, decisions about, 114–117, 115 (box, table), 117 (box)
task design, 105, 106–113, 107 (form), 110 (form), 112 (form)
task prompt, 106, 108, 113 (box)
whole-class task, 103
See also Authentic tasks/assessment
Personalized learning, 27
Phiffer, J., 42
Pickering, D. L., 46, 49, 99, 113
Planning process, 58–59
Poem Discussion Rubric Form, 161
Poem Reading Techniques Form, 160
Pollock, J. E., 99
Portfolios, 48–50, 57, 58, 60, 85, 127–128
Presentation Rubric Form, 181
Principals, ix, x, 74
See also Administrators; Professional development; Teaching practices
Prior knowledge, 63–64
Process. *See* Content-process teaching
Producing evidence of learning, 78, 85, 108, 109 (figure), 124, 126, 134
Professional development, x
administrator support of, 17–20, 18 (figure), 19 (box)
maximizing impact of, 19, 19 (box)
professional portfolios, 57, 58, 60
professional study/discussion groups, 20
questioning skills, development of, 9
reflection on teacher learning, 60
reflective practice, training for, 57–58, 57 (box)
Staff Development Survey, 18–19, 140–141
staff meetings and, 19–20
standards-based classroom practices and, 15–16, 15 (box)
training programs, 18–19, 55, 58
workshop note taking, 16

Professional Development Reflection Form, 143
Professional Development Request Form, 142
Program for Student Achievement (Edna McConnell Clark Foundation), 2

Quality: Opening the Discussion Template, 148
Quality: Quotes for Discussions Form, 149
Quality Coupons, 46, 150
Quality-focused learning, 13, 23, 37–38
    barriers to quality work and, 41–43, 42 (box)
    competitive environments and, 52
    continuous improvement and, 38, 40–41, 126
    dilemmas related to quality work, 43, 43 (box), 50
    discussions about quality and, 38–39, 38 (box)
    grades/percentages, inadequacy of, 47–48, 47 (box)
    grading model for improvement, 44, 45 (box)
    mistakes, role of, 43–46
    performance tasks and, 102–103, 102 (figure), 103 (box)
    portfolios/student-led conferences and, 48–50
    Quality Coupons and, 46
    quality cycle and, 40–41, 41 (box)
    risk taking and, 44, 46
    rubrics for quality-scoring, 44, 46, 46 (figure), 48, 49 (figure)
    substance/presentation, teaching methods for, 51–52
    supportive community of learners and, 38
    time element and, 50
    vision of quality, creation of, 39–40, 40 (box), 52, 53 (box)
    See also Authentic tasks/assessments; Communities of learners; Learning; Reflective practices; Student achievement
Quality worksheet, 39
Questioning strategy, 8, 9
    assessment questions, 122–123
    reflective practices and, 58
    student reflection questions, 67
    Think Pads strategy, 29, 31–32, 32 (box)

Reading Cards rubric, 44, 46 (figure)
Reagan, T. G., 62
Real-world problems, 5–6, 7, 7 (box), 101, 104–105
    See also Authentic tasks/assessments
Reflection forms, 60, 73, 74, 143

Reflective practices, 13, 56–57, 57 (box), 73
    administrator strategies for, 74–75, 75 (box)
    assignments, reflection on, 67, 70
    basic questions in, 58
    benefits of, 62
    classroom incidents, reflection on, 60, 61 (box)
    content area skills, reflection on, 69
    Cycle of Reflective Practice, 74
    Double Windows strategy and, 67–68, 74
    final projects, reflection on, 70
    guided-reflection, 60, 61 (box)
    Into-Through-and-Beyond strategy and, 63, 68, 74
    K-W-L strategy and, 63, 68, 74
    learning strategies and, 64–68
    planning process and, 58–59
    post-lesson reflection, 59, 68–70
    professional portfolios and, 57, 58, 60
    protocols for, 60, 61 (box)
    rigorous nature of, 58
    sharing strategy, reflection letters and, 71–72, 72 (figure)
    standards, implementation of, 57
    student-centered classrooms and, 58
    teacher learning, reflection on, 60
    teacher strategies for, 60, 62, 73–74
    teacher training programs and, 57, 58
    tests, reflection on, 69–70
    Tickets Out/In the Door strategy, 64–67, 65 (box), 66 (figure), 74
    Web of Knowledge and, 63, 68, 74
    See also Lesson reflection form; Student reflection
Regents/non-Regents diplomas, 8, 131
Remediation, 32
Reproducible forms:
    Audience Response Sheet Questions Form, 180
    Big-Picture View of Standards, 137–139
    Class Observation Forms, 162–163
    Curriculum and Instruction Corner Form, 175
    Discussion Appointments Form, 146
    Double Windows, 156
    Goal Card, 145
    Group Task Sheet, 147
    Idea Rolodex, 144
    Kindergarten Science Task Rubric Form, 174
    Learner Actions: The Heart of a Task Form, 164–165
    Lesson Planner Form, 159
    Lesson Reflection Form, 151
    Looking Ahead to Next Year Form, 152
    Look What We Learned This Week Form, 158

Math Reflection Form, 157
Performance Task Design Assessment
    Form, 176–179
Poem Discussion Rubric Form, 161
Poem Reading Techniques Form, 160
Presentation Rubric Form, 181
Professional Development Request
    Form, 142
Quality: Opening the Discussion
    Template, 148
Quality: Quotes for Discussions
    Form, 149
Quality Coupons, 150
Staff Development Survey, 140–141
Student Reflection Questions Form, 155
Student Task Design Paths Form, 169
Task Design Template, 166–168
Task Design Template for Kindergarten
    Science Task, 171–173
Task Prompt for Kindergarten Science
    Form, 170
Tickets In/Out the Door Form, 154
Web of Knowledge, 153
Research-based methods, 1, 15, 85, 101
Resources. See Internet resources;
    Reproducible forms
Responsible students. See Engaged students;
    Self-directed learning
Richardson, J., 15, 17
Risk taking, 44, 46
Rogers, S., 31, 46, 99
Rote learning, 6, 8, 77, 126
Rubrics:
    authentic assessment, 123–126, 124
        (box), 127
    performance tasks, 109, 111
    quality scoring, 44, 46, 46 (figure), 48,
        49 (figure)

Sanders, W., 14
Scearce, C., 34
Science Content Standards for California
    Public Schools, 4–5 (box)
Science lesson, 88–90, 89 (figure), 170,
    171–174
Scotia-Glenville High School (New York),
    113–114
Self-assessment, 78–79, 108, 109 (figure), 126
Self-directed learning, 13, 23, 24
    description of, 24–25
    goal setting and, 25–26, 26 (table)
    honest goals/practical strategies and,
        26–27
    realistic goals and, 26, 27
    See also Communities of learners;
        Learning; Self-assessment
Serrano, A., 81, 84, 88
Showcase portfolios, 48–50, 127–128
Simulated tasks, 117, 120, 120 (box)
Sizer, T. R., 27

Sloan Study of Youth and Development, 101
Small schools movement, 85
Smyth, J., 74
Social studies lesson, 94, 95 (figure),
    120 (box)
Southern Regional Education Board, 2
South Kitsap School District
    (Washington), 42
Sparks, D., 15
Staff Development Survey, 18–19, 140–141
Staff meetings, 19–20
Standardized tests, viii
    See also Accountability; High-stakes
        testing; Tests
Standards, viii, ix, 1–2, 1 (box)
    administrator focus on, 16–17
    Application Taxonomy and,
        6–7, 7 (box)
    Big-Picture view of, 2–10, 101
    content knowledge, application of, 6–7, 8
    critical thinking skills and, 6, 8, 9–10
    interdisciplinary/integrated instruction
        and, 5–6
    past vs. contemporary standards, 6 (table),
        7–9
    portfolios/student-led conferences and,
        48–50
    positive view of, 2
    quality rubrics and, 48, 49 (figure)
    questions about, 3–9, 3 (box)
    strategies for standards-based
        teaching, 11, 13
    students, standards-based demands on,
        3–5, 4–5 (box), 6 (table)
    teacher focus on, 13–14
    See also Authentic tasks/assessments;
        Content-process teaching;
        Standards-based classroom
Standards-based classroom, 1–2
    administration practices and, 16–20, 18
        (figure), 19 (box)
    components of, x, 10–13, 10 (figure), 12
        (table)
    contemporary expectations and, 6 (table),
        8–9
    creation of, 14–16, 15 (box)
    standards-based lessons, learner actions
        and, 94–97, 95–96 (figures)
    standards, definition of, 1–2, 1 (box)
    teaching practices and, 13–16, 15 (box)
    See also Accountability; Authentic
        tasks/assessments; Communities of
        learners; Content-process teaching;
        Quality-focused learning; Reflective
        practices; Standards; Teaching
        practices
Steinbruck, L., 118
Stiggins, R. J., 48, 121, 122, 131, 132, 136
Stigler, J. W., 81, 84, 88
Stone, S., 118

Student achievement:
  emotional safety, learning and, 22, 23,
      24 (box)
  expectations for, x, 7–9
  ownership of learning and, ix, 1, 8, 11, 23
  personalized learning and, 27
  standards-based learning and, 11–13,
      12 (table)
  teacher effectiveness and, 15–16, 15 (box)
  See also Accountability; Authentic
      tasks/assessments; Communities of
      learners; Content-process teaching;
      High-stakes testing; Learning;
      Standardized tests; Standards;
      Student reflection; Teaching practices
Student reflection, 62
  active information processing and, 62
  assignments, reflection on, 67, 70
  Into-Through-and-Beyond strategy
      and, 63
  K-W-L strategy and, 63
  long-term memory and, 62
  new learning, reflection before, 62–64
  post-lesson reflection, 59, 68–70
  student work, reflection on, 59–60, 67, 70
  teacher learning and, 70–71
  tests, reflection on, 69–70
  Think Pads strategy and, 63
  Ticket Out/In the Door, 64–67, 65
      (box), 66 (figure)
  Web of Knowledge strategy and, 63
  See also Reflective practices; Student
      achievement
Student Reflection Questions Form, 155
Student Task Design Paths Form, 169
Student-centered classrooms, 10, 35, 58
Student-led conferences, 48–50
Study groups, 20
Support groups, 20
Sylwester, R., 22

Task Design Template, 107 (form), 110
      (form), 111, 112 (form), 166–168
Task Design Template for Kindergarten
      Science Task, 171–173
Task Prompt for Kindergarten Science
      Form, 170
Task sheets, 36, 147
Tasks. *See* Authentic tasks/assessments;
      Performance tasks; Reproducible
      forms; Task sheets
Teacher training. *See* Professional
      development; Training programs
Teaching practices, viii, ix, 23
  best practices and, 1, 10

collaborative practices, 15 (box), 16
  flexibility in, 9
  planning process, 58–59
  reflective practices, 60, 62
  research-based methods and, 1, 15
  re-teaching/remediation, 32
  standards/accountability and, 1–2
  standards, focus on, 13–14
  standards-based classroom, creation of,
      14–16, 15 (box)
  standards-based classrooms and, x, 9–13,
      10 (figure), 12 (table)
  training programs and, 18–19
  See also Accountability; Communities
      of learners; Content-process
      teaching; Instructional strategies;
      Professional development; Quality-
      focused learning; Reflective practices;
      Reproducible forms; Standardized
      tests; Standards; Student
      achievement; Tests
Technology, 8, 9
Tests:
  assessment, definition of, 121
  reflection on, 69–70
  See also Accountability; High-stakes
      testing; Standardized tests
Texas Assessment of Academic Skills II
      (TAAS), 131, 135
Texas Essential Knowledge and Skills for
      Health Education, 5 (box), 6 (table)
Think Pads strategy, 29, 31–32, 32 (box),
      63, 74
Ticket Out/In the Door, 64–67, 65 (box),
      66 (figure), 74, 94, 154
Tomlinson, C. A., 121
Training programs, 18–19, 55
  Cycle of Reflective Practice, 74
  induction programs, 58
  portfolio documentation and, 57
  reflective practice, training in, 57–58,
      57 (box)
  See also Professional development
Tribes materials, 54

Viadero, D., 122, 132
Vision, ix
  quality work, vision of, 39–40, 40 (box),
      52, 53 (box)
  See also Standards-based classroom

Web of Knowledge, 63, 68, 74, 153
Wiliam, D., 135
Wong, H. K., 11, 21, 81
Wong, R. T., 11, 21, 81

CORWIN PRESS